SIMPLICIUS

On Aristotle Categories 1-4

SIMPLICIUS

On Aristotle
Categories 1-4

Translated by
Michael Chase

B L O O M S B U R Y
LONDON · NEW DELHI · NEW YORK · SYDNEY

Bloomsbury Academic
An imprint of Bloomsbury Publishing Plc

50 Bedford Square
London
WC1B 3DP
UK

1385 Broadway
New York
NY 10018
USA

www.bloomsbury.com

First published in 2003 by Gerald Duckworth & Co. Ltd.
Paperback edition first published 2014

British Library Cataloguing-in-Publication Data
A catalogue record for this book is available from the British Library.

ISBN: HB: 978-0-7156-3197-3
PB: 978-1-4725-5738-4
ePDF: 978-1-4725-0107-3

Typeset by Ray Davies

Contents

Acknowledgments

I would like to thank Richard Sorabji for his patience and sound advice; Ilsetraut Hadot, Pierre Hadot and Philippe Hoffmann for teaching me whatever I know about Neoplatonism in general and the Commentators in particular; and John Dillon and Frans de Haas for their useful comments on the translation.

Research cannot be done without good libraries, and I thank M.-O. Goulet-Cazé, M. Narcy, and C. Robine for access to the library of the CNRS Fédération 33 (Villejuif, France), and P. Petitmengin for access to the Bibliothèque des Lettres of the École Normale Supérieure.

This work is dedicated to the memory of my grandfather, Jack Stephens.

M.C.

Abbreviations

AEPHE   *Annuaire de l'École Pratique des Hautes Études*, Vᵉ section – Sciences Religieuses

D-K   H. Diels, *Die Fragmente der Vorsokratiker* revised by W. Kranz, vol. 3, Zürich/Hildesheim: Weidmann, 1987 (reprint of the 6th revised edition, 1952)

DPhA   R. Goulet, ed., *Dictionnaire des philosophes antiques*, Paris: CNRS Éditions (1989-: vol. 1, 1989; vol. 2, 1994; vol. 3, 2000)

KRS   G.S. Kirk, J.E. Raven & M. Schofield, eds, *The Presocratic Philosophers*, 2nd ed., Cambridge: Cambridge University Press, 1983

PLRE   *The Prosopography of the Later Roman Empire*, Cambridge: Cambridge University Press

RE   *Paulys Realencyclopädie der Klassischen Altertumswissenschaft*, Stuttgart-Weimar, Verlag J.B. Metzler

SVF   *Stoicorum Veterum Fragmenta*, ed. J. von Arnim, vol. 4, B.G. Teubner, 1924

Zeller   Eduard Zeller, *Die Philosophie der Griechen in ihrer geschichtlichen Entwicklung*, Leipzig 1919, reprinted Hildesheim etc., Georg Olms Verlag, 1990

Introduction

The Neoplatonic philosopher Simplicius (fl. sixth century AD) was long considered important primarily as a source of fragments of other philosophers. In his immense *oeuvre*, consisting entirely of commentaries, Simplicius quotes the views of dozens of his predecessors, often providing us with the only extant text of many ancient philosophers. His role as preserver of the fragments of the Presocratic philosophers has caused modern scholars on the subject to speak of Simplicius as 'invaluable',[1] and to praise him for his preservation of fragments of Parmenides, Empedocles, Anaxagoras and Diogenes of Apollonia. A glance at the *index fontium* to Von Arnim's *Stoicorum Veterum Fragmenta*[2] suffices to convince us of his importance as a transmitter of Stoic doctrine. His importance as a source for such Peripatetic philosophers as Eudemus of Rhodes, Andronicus and Boethus is second to none,[3] and he is the source for much of our knowledge of such Pythagorean and Pseudo-Pythagorean authors as Moderatus of Gades and Archytas,[4] as well as of philosophers of the Later Academy[5] and the so-called Middle Platonists.[6] Much of the lost commentaries on the *Categories* of his Neoplatonic predecessors Porphyry and Iamblichus may be reconstructed only through Simplicius as an intermediary,[7] while, as we shall see below, his importance for reconstructing the thought of his master Damascius has only now begun to be appreciated.

It is only recently, however, that Simplicius' works have begun to be carefully studied for their own value. The first international Colloquium on Simplicius' life and work was held at Paris in 1985,[8] and new critical editions of most of Simplicius' works are currently in preparation. In Paris, a team led by Mme I. Hadot has begun a French translation, with abundant commentary, of his *Commentary on the Categories*.[9] The more carefully and thoroughly contemporary scholars direct their attention to Simplicius' works, the more they arrive at the conclusion that Simplicius deserves study not only as a source for ancient philosophers, or as an often-helpful guide to the study of Aristotle, the two reasons for which he has hitherto been consulted. These reasons remain as valid as ever, but in addition it has come to be seen that Simplicius also deserves study for his own sake: as a witness of the Late Antique conflict between Paganism and Christianity;[10] an example of Late Antique pagan piety and spirituality,[11] and as one of the initiators of the long, gradually-formed school-tradition of the teaching of philosophy which would eventually solidify into the form we know as Scholasticism.

1. Life of Simplicius

Until about a generation ago, it would have been a brief and relatively simple task to describe the life and works of Simplicius: we knew very little about him, but what little we did know was agreed upon by those few scholars who paid any attention to him. Since then, the situation has changed: as scholars pay closer attention to his works, his thought, and the time in which he lived, received opinions fall by the wayside, new hypotheses sprout, and it is now difficult to think of many aspects of Simplicius' life and work upon which all contemporary scholars could agree. In what follows, I shall rely heavily on the findings of the Paris-based scholar Ilsetraut Hadot, who, together with her research team, has been instrumental in the current revival of Simplician studies. I find most of Mme Hadot's findings convincing, but would not like to give the impression that unanimity reigns among contemporary scholars with regard to all aspects of Simplicius' life and works.

What is known with relative certainty about Simplicius is the following:[12] born in Cilicia in Asia Minor (modern-day Turkey), Simplicius studied initially at Alexandria under the Neoplatonist Ammonius son of Hermeias, sometime before the latter's death in AD 517; this allows us to situate Simplicius' birth somewhere in the very last years of the fifth century AD. He appears not to have met his younger contemporary John Philoponus, then also studying at Alexandria, but after Philoponus' conversion to Christianity, Simplicius would heap scorn upon him as a philosophical *parvenu* in his *Commentary on the De Caelo*.[13] We know also that Simplicius studied, probably at Athens, under the Syrian Neoplatonist Damascius (*c.* 462 – after 538). From this point on, unquestionable facts about Simplicius' life are in short supply.

In 529, the emperor Justinian forbade all those who were 'sick with the madness of the impious Greeks' to teach within his empire;[14] this measure probably had as its effect the closing of whatever philosophical – i.e. Neoplatonic – schools were operating at that time. According to the historian Agathias,[15] Damascius, his pupil Simplicius, and five other eminent Neoplatonists decided to flee the Byzantine empire and seek refuge at the court of the Persian King Chosroes. Agathias tells us that our seven Neoplatonists were quickly disillusioned by the Great King's lack of philosophical acumen, as well as by the immorality of the people, and that they quickly left the Persian empire.

Agathias does not tell us where our seven renegades went after their disappointing Persian adventure. Up until recently, scholars had supposed that they returned either to Athens or to Alexandria. In a series of recent publications, however, Michel Tardieu[16] has suggested, on the grounds of evidence too complex to enter upon here, that instead they retired to the Mesopotamian city of Harran (= ancient Carrhae), where they established a philosophical school which survived at least until 1081, some four centuries after the Arab conquest of the Persian empire. Should this controversial hypothesis be correct, then our seven Neoplatonists – among them Simplicius and his master Damascius – acquire even greater historical importance, since they would thus have been well situated to provide a major conduit for the transfer of Greek science and philosophy to the Arab world. We know nothing of the date or place of Simplicius' death.

We can evaluate Simplicius' life in variety of ways. He can be seen as a pathetic reactionary, vainly attempting to keep a dying paganism alive as he is chased around – and out of – the Byzantine empire by an inexorably triumphant Christianity. On the other hand, however, there is a sense in which he and his Neoplatonist colleagues can be said to have been victorious in their defeat: by virtue of the influence their ideas had upon posterity. Whether or not Tardieu's hypothesis is correct, there is no doubt that Simplicius' works, in particular his *Commentary on the Categories of Aristotle*, were known in translation to the Arab world,[17] where Simplicius had the reputation of an astronomer and mathematician with numerous disciples who called themselves after his name. His influence upon the Byzantine world was immense, and the scholars of eleventh- to thirteenth-century Constantinople possessed and studied more of Simplicius' work than is possible for us today.[18] The conflict between Paganism and Christianity, as reflected in Simplicius' polemic with his younger Christian contemporary John Philoponus, was a dominant factor in Simplicius' life.

2. Works

By the time of Simplicius, philosophy had long since ceased to be what it had been at its inception – the investigation of Being and the world, initiated by an individual of genius (the Presocratics, Plato, Aristotle, etc.) and transmitted to an intimate circle of disciples. Since at least the time of Plotinus (died *c.* AD 270), and probably well before, philosophy had taken on the form of exegesis.[19] Henceforth, it was held that all truth had been discovered long ago by a handful of men sent by the gods – Orpheus, Pythagoras, Aristotle, but above all Plato – and that the task of philosophy was the correct interpretation of the writings of these divine men. This tendency became so systematized that by the time of Proclus (died *c.* AD 485), a complete reading

curriculum had been established which was to last until the end of
Antiquity.[20] All philosophy students were to follow this *cursus stu-
diorum*, which prescribed the reading – after an initial moral purifi-
cation, provided by the study of Epictetus or the Pythagorean *Golden
Verses* – first of Aristotle (beginning with his logic, then his physical
and psychological writings, and finally his *Metaphysics*) and then of
a carefully-chosen selection of thirteen dialogues of Plato, beginning
with the *First Alcibiades* and culminating with the two dialogues held
to be the apex and summary of all knowledge: the *Timaeus* – authori-
tative for matters of physics – and the *Parmenides*, regarded as a
summa of theological wisdom. It is thus no surprise if all of Simplicius'
surviving works took the form of exegesis or commentaries.

As is the case with most ancient Greek authors, many of Simplicius' works have not survived. Those lost works of whose existence
we can be fairly sure, basing ourselves on Greek and Arabic sources,
ancient library catalogues, etc., include the following:[21] a commentary
on the first book of Euclid's *Elements*; another on Aristotle's *Metaphysics*, as well as one on his *Meteorologica*; another on Iamblichus'
work *On the Pythagorean Sect*; a commentary on one of Plato's
dialogues, probably the *Phaedo*; an *Epitome* of the *Physics* of Theophrastus; and a commentary on the *Tekhnê* of the rhetorician
Hermogenes (second-third century AD).

Of the surviving works of Simplicius, we possess his commentary
on the *Manual (Enkheiridion)* of Epictetus, now available in a new
critical edition by I. Hadot,[22] and in this series in an English translation by Tad Brennan and Charles Brittain (2 vols, London & Ithaca
NY 2000), as well as four Aristotelian commentaries ascribed to him,
published by the Berlin Academy in the series *Commentaria in
Aristotelem Graeca (CAG)*. A substantial proportion of these too is
already available in English translation in this series, including the
whole of the *Categories* commentary. They are as follows, listed in the
order in which we know them to have been composed:

(1.) Commentary on Aristotle's *De Caelo*, ed. I.L. Heiberg (= *CAG*
vol. 7), Berlin 1894.

(2.) Commentary on Aristotle's *Physics*, ed. H. Diels (= *CAG* vols
9-10), Berlin, 1882-1885.

(3.) Commentary on Aristotle's *Categories*, ed. C. Kalbfleisch (=
CAG vol. 8), Berlin, 1907.

(4.) Commentary on Aristotle's *De Anima*, ed. M. Hayduck (= *CAG*
vol. 11), Berlin 1882. The authenticity of this last commentary has
been doubted; some scholars[23] attribute it to Simplicius' Neoplatonist
colleague Priscianus Lydus.

For most of this century,[24] it was thought that the Late Neoplatonists could be neatly divided up into two groups, according to the place

where the majority of their teaching and writing activity took place: there was, it was said, a 'School of Alexandria', comprising such philosophers as Ammonius, Philoponus and Olympiodorus, and a 'School of Athens', of which the most outstanding members were Proclus and Damascius. The 'Alexandrian school', it was claimed, confined their interest almost exclusively to Aristotle, whom they explained in a sober, rational way, whereas the Athenians commented primarily upon Plato and constructed elaborate, multi-tiered, hierarchical ontological systems. Simplicius, it was thought, was something of a hybrid: having begun his studies under the sober Alexandrian Ammonius, he took from that school the rational and critical approach to the explanation of Aristotle which he usually displays in his commentaries, while the fact that he had, after all, spent some time in Athens explained some of the more awkwardly prolix and complex metaphysical passages in his works.

Some scholars still hold this view,[25] or a variant thereof; but as the Neoplatonic commentaries and treatises are re-edited and subjected to closer comparative analysis, a new view of things has begun to arise. This new approach, championed by I. Hadot,[26] holds that the differences between the so-called 'Athenian' and 'Alexandrian' schools are to be explained not by any major philosophical or methodological divergences, but by the texts which each individual Neoplatonist set out to explicate. Owing partly to historical accidents of textual transmission, and partly to the political circumstances under which they were composed,[27] the commentaries which have reached us from authors based in Alexandria are indeed largely devoted to Aristotle. However, where 'Athenian' and 'Alexandrian' commentaries on the same text can be compared – Athenian Syrianus and Alexandrian Ammonius on Aristotle's *Metaphysics*, for instance, or Alexandrian Olympiodorus and Athenian Damascius on Plato's *Phaedo* – then we note that there is not much difference at all between the philosophical doctrines and exegetical techniques of the representatives of the two alleged 'schools'.

This discovery has a number of important implications. First, it implies that the doctrines expressed in the Neoplatonist commentaries are not comprehensible when taken out of context. If we do not find complex metaphysical doctrines in, say, Ammonius' commentary on Aristotle's *Categories*, then we can no longer explain this by stating that Ammonius was an Alexandrian, and therefore did not hold such doctrines. On the contrary, we must first look towards the work being commented for an explanation of the kind of commentary given: since the *Categories* was the first work read by beginning students in the Neoplatonic curriculum, a commentary on it will necessarily lack lengthy and complex expositions on topics which such students could not understand. A commentary on Aristotle's *Physics* or *De Anima*, by contrast, can be expected to contain more expositions of metaphysical doctrines, and the commentaries on the *Timaeus* and the *Parmenides*, intended as they were for the most advanced students of all, could expound late Neoplatonic ontology in all its grandiose architecture and complexity. The fact that tradition happens to have preserved commentaries on the *Parmenides* only by Athens-based philosophers – if we leave to one side the case of Porphyry of Tyre[28] – is, then, of much less explanatory value than the place occupied by this Platonic dialogue in the Neoplatonic school curriculum.

An important finding of recent research has been the extent to which Simplicius was influenced by his master and fellow-exile Damascius.[29] This does not mean than we will find, in the commentaries by Simplicius, lengthy expositions of Damascius' complex metaphysics of the Ineffable, the Second One, the One-which-is-Many and the Many-Which-are-One, from which arises the Unified (*to hênômenon*), which then gives rise, through a series of intelligible triads, to the nine levels of reality which Damascius discerned in Plato's *Parmenides*.[30] Given what we now know of Neoplatonic commentaries, we would not expect such doctrines, expounded at length in Damascius' treatise *On the First Principles* and in his *Commentary on the Parmenides*, to be set forth in the course of an exposition of works by Aristotle or Epictetus; Neoplatonic teachers did not attempt to explain ultimate reality to beginning philosophy students. Instead, Damascius' doctrines underlie Simplicius' work as a kind of *toile de fond*: they occasionally rise to the surface in the form of particularly abstruse passages, quotations, or allusions, but they are never pursued or made explicit. It was only after the student had digested Aristotle – Proclus took just over two years to accomplish this – and the introductory dialogues of Plato, that the ultimate truth – that, *grosso modo*, the metaphysical system of Damascius, slightly modified – would gradually be revealed to those of Simplicius' students who had shown the talent and tenacity to last long enough.

3. Simplicius' commentary on Aristotle's *Categories*

Simplicius' commentary on the *Categories* is a strangely composite entity. At the very outset, the author candidly tells us how he has written his work. He mentions most of those among his philosophical predecessors who have previously commented on the *Categories*: Themistius, Porphyry, Alexander of Aphrodisias, Herminus, Maximus, Boethos, Lucius and Nicostratus, Plotinus,[31] Porphyry again (in his lost *Commentary to Gedalius*), and finally the divine Iamblichus,[32] whose major accomplishments were adducing the writings of (Pseudo-)Archytas,[33] and introducing his 'intellective theory' everywhere he could. Indeed, writes Simplicius,

I myself came across some of these writings, and I made a copy, following Iamblichus' writings with as much care as I was capable of, often using the Philosopher's very words.[34]

Simplicius' commentary on the *Categories* is, then, at least to some degree, a copy of the (lost) commentary of Iamblichus on the same Aristotelian work. Shortly before this, however, Simplicius had told us that Iamblichus, in turn, had based himself very closely on Porphyry's (lost) *Commentary to Gedalius*, making a few corrections, additions and improvements along the way.[35] Thus, Simplicius' work turns out to be a copy of a copy of a (lost) original! Yet we know it was not merely that, for Simplicius occasionally adds his own judgments on Iamblichus' work, and elsewhere inserts bits of Damascian doctrine which can scarcely come from Iamblichus, who died more than two hundred years before Damascius' death.

After an interesting and historically valuable Preface,[36] in which he discusses the work of his predecessors, Simplicius goes on to reproduce the two schemata of questions which I. Hadot has shown are present in all the commentaries on the *Categories*. First comes a ten-point scheme[37] designed as an introduction to the philosophy of Aristotle, which addressed such questions as the classification of Aristotle's writings, the qualities required of a good teacher and a good student, etc. There then follows the traditional six-point introductory scheme to the *Categories*,[38] discussing the goal (*skopos*) of the treatise, its usefulness, its authenticity, its place in the Neoplatonic curriculum, the reason for its title, and its division into chapters. A final point discusses the question 'Under what part of Philosophy should the *Categories* be ranged?', the answer being 'logic'.[39]

Simplicius then proceeds, throughout more than 400 pages of Greek, to discuss Aristotle's text lemma by lemma. The composite nature of Simplicius' work can help to explain some of the more surprising characteristics of Simplicius' *Commentary on the Categories*. His usual procedure is to start from an objection or problem (Greek *aporia*), which he no doubt found attributed in his sources to the Stoico-Platonists Lucius or Nicostratus, or to the Peripatetics Boethos of Sidon and Alexander of Aphrodisias. Simplicius then passes in review the solutions of his various predecessors, and finally comes up with a solution (*lusis*), which may be due to Porphyry, Iamblichus, or Simplicius himself (who may, in turn, be relying on a lost commentary and/or oral instruction by Damascius). When Simplicius quoted or paraphrased an older text, the conventions of his time did not require him to announce the fact,[40] so that it is often next to impossible to tell when he is speaking in his own voice and when he is quoting some earlier authority. As a rule, however, we may assume that the more textually based, 'down-to-earth' solutions are due to Porphyry, while the occasional passages of densely-written metaphysical speculation are quotations or paraphrases – acknowledged or otherwise – from Iamblichus or Damascius.[41]

Given what we have learned about the determination of Neoplatonic commentaries by the text to be commented, we would expect a commentary on Aristotle's *Categories* – the first work studied in the division (logic) of the first author (Aristotle) to be read by prospective philosophers – to be relatively elementary. Simplicius' *Commentary* fits this description, but the operative term here is 'relatively'. While it does not show fundamental doctrinal differences with the other Late Neoplatonic commentaries on the *Categories* – those of Ammonius, Philoponus, Olympiodorus, David, and the Latin commentary of Boethius[42] – Simplicius' work does indulge in occasional flights of Iamblicho-Damascian metaphysics. One thinks, for example, of his discussion of the three-fold nature of the common,[43] or the passages mentioning 'essential participation' (*ousiôdês methexis*).[44] Such passages are perhaps to be explained by the fact that Simplicius' *Commentary* was actually composed and written down as a literary work, while the other Commentaries on the *Categories* – like the vast majority of the Neoplatonic Aristotelian commentaries – have come down to us in the form of students' notes.[45]

Overall, however, one gets the impression of thoughtful, scholarly care, as Simplicius attempts to integrate and assimilate some 800 years of philosophical commentary on the *Categories*. He compares manuscripts,[46] makes textual emendations,[47] and occasionally even goes so far as to correct his beloved Iamblichus.[48] All the reasons for reading Simplicius' commentary which we enumerated above thus still hold true: he provides us with information on the views of otherwise little-known ancient philosophers; helps us to comprehend the *Weltanschauung* of the Late Antique creators of the Scholastic tradition; and he can give us an improved understanding of Aristotle's text itself. Indeed, when one surveys contemporary philosophical debate about the *Categories*, one finds discussions about the following kinds of questions: What is the actual subject-matter of the *Categories*: words, things or concepts? Why does the treatise begin without a proper introduction, but plunge directly into a seemingly irrelevant discussion of synonyms, homonyms, and paronyms? What is the ontological status of the *differentia*? Whence did Aristotle derive his list of ten categories? It is interesting to learn from Simplicius that most of such issues had already, by the sixth century AD, been discussed for hundreds of years. Much contemporary 're-inventing of the wheel' could thus be avoided if modern philosophers were more familiar with the ancient exegetical tradition.

When listing the characteristics required of a good Aristotelian exegete, Simplicius writes:[49]

The worthy exegete of Aristotle's writings must not fall wholly short of the Philosopher's greatness of intellect (*megalonoia*). He must also be acquainted with everything the Philosopher has written, and must be versed in (*epistêmôn*) Aristotle's stylistic habits. His judgment must be impartial (*adekaston*), so that he may neither, out of superficial understanding, show to be unacceptable something that has been well said, nor, if some point should require examination, should he obstinately persist in trying to demonstrate that Aristotle is always and everywhere infallible, as if he had enrolled himself in the Philosopher's school.

On the whole, and if we make allowances for Simplicius' Neoplatonic program to harmonize the philosophies of Plato and Aristotle, it is fair to say that he fulfils these requisites quite admirably. This is perhaps why today – as was the case throughout the Middle Ages and the Renaissance – Simplicius' work continues to be the most widely read and studied of the Neoplatonic Commentaries on the *Categories*.

Notes

1. KRS, 1; 3. See the *Stellenregister von Hermann Diels, ergänzt von Walther Kranz*, in D-K vol. 3, 638-40.

2. *SVF* 216-17.

3. See P. Moraux 1973; 1984. See also the *Stellenregister* to F. Wehrli 1959, Heft X, 169-71. On Theophrastus, see now the *Index of Theophrastean Texts* in W.W. Fortenbaugh et al., 1993, vol. 2, 695-7.

4. On Archytas, see T.A. Szlezák 1972; and on Pseudo-Pythagorean writings in general, H. Thesleff 1965.

5. On Simplicius as a source for Speusippus, see the Index Locorum in L. Tarán 1981, 501-2. For Xenocrates, see the Indice delle Fonti in M. Isnardi Parente, 1982, 454.

6. See J.M. Dillon 1977, index s.v. 'Simplicius'.

7. On Simplicius as a source for Iamblichus, see J.M. Dillon 1973; B. Dalsgaard Larsen, 1972.

8. The Acts of this colloquium were published in I. Hadot 1987a.

9. Two volumes have appeared to date: I. Hadot 1990; C. Luna 1990.

10. On the pagan/Christian conflict as exemplified by Simplicius and John Philoponus, see Ph. Hoffmann 1987b.

11. On writing commentaries as a spiritual exercise in Antiquity, see Ph. Hoffmann, 1987a; I. Hadot 1996, ch. 3; M. Erler 1987. On Neoplatonic spirituality in general, see H.D. Saffrey 1990.

12. See I. Hadot 1987b; 1996, ch. 1

13. See Ph. Hoffmann 1987b.

14. This decree (= *Codex Justinianus*, I, 11, 10, § 2, p. 64 ed. Krüger; cf. *ibid.*, I, 5, 18, § 4, p. 57) has been the subject of much debate: see J.P. Lynch 1972, 165; J. Glucker 1978, 322-9; A. Cameron, 'The Last Days of the Academy at Athens', *Proceedings of the Cambridge Philosophical Society* 195

(1969), 7-29; 'La fin de l'Académie', in *Le Néoplatonisme, Colloques Interna-
tionaux du Centre National de la Recherche Scientifique, Sciences Humaines,
Royaumont 9-13 juin 1969*, Paris 1971, 281-90; H.J. Blumenthal, '529 and its
Sequel: What happened to the Academy?', *Byzantium* 48 (1978), 369-85.
Against the views of Cameron and Blumenthal, see I. Hadot 1978, 22ff.;
1987b, 7ff.; 1996, ch. 2. See also Paul Foulkes, 'Where was Simplicius?',
Journal of Hellenistic Studies, 1992, 112-43; S. van Riet, 'A propos de la
biographie de Simplicius', *Revue philosophique de Louvain* 89, 1991, 506-14;
Frans de Haas in De Haas-Fleet, *Simplicius: On Aristotle Categories 5-6*
(London & Ithaca NY, 2001), Introduction to ch. 5. See also n. 16 below.
    15. Agathias, *Historiarum libri quinque*, II, 30,3-31,4 ed. Keydell; 124,8-
126,10 ed. Costanza.
    16. cf. M. Tardieu 1986; 1987; 1991. [But for a number of important
objections to his hypothesis, see e.g. Lameer 1997, Gutas 1999, and esp. Luna
2001. (Ed.)]
    17. I. Hadot 1987b, 36, citing Ibn al-Nadîm, *Kitâb al-fihrist*, 7, 1, p. 248
ed. Flügel/Rodiger/Müller = vol. 2, p. 598 Dodge. Cf. H. Gätje 1982; F.E.
Peters 1968, 7.
    18. I. Hadot 1987b, 34-5; 1987c, *passim*.
    19. On what follows, see P. Hadot 1995, ch. 2: 'Philosophy, Exegesis, and
Creative Mistakes'.
    20. For the details of this curriculum, see I. Hadot, 1987d; 1990; 1991;
1992; L.G. Westerink 1990.
    21. See I. Hadot 1987b, 39; 1996, 3-7.
    22. See I. Hadot 1996. A second volume, containing French translation
and commentary, will be published within the next few years.
    23. Notably F. Bossier and C. Steel; cf. 'Priscianus Lydus en de "In de
anima" van Pseudo(?)-Simplicius', *Tijdschrift voor Philosophie* 34 (1972),
761-822 and C. Steel, Introduction to *'Simplicius': On Aristotle On the Soul
2.5-12*, published with Priscian in this series (London & Ithaca NY, 2000). I.
Hadot, who had initially tended – very hesitantly – to accept the hypothesis
of Bossier/Steel (cf. her review of their article in I. Hadot 1978, 193-202), now
leans towards restoring the authorship of the *In De Anima* to Simplicius; cf.
I. Hadot 1987b, 25-6 & n. 69; 1996, 5 & n. 12.
    24. This view was pioneered by Karl Praechter; cf. Praechter 1911; 1912;
1927.
    25. Most notably the late H.J. Blumenthal; L.G. Westerink was also of
this opinion, as was Ph. Merlan.
    26. Similar conclusions have been reached independently by A.D.R.
Sheppard; cf. 1980; 1987.
    27. The Neoplatonists in Alexandria may have had to come to an under-
standing with the powerful local Christian authorities. One suggestion by
H.D. Saffrey (*Revue des Études Greques* 67, 1954, 400-1) was that this
included restricting their teaching to Aristotle, whose doctrines were easier
to reconcile with Christianity than were those of Plato; cf. Praechter 1910,
151-4. But Westerink replied with counter-evidence (ch. 14 of Richard
Sorabji, ed. *Aristotle Transformed*). For a new suggestion see Richard Sorabji,
'Magical names and the fate of the Alexandrian Neoplatonist School', in
Andrew Smith, ed., *Proceedings of the conference on Neoplatonism and
Society*, Dublin, forthcoming.
    28. Edited and attributed – no doubt correctly – to Porphyry by P. Hadot
1968.
    29. See I. Hadot 1978; 1996, ch. 4; Ph. Hoffmann 1994.

30. For accounts of the philosophy of Damascius, cf., besides the works cited in the previous note, J. Combès, 'Introduction' to *Damascius, Traité des Premiers Principes, vol. 1: De l'Ineffable et de l'Un, texte établi par L.G. Westerink et traduit par J. Combès*, Paris: Les Belles Lettres, 1986, ix-lxxii.

31. Simplicius, like Dexippus, reproduces many of the views expounded by Plotinus in his treatises *On the Genera of Being* (= *Ennead* VI,1-3), but in such a distorted form that Paul Henry was led to believe Simplicius was drawing on Plotinus' *ungeschriebene Lehre*. It seems more likely that Simplicius is quoting Plotinus at second- or third-hand, via the lost commentary *Ad Gedalium* of Porphyry; cf. P. Hadot 1974.

32. Simplicius appears to have inherited his fondness for Iamblichus from Damascius; see Simplicius *In Phys.* vol. 1, 795,11-17 Diels: 'All the philosophers from Proclus down to about my time followed Proclus ... except ... our Damascius ... Damascius, because of his love of hard work and his sympathy for Iamblichus, did not hesitate to reconsider many of Proclus' dogmas'.

33. See n. 4 above. Like Iamblichus, Simplicius was convinced that Aristotle had plagiarized the *Categories* from a work by Plato's Pythagorean acquaintance Archytas of Tarentum. Modern research has shown this work to be a Hellenistic forgery.

34. Simpl. *In Cat.*, 3,2-4 Kalbfleisch.

35. *ibid.* 2,10-15.

36. *ibid.* 1,3-3,7.

37. *ibid.* 3,18-9,3.

38. *ibid.* 9,4-20,12.

39. On this section of Simplicius' commentary, and the question of whether logic was a part or merely an instrument (*organon*) of philosophy, see P. Hadot, *Appendice* I, in I. Hadot, 1990, 185-8.

40. It would be anachronistic to speak of 'plagiarism' here: in late Antiquity, it was customary to cite one's main source only where one disagreed with it.

41. On the different methodological approaches of Porphyry and Iamblichus, see J. Pépin 1974; J. Dillon 1997.

42. I omit from this list Porphyry's minor *Commentary by Questions and Responses* (ed. A. Busse, *CAG* 4.1 [1887]; English translation in this series by S. Strange, London & Ithaca NY, 1992), as well as the commentary by Dexippus (ed. A. Busse, *CAG* 4.2 [1888]; English translation in this series by J. Dillon, London & Ithaca NY, 1990). Both of these works, written in dialogue form, contain peculiarities of form and content largely attributable to their role as elementary introductions.

43. Simpl. *In Cat.* 83,1ff. Kalbfleisch.

44. Simpl. *In Cat.* 254,3ff.; 288,34ff. Kalbfleisch. On these passages and their Damascian origin, see I. Hadot 1996, 77ff.

45. The only other Commentary which was not 'taken down by dictation' (*apo phonês*) would seem to be Ammonius *In De Interpretatione*, ed. A. Busse (= *CAG* 4.5), Berlin, 1897. This commentary, similar in density and difficulty to Simplicius' *In Cat.*, has recently been translated in this series by David Blank (London & Ithaca NY, 1996).

46. e.g. 34,29ff. Kalbfleisch.

47. Simplicius' proposed emendation (88,24ff. Kalbfleisch) of Aristotle *Categories* 5, 2b6f., was accepted by all modern editors except Minio-Paluello;

see the *apparatus criticus* to the latter's text in the series Oxford Classical Texts (Clarendon Press, 1949, 7).

   48. At 41,22ff. Kalbfleisch, for instance, Simplicius corrects Iamblichus' faulty reading of Alexander, and he even confesses (107,5ff.), that he cannot understand him.

   49. 7,23-8 Kalbfleisch.

Textual Emendations

Simplicius
On Aristotle Categories 1-4

Translation

Simplicius' Commentary on
Aristotle's *Categories*

Many authors have set forth many speculations on Aristotle's book of *Categories*. This is so not only because it is the prologue to the whole of philosophy (since it is the beginning of the study of logic, and logic, in turn, is rightly taken up prior to the whole of philosophy[1]), but also because the *Categories* is, in a sense, about the first principles (*arkhai*), as we shall see in our discussion of the goal (*skopos*).[2]

Different authors have carried out studies of this book from different standpoints. Some, like the eloquent Themistius,[3] and whoever else was like him, have been anxious only to make the actual wording (*lexis*) itself more clear; others strove concisely to unveil the concepts (*ennoiai*) proposed by Aristotle as well, as Porphyry did in his commentary by questions and responses.[4] Others, in addition to this, touched at least moderately upon specific subjects of inquiry (*zêtêmata*),[5] as was the case with Alexander of Aphrodisias,[6] Herminus,[7] and other such men. In this latter group I also place Maximus,[8] who, although a student of Aidesius,[9] the student of Iamblichus, concurred with Alexander on almost every point in his *Commentary on the Categories*.[10] Some commentators, however, also applied deeper thoughts to the work, as did the admirable Boethus.[11] Others were content to write only puzzles (*aporiai*)[12] against what is said: this is what Lucius[13] did, and after him Nicostratus,[14] who appropriated the considerations of Lucius. These two vied with each other in providing objections (*enstaseis*) to nearly everything said in the book, and they did not go about their task with respect, but rather in a violent and shameless manner. Nevertheless, we must be grateful to them, too, both because the puzzles they set forward were, for the most part, substantial, and because they provided their successors with starting-points both for the resolution of the puzzles, and for the development of many other excellent theories.[15]

After these, the great Plotinus applied the most substantial examinations to the book of the *Categories*, in three entire books entitled *On the Genera of Being*.[16]

After these men it was Porphyry, cause of all that is good for us, who composed – not without labour – a complete explanation of the book, containing the resolution of all objections, in seven books addressed to Gedalius.[17] He also included in this work an account of

1,5

10

15

20

2,1

5

many of the doctrines of the Stoics, in so far as they were dealing with the same themes.[18]

After Porphyry, the divine Iamblichus[19] also devoted a lengthy
10   treatise to this book. For the most part, he followed Porphyry right
down to the letter, but he picked out some things and articulated them
in order to make them more clear. At the same time, he contracted the
scholastic long-windedness Porphyry had used against the objections;
and he applied his Intellective Theory[20] everywhere, to almost all of
the chapter-headings. In addition, he also added something else to his
15   writing which was useful: for even before Aristotle, the Pythagorean
Archytas, in the book he entitled *On the All*, had already divided the
primary genera into ten, and had clearly explained, with the help of
examples, their distinctive tokens (*gnôrismata*), and had indicated
the order (*taxis*) they occupy with regard to one another, and the
specific differences of each [genus], as well as their common and
20   individual properties.[21] Iamblichus, then, adduced the considerations
of Archytas in the appropriate places, unfolding that which had been
intellectively concentrated,[22] and demonstrating their accord with the
doctrines of Aristotle. If there happened to be anything discordant
between them – there are few such instances[23] – then he brought
these differences, too, to the attention of lovers of knowledge; nor did
he leave the cause of the discord unexamined. Rightly so, for it is
25   obvious that Aristotle always wants to remain faithful to Archytas.[24]

Dexippus, the student of Iamblichus, also gave a concise explanation of Aristotle's book,[25] but he proposed mainly to resolve the
problems (*aporias*) raised by Plotinus, which he set forth in dialogue
form. Dexippus, however, added virtually nothing to the considerations of Porphyry and Iamblichus. Since, then, there has been so
30   much interest in the *Categories* on the part of the most illustrious
philosophers, I should straight away appear ridiculous for having
dared to have written something myself as well, unless I were to show
3,1   that the cause of my audacity was reasonable. Now, I have read[26]
some of the aforementioned writings,[27] and, following Iamblichus as
carefully as possible, I wrote them down, often even using the philosopher's very words.

My goal (*skopos*) in making this copy was, in the first place, to
5   obtain, through the act of writing, as accurate a comprehension
(*katanoêsis*) as possible of what had been said.[28] At the same time, I
wished to reduce this man's lofty spirit, inaccessible to the common
people, until it was more clear and commensurate [with the common
understanding].[29] Thirdly, I also wanted to reduce somewhat the vast
multitude of variegated writings; not, as the most philosophical Syri-
10   anus did, to an absolute minimum,[30] but as far as was compatible
while leaving out nothing necessary.

If I, too, have been able to add something, then I owe gratitude to
these men for this as well, after the gods; for it was guided[31] by them

that I have added the occasional problem (*aporia*) of some value, or some articulation worthy of what has been said which is worthy of the rational principle *logos*.[32] Nevertheless, I advise my readers never to disdain the writings especially of Porphyry and Iamblichus in favour of these little scholia, but rather, if at all, to use them as an introduc- 15 tion and training[33] for a clearer comprehension of what those men have said.

Since the *Categories* is the first book of Aristotle's which we encoun-ter,[34] and Aristotle's school – the so-called Peripatetic – is one of the schools of philosophy, we ought first to say how and in how many ways the philosophical schools received their appellations. Secondly, what 20 is the division of the Aristotelian writings, so that the class to which we shall assign the present work shall be clear. Third, whence should one begin [the study of] Aristotle's writings? Fourth, what is the goal of Aristotle's philosophy? Fifth, which things lead us towards this goal? Sixth, what is the form[35] of the Aristotelian writings? Seventh, 25 why did the Philosopher practise obscurity? Eighth, what must the exegete of accounts (*logoi*) such as these be like? Ninth, what kind of student should be accepted? Tenth, in the case of each Aristotelian treatise, how many main points (*kephalaia*) should be taken up, which are they, and for what reason?

Now, the philosophical schools are named in seven different ways:[36] 30
1. After the founder of the school, like the Pythagoreans or the Platonists;[37] 2. or after the native land of the head of the school;[38] thus 4,1 the followers of Aristippus are called Cyrenaics,[39] the followers of Euclides[40] are called Megarians, and the followers of Xenophanes and Parmenides are called Eleatics;[41] 3. or after the place in which they spent their time philosophizing, as the Academics and the Stoics;[42] 4. or after some incidental activity, like the Peripatetics;[43] 5. or after the criterion they used while philosophizing,[44] as the followers of Pyrrho 5 are called *Ephektikoi*;[45] 6. or after the goal which they propose for their philosophy, as the Epicureans are [called] Hedonists;[46] 7. After their form of life, like the Cynics;[47] for the goal at which they aim is one thing, and another is their form of practising it (*epitêdeusis*). For instance, it was not through pleasure that the Epicureans used to hunt after pleasure, but rather through effort and self-mastery (*dia ponôn malista kai enkrateias*).

Of the Aristotelian writings,[48] some are particular (*merika*),[49] like 10 the *Letters* written to one individual about some particular reality,[50] while others are general (*katholou*).[51] Still others are intermediary,[52] like the investigations on plants and on animals, which are about things which are not entirely particular, since they are about the species (*eidê*) of animals. For the moment, however, let the particular and intermediary works remain undivided.[53]

Of the general works, those which the Philosopher composed in 15 order to remind himself of certain things, and in order to carry out further scrutiny, are hypomnematic;[54] and of these, some are uniform (*monoeidê*), as if to remind about one particular thing, while others are manifold (*poikila*),[55] as being about many things. Now, the hypomnematic writings do not quite seem worthy of attention; this is why the Philosopher's doctrines do not receive any confirmation from them. Alexander, however, says that the hypomnematic writings were

20   put together at random, and do not relate to one goal (*skopos*); that is why, he says, the others are said to be syntagmatic[56] in contradistinction to these writings.

Of syntagmatic writings, some are in dialogue form,[57] while in others the author speaks in his own name (*autoprosôpa*).[58] Of autoprosopic writings, some are theoretical (*theôrêtika*), others practical (*praktika*), and others instrumental (*organika*). Of theoretical writings, some are theological (*theologika*), like the *Metaphysics*, while others have to do with the study of nature (*phusiologika*), like the

25   *Physics* and the treatises following upon the *Physics*.[59] Still others are mathematical, such as the geometrical and mechanical books he wrote.

Of the practical works, some are ethical, such as the *Nicomachean*, the *Eudemian*, and the so-called '*Great*' *Ethics*.[60] Others are economic, and still others are political, like the discourses (*logoi*) entitled *Economics* and *Politics*.[61] Of instrumental works,[62] some are about the demonstrative method itself, while others are about what precedes it,

30   like the *Prior Analytics*, *De Interpretatione*, and the *Categories*. Still

5,1   others are about those things that take on the appearance of demonstrations,[63] like the *Topics*, the *Sophistical Refutations*, and the *Rhetorical Arts*. This, then, is the more complete (*holoskherestera*) division of Aristotle's writings.

About the third [point], we should say where one should begin [the study of] Aristotle's writings,[64] for the discussion of this follows logically after the division. Now, some say one should begin with the

5   instrumental writings,[65] because they create within us the faculty of judgement (*to diakrinein*): in actions, between good and evil; and in knowledge, between the true and the false. It is thus necessary that practical and epistemological (*gnôstika*) writings be preceded by those which provide us with the faculty of judgement. Moreover, if knowledge of instruments obviously comes first in the other arts as well,

10   such as building, metal-working, and even medicine, how much more is this the case with philosophy, which undertakes to transmit everything with a demonstration (*apodeixis*), and which entrusts our lives and our knowledge to demonstration alone? If, then, we encounter practical or theoretical discourses (*logoi*) without demonstration, how can we avoid having the same thing happen to us as occurred to those

15   who went to Circe without the *môly* of Hermes, and being bewitched by what each person says in a convincing manner?[66]

Some instruct us to begin with the ethical writings[67] for they say that instruments (*ta organa*)[68] belong to the category of intermediary things,[69] and it is possible to use them either well or badly, as is illustrated by the majority of Sophists and rhetoricians. Thus, people who are going to use instruments first have need of a life which is moderately prepared, for the knowledge of philosophy is not like that of architecture or navigation; rather, it has to do with life itself   20 (*zôtikê*). We first require the training which comes from the ethical works,[70] in which we receive ethical teachings not demonstratively, but in conformity with correct opinion,[71] in accordance with the natural innate concepts we have concerning beings.[72] If Aristotle's *Ethics* were merely hortatory and undemonstrated catechisms,[73] of the kind that used often to be uttered by the Pythagoreans,[74] it would   25 be correct to start with them and use them to give preliminary training to our characters.[75] If, however, Aristotle handed down these things, too, by means the most scientific of divisions and demonstrations, how could we hope to make any progress by approaching these writings without the demonstrative methods? Perhaps, then, some previous ethical instruction *is* necessary after all, but it should not be transmitted by means of Aristotle's ethical writings.[76] Rather, [such   6,1 instruction should be provided] through unwritten habituation[77] and non-technical exhortations, which rectify our characters by means both written and unwritten.[78] It is only then that we shall need the logical and demonstrative method.[79] After such studies, we shall be capable of comprehending scientific discourses (*logoi*) about ethics, as well as those pertaining to the theory of beings, in a scientific way.   5

The fourth point of those put forward was to discover the goal of Aristotle's philosophy,[80] for from the goal, we shall clearly also discern the venerability (*to semnon*) of his philosophy. Now, the goal of this man's philosophy, too, is, with regard to character, perfection by means of the virtues; with regard to knowledge, the ascent (*anadromê*) towards the one principle of all things.[81] For Aristotle   10 knew this Principle scientifically (*epistêmonikôs*), and he was awestruck[82] and cried out with a clear voice, 'The rule of many is not good!'[83] The goal common to both is the most complete happiness which can befall mankind. When it came to describing this happiness, Aristotle did not yield to any of the most eminent philosophers; nor did he think it right that one who had risen (*anadramonta*) to such happiness should even be called a man, but a god. Such are Aristotle's lofty words in the last part of the *Nicomachean Ethics*.[84]   15

What leads us to such a goal are all the Philosopher's writings.[85] Some of his works prepare for the method of demonstration, others adorn our characters (*êthê*) by means of virtue; while still others lead our [faculty of] knowledge, through [the study of] natural things, on up to that which is above nature.

The type of Aristotle's expression[86] is condensed, intellective, and rapid-fire,[87] with regard both to content and to style: either he ad-

20   duces the solution to a given problem (*aporia*) immediately; or else he
joins together several problems (*aporiai*) and resolves them all with
a single solution, and a concise one at that. Yet he never intentionally
departs from vividness (*tês enargeias*).[88] Vividness used for persuasion is of two kinds: one which comes from the intellect, and one which
comes from sensation. Now, since he is conversing with people living
on the level of sensation, he prefers that vividness which derives from
sensation. This is why his demonstrations have such constraining
25   force, which is such that even if, because of some unfortunate precon-
ceptions, one is not persuaded [by his arguments], he is never the less
obliged to hold his peace.

[Aristotle] always refuses to deviate from nature; on the contrary,
he considers even things which are above nature according to their
relation to nature, just as, by contrast, the divine Plato, according to
Pythagorean usage, examines even natural things insofar as they
30   participate in the things above nature.[89]

To be sure, unlike some of his predecessors, Aristotle did not
make use of myths or of symbolic riddles,[90] but preferred obscurity
(*asapheia*) to all other kinds of veiling.

7,1   Now, our line of inquiry (*logos*) was seeking for the reason for this
[obscurity], too, in the context of the seventh of the things set forth
previously, and it has nicely come across the solution spontaneously.[91]
For the more ancient [philosophers] considered that they should not,
by using obvious clarity, expose their wisdom to the superficial apprehension of shoemakers,[92] thus some hid their wisdom by myths, and
5   others by symbols, as the more ineffable sacred objects of temples
are hidden by curtains.[93] Aristotle, for his part, preferred obscurity
(*asapheia*); perhaps because he rejected the indeterminate hidden
meaning (*huponoia*) of myths and symbols – such things can, after all,
easily be understood differently by each interpreter – or perhaps also
because he supposed such obscurity was better training (*gumn-
astikôteron*) for quick-wittedness.[94]

10   Nevertheless, Aristotle accomplished what he set out to do: considering that it was not worthwhile to offer even mythical guidance
(*psukhagôgia*) to the frivolous, he discouraged them to such an extent
that he gained the reputation of being the most obscure of all writ-
ers.[95] But everyone who can follow a line of argument (*logos*) even
passably well knows that it was not owing to some weakness in
reasoning (*logos*) that Aristotle's works were afflicted with obscurity.
Indeed, Aristotle's style (*hermêneia*) displays a great deal of literary
15   power, to the extent that he could often, in a few syllables, transmit
more than one could teach in entire periods. This is evident from those
writings in which he wanted to teach as clearly as possible, as for
example in the *Meteorologica*, the *Topics*, and in that version of the
Constitutions which is genuinely by Aristotle. Because of the more
commonplace character of their theories, he was able to report them

with more clarity. That Aristotle was capable of expressing himself clearly is especially shown by the style (*kharaktêr*) of his *Letters*. As is appropriate for letters, they give a plausible reproduction of famil- 20 iar conversation, and none of the known authors comes close to Aristotle as far as epistolary style is concerned.

The worthy exegete of Aristotle's writings[96] must not fall wholly short of the latter's greatness of intellect (*megalonoia*). He must also have experience of everything the Philosopher has written, and must be a connoisseur (*epistêmôn*) of Aristotle's stylistic habits. His judge- 25 ment must be impartial (*adekaston*), so that he may neither, out of misplaced zeal, seek to prove something well said to be unsatisfactory, nor, if some point should require attention, should he obstinately persist in trying to demonstrate that [Aristotle] is always and every- where infallible, as if he had enrolled himself in the Philosopher's school. [The good exegete] must, I believe, not convict the philo- 30 sophers of discordance by looking only at the letter (*lexis*) of what [Aristotle] says against Plato; but he must look towards the spirit (*nous*), and track down (*anikhneuein*) the harmony which reigns between them on the majority of points.[97]

The auditor[98] must also be sufficiently good (*kalos*) and virtuous (*spoudaios*),[99] and above all he must frequently carry out, both by 8,1 himself and in the company of others as avid for learning (*phi- lomathoi*) as himself, the in-depth examination of Aristotelian concepts (*noêmata*).[100] He must, however, guard against disputatious twaddle,[101] into which many of those who frequent Aristotle tend to fall. Whereas the Philosopher endeavours to demonstrate everything by means of the irrefutable definitions of science, these smart- alecks[102] accustom themselves to contradict even what is obvious, blinding the eye of their souls.[103] Against such people, it is enough to 5 speak Aristotle's words: to wit, they need either sensation (*aisthêsis*), or punishment.[104] If they are being argumentative without having paid attention, it is perception they need. If, however, they *have* paid attention to the text, but are trying to show off their discursive power, it is punishment they need.

Finally, the tenth of the matters set forth[105] was: how many, and of what kind, are the preliminary points (*kephalaia*) we must articulate 10 prior to the study of each Aristotelian treatise. They are the following: the goal (*skopos*), the usefulness, the reason for the title, its place in the order of reading,[106] whether the book is a genuine work of the Philosopher, its division into chapters. It may also not be inappropri- ate to inquire under what part of his philosophy the work is placed.[107]

For the goal,[108] once correctly identified, defines and rectifies our thought (*dianoia*), so that we are not vainly transported about in 15 every direction,[109] but refer everything to it.

The work's usefulness,[110] once it has come to light, makes us more zealous and enthusiastic.[111] The reason for the work's title, when it

happens to be clear, is not an obstacle;[112] and if it is made clear
beforehand,[113] it reinforces the goal. As for authenticity[114] – which, it
seems to me, ought to be closely examined (*basanizesthai*) before any
other question – it is necessarily taken up beforehand;[115] for we are
20   not left unaffected by the renown of an author's personality.[116] Nor is
this absurd; since we are not totally prepared for discerning the truth,
we are satisfied, in some matters, to follow the authority of the great.
For many spurious books were also written, especially at that time
when many kings were anxious to improve their libraries, and used
to buy hard-to-find (*apexenômena*) books[117] at high prices. The divi-
25   sion of books into chapters (*kephalaia*), which cuts up [a work], as it
were, according to its articulations, imitates the anatomical theory [in
use] among doctors.[118] Just as anatomy uses dissection to discover the
usefulness which each limb contributes to the whole, providing us
with more accurate knowledge of the composite whole by laying bare
the simple [parts], so dividing a work brings the whole better into
30   view, and presents the usefulness of each element towards the overall
goal. [Finally], showing under which part [of philosophy] the work is
reduced exhibits the organization of the part and the whole.

    It is to be noted, however, that all these things do not always
9,1   require articulation, for often, the usefulness becomes clear at the
same time as the goal, while the title is obvious to everyone, as [in the
case of] the *On the Soul*.[119] Authenticity, for its part, does not need to
be established in every case, but in general only when there is some
starting-point for controversy.

    Let us examine, then, each of the proposed preliminary points in
5   the case of the present book. Let us first consider what is the goal
(*skopos*), since this point has obviously been a point of contention even
among the most distinguished.[120] It is clear at the outset that it is
about some ten simple things, which, since they are most universal
(*holikôtata*), they call 'genera' (*genê*). Now, some say that they are
words (*phônai*), and that the goal (*skopos*) is about simple words, and
10   that it is the first part of logic. Just as the book on propositions[121] is
about composite words, but not about realities (*pragmata*), so this
[book], being about the parts of the proposition,[122] would be about
words. Moreover, Aristotle begins his discussion (*logos*) with the
words: 'Of things that are said, some are said in combination, others
are said without combination'[123] and again: 'Of things said with no
combination, each signifies either substance …',[124] as if the goal
15   (*prothesis*) were about significant words. After enumerating the ten
genera, he says: 'None of the aforementioned is said by itself in any
affirmation, but it is by the combination of these with one another
that an affirmation comes about'.[125] For it is the combination of words
(*phônai*), not of realities, that becomes an affirmation.[126]

20   Others, however,[127] do not accept this goal (*skopos*). It does not,
they say, pertain to the philosopher to theorize about words, but

rather to the grammarian, who investigates their modifications,[128] configurations, and changes in word-endings,[129] as well as their proper usages (*kuriotêtes*) and their types.[130] They say the goal (*skopos*) is about the very beings which are signified by words; and that these are what is said (*to legomenon*). These critics also bring forth Aristotle as a witness, when he says 'of beings, some are said of some substrate',[131] as if the division was about beings, and again: 'substance is that which is so called in the strictest sense, primarily, and most of all',[132] so that the discussion (*logos*) is about existent substance and the other beings.

In opposition to these considerations too, however, is [the fact that] the present book is a part of the study of logic, whereas to occupy oneself with beings *qua* beings is to engage in that philosophy which is metaphysical, and in general primary.

Others[133] say that the goal (*skopos*) is neither about significant words nor about signified realities, but rather about simple notions (*noêmata*). For if, they say, the discussion (*logos*) in the [*Categories*] is about the ten genera, and the latter are posterior and conceptual,[134] then the discussion is about notions. Moreover, Aristotle has stated clearly[135] that it is about things said, and things said and 'sayables' (*lekta*)[136] are notions, as was also the view of the Stoics.[137] These people, however, should have considered that to speak about notions *qua* notions does not pertain to the study of logic, but rather to that of the soul.[138] Of these people, each one had an imperfect grasp of the goal (*skopos*), and this is why they all call on Aristotle as a witness with, so to speak, partial justification; they accuse each other with just cause, and are, in turn, justly called to account themselves. Let us, however, also consider those who had a more complete grasp [of the goal], among the foremost of whom, in my view, was Alexander of Aphrodisias, who said that this book is the principle (*arkhê*) of the study of logic. 'Since,' he says, 'speech (*logos*) signifies by virtue of the fact that its primary parts are significant.[139] Now, because [Aristotle] wanted to indicate what these notions (*noêmata*) were which are signified by the primary and simple parts of speech, he carries out a division (*diairesis*) of being, not into individuals – for these are uncircumscribable (*aperilêpta*) and unknowable,[140] owing to their multiplicity and the fact that they undergo all kinds of changes. Instead, he divided [being] into these ten highest genera, which he called "categories", since they are most generic and, while they themselves do not act as the substrate for any other thing, they are predicated of the others. Thus, the goal (*skopos*) would be about the simple and most generic parts of speech which signify simple realities, and the simple notions which exist in conjunction with these simple realities.' Alexander of Aigai[141] had also arrived at same opinion. Porphyry,[142] for his part, both in his [commentary] *To Gedalius* and in his [commentary] *By Questions and Answers,* says that the

goal (*skopos*) of the book is about predicates. These are simple words
significant of realities, *qua* significant, and not *qua* simple expressions. For *qua* expressions, they have other fields of study, which are
dealt with by Theophrastus in his work on the elements of speech,[143]
25   as well as by his followers, who wrote [on such topics as] whether
nouns and verbs are the [sole] elements of speech, or whether articles,
conjunctions, and other such things are also – these, too, are parts of
the vocabulary (*lexis*), but the parts of speech (*logos*) are nouns and
verbs.[144] [They also wrote on] what are literal and metaphorical
expressions, and what are their modifications (*pathê*); for instance,
what is apocope[145] and aphaeresis;[146] what are the simple and compound [expressions], quasi-compound expressions,[147] and all such
30   things; and whatever has been said about styles (*ideai*): what is
clarity (*to saphes*) in expressions, what is majesty (*to megaloprepes*),
11,1   the agreeable (*to hêdu*), and the persuasive (*to pithanon*).[148]

Insofar as an expression is significant, however, it is defined in
accordance with the genera of beings. An expression (*lexis*) is called a
'category' as applied (*agoreuomenê*) to a reality,[149] whereas the reality
(*pragma*) is called a predicate (*katêgorêma*). Now, a category is either
a reality taken together with the expression which signifies it, or the
5   signifying expression, in so far as it is significant; in either case, the
category has something to do with realities (*pragmata*) as well. But
since particular things are infinite[150] and incomprehensible, Aristotle
reduced the infinite particulars to ten genera, having concentrated all
the substances together into one highest substance. The expression
(*lexis*) which signifies this highest substance is 'substance itself' (*autê
hê ousia*), which is a symbol of the substance found within beings,
whether this substance is something substantially existent (*hupo-
10   stasis*), or whether it subsists merely as far as [the level of] our
conceptions (*akhri epinoias*). This makes no difference for predication, because it is not *qua* having substantive existence that realities
are indicated by the category, but insofar as they are conceived of
(*epinoeitai*), either as beings or as if they were beings. Likewise, when
individual quantifieds are referred to the most generic Quantified,
there comes about another category, the highest expression (*lexis*) of
'the quantified', which is said of (*agoreuomenê kata*) the highest
15   reality (*pragma*). The same for the qualified (*to poion*). Another genus
is [that of the] relative (*to pros ti*), under which are referred all those
things which are disposed in a certain way towards something else,
and there is another category: that of the expression (*lexis*) 'relative'
(*pros ti*), under which are 'double' and 'half', 'slave' and 'master',
'father', 'son', and things such as these. 'Sitting', 'standing', and 'lying
down' make up another genus, that of 'posture' (*to keisthai*). 'Being
clothed' and 'being armed' are referred under 'having' (*to ekhein*),
20   while 'in the Lyceum' and 'in the Academy'[151] are under the single
genus of 'where' (*pou*). 'When' (*pote*) is another genus, which contains

the parts and species of time. 'Cutting' and 'burning' are in [the category of] 'doing' (*to poiein*), just as 'being cut' and 'being burned' are in 'being affected' (*to paskhein*).

Porphyry also adds the remarks of Boethus, which are full of sharp-wittedness (*ankhinoia*) and tend in the same direction as what has been said. He too says that with regard to nouns and verbs, the division takes place as far as the elements of speech (*logos*), but according to the categories the division takes place in so far as expressions (*lexeis*) have a relation (*skhesis*) to beings, since they are significant of the latter. 'This,' he says, 'is the reason why conjunctions (*sundesmoi*), although they are to be found within the vocabulary (*lexis*), fall outside of the categories. For they do not indicate any being, not substance, nor the qualified, nor anything of the kind'.[152] It is thus clear from what has been said that these men do not define the goal (*skopos*) as being about mere words (*phônai*), nor about beings themselves in so far as they are beings, nor about notions (*noêmata*) alone. Instead, because it is a prelude to the study of logic,[153] [the *Categories*] is about simple words (*phônai*) and expressions (*lexeis*); but [it deals with these] *qua* significant of primary and simple beings, and not in so far as they decline[154] or are transformed in order to accord[155] [with certain words], or undergo such-and-such modifications (*pathê*) and have such-and-such forms (*ideai*),[156] all of which the domain of the investigation of expressions *qua* expressions. It is clear, however, that if [the goal of the *Categories*] is about expressions insofar as they signify, it is necessary that the signified realities (*pragmata*) and the notions (*noêmata*) which come about in accordance with significations also be involved. This is why [Aristotle] teaches us what each expression signifies, and defines realities in accordance with each category. Moreover, he uses the same division both here, where the goal (*skopos*) is primarily about significant expressions, and in the *Metaphysics*, where he teaches about beings *qua* beings.[157] His procedure is similar in his logical works, for instance the *Topics*[158] and in the *Nicomachean Ethics*,[159] and in his other treatises, he uses the same division of the primary genera into these ten. This is because the division is the same everywhere, but it is taken here with regard to significant expressions, in a manner appropriate to the study of logic, whereas elsewhere it is taken in accordance with the substantial existence (*hupostasis*) of beings, in a manner appropriate to the theory of beings. For neither are significant expressions wholly separate from the nature of beings, nor are beings detached from the names which are naturally suited to signify them. Nor, finally, are notions extraneous to the nature of the other two; for these three things were previously one, and became differentiated[160] later. For Intellect, being identical with realities and with intellection,[161] possesses as one both beings and the notions of them,

25

30

35
12,1

5

10

15

by virtue of its undifferentiated unity,[162] and there [*sc.* in the intelligible world] there is no need for language.[163]

As for the soul, when it is converted towards the Intellect, it possesses the same things [*sc.* as the Intellect] in a secondary way, for
20 then the rational principles (*logoi*) within it are not only cognitive, but generative. Once, however, the soul has departed from there [*sc.* the intelligible world], it also separates the formulae (*logoi*) within itself from beings, thereby converting them into images instead of prototypes, and it introduces a distance between intellection and realities. This is all the more true, the further the soul has departed from its similarity to the Intellect, and it is henceforth content to project
25 (*proballesthai*) notions which are consonant with realities.

When, however, the soul has fallen into the realm of becoming, it is filled with forgetfulness,[164] and requires sight and hearing in order to be able to recollect.[165] For the soul needs someone who has already beheld the truth,[166] who, by means of language (*phônê*) uttered forth from the concept (*ennoia*), also moves the concept within [the soul of the student], which had until then grown cold.[167] This, then, is how the need for language (*phônê*) came about: on the one hand, it strives immediately to assimilate itself to notions (*noêmata*), while, on the
30 other, by means of them it adjusts to realities and becomes of one nature with them, in order that words (*phônai*) might not be spoken in vain – as in the case of 'blituri' – but might rather set in motion within the listener those [notions] which are similar to the kinetic notions.[168] For intellections (*noêseis*) which proceed forth from other
13,1 intellections[169] also set in motion immediately, and they join the learner's notions to those of the teacher, by becoming intermediaries (*mesotêtes*) between the two. When intellections are set in motion in an appropriate way, they adjust themselves to realities, and thus there comes about the knowledge of beings, and the soul's spontaneous *erôs*[170] is fulfiled.

5 Language (*phônê*) is, moreover, the limit of psychic activity, and it pertains to limits to convert things towards their principles. Therefore, language takes those souls which have departed from the Intellect and from beings, and have become distinguished from one another, and gathers them together into unanimity of thought (*homonoia*); it makes them adjust to realities, sends them back up to the Intellect, and prepares them not only to wish to be without language (*aphônoi*), but to wish no longer even to have concepts (*ennoiai*) which
10 are other then realities. Thus, the soul has particularized (*emerisen*) those things which were pre-contained in a state of unity within the Intellect, yet not without maintaining, even in their state of division, their mutual connection (*allêloukhia*).

It is thus clear from the preceding considerations that the goal (*skopos*) [of the *Categories*], appropriate to the study of logic, is about simple, primary, and generic words (*phônai*), in so far as they are

significant of beings. Instruction is, at any rate, also given about the
realities which are signified by them, and about notions (*noêmata*), in   15
so far as it is realities that are signified by words.[171] This is also the
view of the Alexanders,[172] Herminus, Boethus, and Porphyry; it was
seconded by the divine Iamblichus, clarified by Syrianus, and accepted by our teachers.[173]

Since it has been shown that the goal (*skopos*) is about words
(*phônai*), but some words are simple and others compound, it is about
simple, primary words which signify the primary and most generic of   20
beings by means of simple, primary notions.[174] Now, the Pythagoreans
gathered together the simple entities into the decade, as was taught
by Archytas, with whom Plato, too, was acquainted, in his book *On
the Universal Formulae* (*Logoi*). Aristotle, too, followed him right
down to the names [he gave to his categories]; according to some
people, the only point at which Aristotle deviated [from Archytas] is
that he did not take into consideration the One, which contains the   25
ten [categories], and that he rejects the natural character of names.[175]

Instruction about these things is useful for the introduction both to
the whole of philosophy, and to the study of logic. For it is clear that
simple things are suitable for elementary teaching (*stoikheiôsis*).
Thus it is that geometers start with what is more simple: they first
teach about triangles and squares, and then about pentagons and the   30
following polygons. Those who devote their studies to number, for   14,1
their part, [begin by teaching] what is odd and what is even, and thus
they progress to [teaching] what are the even/odd and odd/even
numbers.[176] With regard to the study of logic, that beginning from the
simplest utterances is useful will be clear from the following considerations. Theory and practice (*praxis*) proceed in opposite directions: 5
for theory begins with the end (*telos*), and proceeds along its way as
far as the starting-point (*arkhê*), while practice proceeds from the
starting-point as far as the end, as in the case of a house. Theory
immediately conceives the need for the house, through which it exists:
it serves as a shelter from winds, storms, and burning heat. Starting
from the end, then, and theorizing as to how it might be brought
about, theory discovers that it is impossible to put up a shelter   10
without walls, and that walls cannot be established without foundations. Even these, however, cannot be laid until the earth is dug up,
and this is where theory leaves off: precisely where practice begins. It
first digs up the earth, then lays the foundations, builds walls over
these and, finally, it sets the roof in place. Try to maintain the analogy:
just as we need a house to prevent the destruction caused by wind,   15
storms and burning heat, so we need demonstration to prevent both
the destruction caused by falsehood in our theory, and that destruction – which could indeed be properly called 'destruction'[177] – which
comes from evil in our practice. For just as in theory, falsehood is
opposed to truth, so, in practical philosophy, evil is opposed to good.   20

We need some instrument to distinguish between them, lest we fall into falsehoods instead of truth, and evil instead of good. This is demonstration (*apodeixis*): the criterion of each thing, which does not permit deception by means of some trace of the truth or of the Good, albeit murky; rather, it lays all things bare and submits them to the test.[178] Thus, just as in examining the question of how to build a house, we stop when we get to the point of digging up the earth, the same thing happens when we examine how demonstration comes about. Since demonstration tells us what is a property[179] of what and what is not a property of what – and not simply [this], for it also adds the reason *why* something is or is not a property – it is clear that demonstration is not a simple formula (*logos*), but is a collection (*sullogê*) of several: where that which is a property; that of which it is a property; and the reason [why one is a property of the other] are gathered together into at least two premises (*protaseis*). For instance, he who shows that the soul is immortal by means of 'self-moving' says the following: 1. The soul is self-moving. 2. What is self-moving is immortal – and he thus draws the conclusion, namely 3. that the soul is immortal.[180]

Thus, demonstration is a demonstrative syllogism. Yet how could we learn the demonstrative syllogism without previously having learned about the syllogism *tout court*? For we shall not be able to write this or that particular grammatical form (*tupos*) unless we have previously learned simply to write! Yet how could we learn about the syllogism *tout court*, except by learning the elements of which it is made up?[181] Now, these are premises; but these in turn are made up of nouns and verbs, some of which are substrates and some of which are predicates; we therefore require knowledge of these things too. But the analysis does not stop here, for they are preceded by the consideration of simple words (*phônai*). According to this, they are all considered to be names (*onomata*), since the first imposition[182] is that of words *qua* names.

Once men felt the need to signify realities to each other – since they had strayed from common intellection – they imposed the name 'body' on such-and-such a thing, 'on the right' on another, and 'to do' or 'to undergo' on yet another, since there was as yet no difference according to which some names act as substrates, while others are predicated, and some additionally signify time, while others do not.[183] What comes first, then, is the consideration of simple words (*phônai*), and anyone who intends to create a demonstration must start from there. We are thus right to start with the *Categories*, since through them we are introduced both to the meaningful formula (*logos*) and to signified realities (*pragmata*), starting with simpler things [and proceeding] to what is more composite. For after simple words, we learn what a noun is, and a verb, and then – in the *On Interpretation* – about affirmations and denials, and what are the differences between them. Later, in the *Prior Analytics*, [we learn about] terms (*horoi*), premises and syllogisms; what are the kinds of syllogism, how many figures there are for each kind, and how many moods there are to each figure. Thus we come to the study of demonstration, to which Aristotle gave the title of the *Posterior Analytics*.

We are thus right to begin both the study of logic and of the whole of philosophy with the book of the *Categories*, and from the preceding considerations the place occupied by the present book in the order of reading is also handed down to us.

It is, however, also worthwhile to inquire about the reason for the title. In the first place, we shall inquire how many different titles it has been given, and which of these titles is the most acceptable. Now, some people entitled the book 'The Pre-Topics';[184] others 'On the Genera of Being';[185] others 'On the Ten Genera'; others 'The Ten Categories', and still others 'The Categories', under which title it still circulates today. Yet those who entitled the book 'Pre-Topics', and ascribed to it a corresponding place in the reading order, are absurd. For it is not only the *Topics* that it precedes: rather, in logic, it precedes the entire theory of syllogistics or analytics, and that of premises, which they entitle *On Interpretation*; while in ontology, instruction about simple things precedes the whole of philosophy, since it teaches about what is most elementary.

Since, however, it was not just anyone who placed the books of the *Topics* immediately after the *Categories*; but Adrastus of Aphrodisias,[186] who was one of the genuine Peripatetics, and who, in his book *On the Order of Aristotle's Philosophy*,[187] wants the *Topics* to be placed after the *Categories*, [let us see] what reason – even if it were only plausible – the judgement of this eminent man could possibly have had. It is because that knowledge of simple words, as provided by the book of the *Categories*, must at any rate come first. Before proceeding to the demonstrative method, however, and the syllogisms and premises which necessarily precede it, he transmits to us the method which reasons syllogistically from widely-held and plausible beliefs.[188] But since this method also proceeds according to syllogisms, in the case of this method too, he teaches us beforehand what the common syllogism is, just as he did in the case of the *Prior Analytics*. For if we must proceed from the widely-held to the demonstrative, and from the plausible to the unconditionally true, then, Adrastus would say, it is right that the study of the *Topics* should precede the study both of demonstration and of those matters which are necessarily taken up before demonstration. Now these considerations are plausible – if, that is, they have been plausibly expressed – but entitling the book 'The Pre-Topics' is truly absurd: for simple words immediately precede both the premises which are made up of them and the syllogisms which are made up of the premises.

As for those who entitle the work 'On the Genera of Being', or 'On

20

25

30

35

16,1

5

10

15

the Ten Genera', as Plotinus seems to do in his refutation of them:[189]
they take only realities (*pragmata*) into consideration, and not the
logical goal (*skopos*).[190] For the genera of being are realities themselves.

20   That the goal (*skopos*) is not about beings, but about the words
which signify them, *qua* significant, has been stated previously; but
he [*sc*. Aristotle] himself also indicates it clearly by saying: 'Of the
aforementioned things, none is said by itself in any affirmation, but
it is by the combination of these with one another that an affirmation
comes about.'[191] For if affirmations consist in words (*phônê*) and
25   phrases (*logos*), the goal could not be about beings; for it is not the
combination of realities that becomes an affirmation, but that of
meaningful words. Since, moreover, he says[192] that each of the things
transmitted here signifies either substance or quantity or quality or
another such thing, but what signifies is not realities – for they are
30   what are signified – but words, it is clear that the treatise is not about
beings, but about the words which signify beings.

Since, however, it has been entitled 'Categories' by most, we must
seek the reason for this.[193] Indeed, what we are taught by this book is
17,1   not how we are to go about constructing accusations, complete with
the motive; for this is the concern of rhetoricians, not philosophers.
The opposite of this sense of 'to accuse' (*katêgorein*), moreover, is
apêgorein, that is, to give a speech for the defence (*to apologeisthai*).
Porphyry, however, gives a simpler explanation, saying that address-
ing (*agoreuein*) realities in accordance with some meaning, and, in
5   general, saying a significant expression of a reality, is called 'predicat-
ing' (*to katêgorein*), 'so that,' he says, 'every simple meaningful
expression, when it is addressed to and said of the reality which it
signifies, is called a category'. These are his very words.[194] However,
according to this line of reasoning (*logos*), both the simple expression
'Socrates' and the expressions which signify each individual would be
called a 'category', and thus the discussion (*logos*) would not be about
10   the most generic expressions, but about those which are simple. The
others have thus done better to say that [the book] has been entitled
'Categories', since it is about the things which are most generic, which
are always naturally suited to be predicated.[195] For of the assertoric
proposition,[196] in which the true and the false are constituted, one
part is the substrate – that which is defined – and another part is
what is said *about* the substrate; this latter is called the 'predicate'
(*katêgoroumenon*), since it is said of (*kata*) the substrate. For exam-
15   ple, [let us consider the statement] 'Socrates is a man'. 'Socrates' acts
as the substrate, while 'man' is what is predicated. That which is more
particular (*merikôteron*) acts as the substrate, while what is predicated is what is more universal (*katholikôteron*), and in the case of
things predicated in the proper sense, it is impossible to reverse the

terms. For it is impossible to say that 'man is Socrates', or that 'animal is man'.[197]

As has also been said in Porphyry's *Isagoge*,[198] some things are exclusively predicated, *viz.* the most generic genera,[199] and others are 20 exclusively substrates, *viz.* individuals (*ta atoma*). After all, everything else participates in the former, and this is why they are 'said of' (*kata*) their participants. They themselves, however, do not participate in other things, and therefore they do not serve as substrates for any other thing for the purpose of predication. Individuals, for their part, participate in those things which are above them, and therefore serve as substrates[200] for them, but they are not participated by any other thing as if they were more universal,[201] and it is for this reason that they are not predicated of anything. If, however, the goal (*skopos*) 25 of the book is about the highest genera, it was reasonable to entitle it 'The Categories'. After all, Archytas, who had the same goal (*skopos*), [as Aristotle], entitled his book 'On The Universal Formulae (*Logoi*)', since universals (*ta katholou*) are always predicated of what is beneath them, but never act as substrates.

It is not surprising if the name [*sc.* 'Categories'] strikes people as foreign, because it is alien to common usage. For since names are deficient with regard to realities, philosophers – who do not merely 30 wish to gain knowledge of realities which are unknown to others, but also to reveal them to those who want to learn – are sometimes obliged to make up names, as Aristotle himself created the name 18,1 'entelechy'. They have also sometimes used names which designate one set of things in an extended sense of other things, transferring them appropriately, as in this case was done with the name 'category'.[202] The book was entitled 'Categories', and not 'On the Categories', because it is often customary to preface a work by writing the name of what the discourse is about in the nominative case.[203] 5 Thus the discourse about Themistocles was entitled 'Themistocles',[204] and that about the republic was entitled 'Republic'.[205]

That the book is a genuine work of the Philosopher[206] is shown, first and foremost, by the density (*puknotês*) of its concepts (*ennoiai*) and the concentrated[207] nature of its phraseology, which proceeds in accordance with Aristotle's intellective power. Aristotle himself, moreover, alludes to the book elsewhere, calling it the 'Ten Catego- 10 ries', lest we suspect that he is mentioning the work by Archytas, which bears another title. Thus, either we must also reject the works in which Aristotle makes mention of this book as spurious, or else we must not athetize the *Categories*. Moreover, the most serious of Aristotle's companions[208] also accepted the book as authentic. In addition, if Aristotle had not written this book first, not only would his philosophy as a whole have been without a beginning (*anarkhos*) and without a head (*akephalos*), but this is especially true of logic. 15

Adrastus, in his work *On the Order of Aristotle's Writings*, reports

that there is also another book of the categories which circulates under the name of Aristotle:[209] it, too, is brief and concise in expression, and it differs [*sc.* from Aristotle's authentic *Categories*] only by a
20 few divisions, but it begins with the words 'Of beings, some are ...'.[210] He records the same number of lines for each work, so that in saying 'brief in expression', he means that the arguments of both are set forth concisely.

It remains for us to speak about the book's division into chapters.[211] Some commentators, paying no attention to how the chapters have been divided according to their articulations[212] and to how well they fulfil the purpose of the overall goal (*skopos*), nor to how they main-
25 tain their mutual continuity, consider that the chapters just lie there in the haphazard manner[213] typical of hypomnematic writings.[214] What is more, some contradict Aristotle and reject his division: of these, some claim that it is uselessly redundant, others that it omits many things, like Athenodorus[215] and Cornutus,[216] who believe the goal (*skopos*) is about expressions (*lexeis*) in so far as they are expressions. They bring forward many expressions as examples, some literal
30 and others figurative, and thereby think they refute the division,
19,1 since it has not included all possible expressions.[217] These people also think that there is a division of names into homonyms, synonyms, and paronyms, and suppose that the book is a motley heap of logical, physical, ethical, and theological speculations. For them, the specula-
5 tions about homonyms, synonyms and paronyms are logical, as is, moreover, the one about opposites.[218] Those about movement, they say, are physical, while those about virtue and vice are ethical, just as the philosophical considerations about the ten genera are theological.[219] In fact, however, the truth is otherwise. [Aristotle] is not carrying out a division of names, for if he were, he would not have omitted heteronyms or polyonyms.[220]

If we are to divide it into large parts, the book is tripartite. In the
10 first part, Aristotle articulates a few matters which will be useful for the categories: for instance, what are homonyms, synonyms, and paronyms. After all, he intended later to state[221] that what is *in* a substrate is predicated *homonymously*, whereas what [is said] *of* a substrate is predicated *synonymously*. He also intended to state[222] that qualified things (*ta poia*) are so called paronymously from Quality (*apo tês poiotêtos*), and quantified things (*ta posa*) likewise from Quantity (*apo tês posotêtos*). Nevertheless, in order that the continuity of instruction might not be interrupted by his teaching about these
15 things in the middle of his exposition, nor that, should they remain unexplained, they might make the entire discussion (*logos*) unclear, he rightly took up the articulation (*diarthrôsis*) of them beforehand.[223] The second heading goes through the ten genera themselves.[224] The third heading also deals with some matters which Aristotle had already mentioned in his discussions of the categories; here, however,

he transmits to us a clearer conception of them.[225] Since, for example, he had said[226] that the relatives subsist (*huphistanai*) simultaneously, 20 he tells us what 'simultaneous' means.[227] Since he states here that one substance is prior, while elsewhere he states that another one is prior,[228] he also tells us in how many senses the term 'prior' is used,[229] so that we should not suspect him of contradicting himself,[230] but rather should realize according to which meaning of 'prior' the first-mentioned substance was said to be prior, and according to which meaning the latter substance [was said to be prior].

He also speaks about motion, since he had mentioned it in the [discussion of] 'Doing' and 'Being-Affected',[231] and he divides the opposites,[232] having made mention of them, too, both in [the discus- 25 sion of] the relatives,[233] and in that of some of the qualifieds.[234]

Porphyry raised the following difficulty: why did Aristotle not also place [the discussion of] these matters as well before that of the categories, or else why did he not introduce the first-mentioned matters, too, after the categories?[235] He gives an excellent solution to the difficulty: the former matters [sc. homonyms, synonyms and paronyms] were completely unknown to common usage, whereas of the latter[236] we at least have some conceptions (*ennoias*), albeit we lack a clear differentiation of them, too. Thus, it was because he did 30 not wish to delay for long the discussion of the categories themselves 20,1 that he postponed them until later. Because of the kind of pre-existing conception we have of them, he was not obliged to give us preliminary instruction about them; but on the other hand, he would not consent to the auditor's being left with a non-technical knowledge of them. For although we do use some names which are in common usage, we do not have a precise awareness of their natures; yet it was these natures 5 which the namers (*onomatothetai*) had in view when they imposed names [upon things].[237] Let this be enough, then, on the book's division into its own chapter-headings.

If anyone also desires to learn under which part of Aristotle's philosophy [sc. the *Categories* should be placed], it is clear that it is under the instrumental part. It has been shown that instruction about simple words (*phônai*) occupies the first part of the study of 10 logic, whereas logic as a whole is the instrumental part of philosophy, like the rulers and plumb-lines used by carpenters and architects.[238]

Cat. 1a1 'Those things are called homonyms of which only the 21,1 name is common.'[239]

Nicostratus and his followers[240] raise the following problem: 'Why is it that Aristotle, having proposed to speak about the categories, does not teach us about them right away, but rather about the other things; *viz.* homonyms, synonyms, and paronyms?'

Porphyry[241] gave a fine reply to these objectors, saying that in the 5

case of almost every theoretical field of study, some things are written beforehand, which tend to clarify what is to follow, as for instance, definitions, axioms and postulates in geometry. Here, then, he proposes to speak about the primary expressions,[242] which are indicative of the primary and simple realities, under which all other realities had to be reduced. If there were one particular name for each reality,
10   each one would be reduced under one category. If, however, the same name belongs to several realities which differ substantially,[243] then a distinction had to be made. Sometimes, it is obvious that they are reduced under the same category; in other cases it is not. Man, for example, is called 'animal', as is the horse. Again, Socrates is an animal, and so, too, is an image of Socrates, even though the latter is
15   a configuration of colours. Now, of these, 'man' and 'horse' participate in the same substance, that of 'animal', which is predicated of them synonymously, and they are therefore reduced under the same category. Socrates and the painted Socrates, however, do *not* both participate in the substance of 'animal': but one participates in substance, while the other participates in 'colour' or 'surface figure'. Thus, they are not reduced under the same category, but Socrates comes
20   under the category of Substance, while the painted Socrates comes under the category of the Qualified.

It was thus necessary to give preliminary teaching about homonyms and synonyms. The necessity of having a preliminary notion of homonyms was also shown by Andronicus,[244] who made the initial phrase of the *Categories* read as follows:

Of things said, some are said without combination, others with combination. Of those without combination, those which have the name alone in common are called homonyms.[245]

25   Thus, a preliminary notion of homonyms is clearly necessary, both for the above-mentioned reasons, and because, since there is a great deal of controversy about whether or not Being is a genus,[246] [the answer]
22,1 can be known by means of homonyms and synonyms.

The divine Iamblichus,[247] for his part, says: 'It seems to me that he who makes a thorough study of the *Categories* can do no better than to begin with homonyms. After all, the categories themselves have the name "categories" homonymously,[248] for they are different with regard both to their realities and to their entire genera, and have nothing in
5   common but the name alone. Even [the verb] "*katêgorein*"[249] is also said homonymously. Since, then, unless one defines homonyms, it is not possible even to understand the category's characteristic particularity (*idiôma*) itself, nor to find out how it is possible for it to belong in common to several things, and to have a relation (*skhesis*) to all beings, Aristotle was right to carry out the discussion (*logos*) of them at the beginning.'

In addition, there is nothing as effective as a precise definition of   10
names to counteract sophistical quibbling.²⁵⁰ This is also said by Plato
in the *Euthydemus*,²⁵¹ and everyone else agrees that the double
nature of names has transmitted a powerful incentive to dialectics.

Let us now see how Aristotle has indicated the nature of homonyms,²⁵² clarifying the letter of his text in the following way. Of
realities, each one is indicated both by its name and by its account   15
(*logos*), which may be descriptive or definitory.²⁵³ For example, man is
indicated both by this name 'man' and by the definitory account,
which says 'rational, mortal animal'. The name indicates him in a
unitary mode (*kata to monoeides*), whereas the account designates
him insofar as he is composed of a plurality of parts (*kata to
polumeres*). The name, however, being a symbol, can remain the same
and yet be the name of some other thing, even if the latter differs   20
essentially.²⁵⁴ For instance, it can be of a painted image of a man, for
it becomes the symbol of it, too.²⁵⁵ The account which explains the
substance,²⁵⁶ however, cannot be the same and yet belong to some
other thing which is essentially different.

It should be known, then,²⁵⁷ that whatever things share a name but
differ with regard to their account, are called *homonyms*, and conversely, those which share an account, but differ with regard to their
names, are called *polyonyms*.²⁵⁸ For example, the definition (*horis-*   25
mos) of man is one, but his names are many: *merops*, *brotos*,²⁵⁹ and so
on. Things which share in both the same name and the same account
(*logos*) are called *synonyms*: for instance, both man and horse have in
common their name, *viz.* 'animal', and they also share the same
definition (*horismos*), since both are 'animals' and animate, sensitive
substances. Therefore 'animal' is predicated of both of them synony-   30
mously.²⁶⁰ Those things which do not have in common either their
name or their account are called *heteronyms*; but in truth they are
really [merely] different (*hetera*), especially when they do not even
have the same substrate in common, as for instance the ascent and
the descent share [the common substrate of] the same ladder. It is
rather such things [as the ascent and the descent] that ought to be
called *heteronyms*.²⁶¹ There are also things which share in both [name   23,1
and account] in a certain sense, but also differ in another sense, such
as the so-called paronyms. Thus, for example, an instance of white
(*leukon*) is so called after 'whiteness' (*leukotês*), and 'grammarian'
after 'grammar'.

Five varieties of these things have thus appeared as a result of our
division: homonyms, synonyms, polyonyms, heteronyms and
paronyms.²⁶² Aristotle here takes up only three for discussion, namely   5
homonyms, synonyms and paronyms. This is perhaps because he
made use of only these three in his discussion of the categories,²⁶³ or
perhaps also because, from two of these, it is easy to obtain knowledge
about what are opposed to them. For once one has recognized as

homonyms those things which have their name in common, but differ
according to their account, he will know that those things which have
10   their account in common, but differ in their name, are polyonyms.
Again, once he knows that those things which share in both are
synonyms, he will also know that heteronyms are those which differ
in both respects.

This last solution might be correct, if we have in view Aristotle's
habitual conciseness. It is more correct, however – and this is also the
view of the philosopher Syrianus – to say that polyonyms and hetero-
15   nyms, the two omitted kinds, are more suitable to linguistic studies
than to the consideration of realities[264] themselves. This is why
Aristotle will deal more appropriately with them in his treatises on
rhetoric and other such subjects, where he will teach both how to say
the same thing in many different ways by means of polyonymy, and
how to express things which are different by nature by means of
different names, so that one's discourse (*logos*) may appear clear and
free from confusion.[265] Here, however, he discusses homonyms and
20   synonyms because the difference between them is of serious import.
He begins with the discussion of homonyms[266] because they require a
simpler kind of knowledge, and they have only one thing in common,
viz. their name. He then proceeds to discuss synonyms, which have
both their name *and* their account in common, and then goes on to
deal with paronyms, which do not completely fulfil either condition;
that is, they share both their name and their reality, but are interme-
25   diate between homonyms and synonyms. It is because it deals with
simpler things that the divine Iamblichus says the discussion of
24,1   homonyms comes first, because the categories are categories homonymously, although they have synonymously the fact of being predicated
of the things beneath them. What is more, they have in common the
very fact of being categories and most generic genera, not only as far
as names are concerned, but the very nature of being predicated –
5   that is, of being most generic – is common to them.[267]

Some people raise the following problem:[268] Why, although Aristotle had proposed to speak about expressions (*lexeis*), and not about
realities themselves, does he nevertheless say nothing about homonymy, but rather teaches us about homonyms, although the
concept (*ennoia*) of homonymy comes first, since it is from this concept
10   that homonyms derive?[269] They rightly say that it is from realities
(*pragmata*) that homonyms become clear to us: *viz.*, when the same
name is spoken, I project one concept in conjunction with the name,
while you project a different one.[270] For example, if someone says the
name 'dog', I might conceive of the land-animal, while you might
conceive of a sea-dog.[271] This is why the dialecticians recommend that
we keep silent when faced with syllogisms based on homonymy, until
15   the questioner transfers the name to one of the significata.[272] For
example, suppose some one asks whether tunics are masculine: we

shall agree, if in fact they happen to be masculine. And if he asks whether that which is masculine is animate, we shall also agree, for it is true. But if he should then conclude that tunics are animate, at this point we must define the homonymy of the term 'masculine', and show that 'masculine' is said of tunics in one sense, but in another sense of a person possessing masculinity. Thus, properly speaking, it is realities and not names that create homonymy.   20

Moreover, Aristotle himself presents his teaching upon homonyms because the discussion (*logos*) of homonymy is also, at any rate, immediately consequent upon the goal (*skopos*) of the *Categories*.[273] For his part, Plato states that it becomes clear from realities whether the same name is borne by different things homonymously or synonymously, for he says in the *Sophist*,[274] 'for now, you and I have the name   25,1 in common with regard to this matter, but perhaps we each privately keep the fact (*ergon*) which we are naming to ourselves'. Thus, it is when it becomes known that each individual has his own particular conception (*ennoia*) of a common name that it becomes clear that the name is homonymous. For homonyms and synonyms are not such in   5 and of themselves; rather, the nature of homonyms and synonyms is in the conceptions (*ennoia*) – be they perverted or in agreement – of human beings as they converse and name things. Aristotle was, moreover, right to say 'they are called', since the discussion (*logos*) is not about realities themselves, but about significant expressions.

They also raise the following problem:[275] Why did Aristotle call   10 homonyms only those things 'of which only the name is common[276]', even though homonymy is also in verbs, as in the case of *êndrapodis-tai*[277] and in participles, as in the case of *êndrapodismenos*,[278] and in conjunctions? After all, the dialecticians hand down to us many different meanings of 'or' and of 'either'.[279] They also say that 'name' (*onoma*) is said in three senses: (i) as denoting the proper noun (*to*   15 *kurion*); (ii) as denoting the appellative noun (*to prosêgorikon*);[280] and (iii) as extending to every part of speech, as, for example, when we say that Plato used beautiful names, Xenophon common ones. There is, therefore, nothing absurd about the fact that the sense which extends in common to all the parts of speech should be said here.

Boethus says that 'name' has two meanings: one in which it takes a preceding article, which is called 'name' in the more particular sense, and one which extends to all the elements of speech (*logos*).   20 When, therefore, we ask of any expression whatsoever whether it is homonymous, we place the article first, just as much in the case of names in the proper sense of the word as in that of other expressions. We say 'dog is homonymous', and 'he was enslaved[281] (*to êndrapodis-tai*) is homonymous' (for [this phrase] signifies both 'he was taken prisoner' and 'taking someone else prisoner'). Boethus is thus right to say that homonyms have the name in common, for they all have the   25 proprium of names, insofar as they are preceded by the article.[282]

Things which are enunciated in this way are similar to the so-called indeclinable names: [they are declined as follows]: *to andrapodizesthai, tou andrapodizesthai, tôi andrapodizesthai*, etc.[283] By saying 'name/noun' (*onoma*), Aristotle indicated at the same time how the differentiation of homonyms should be enunciated: we should place the article before them and say, '*to êndrapodizesthai* means such-and-such, but it also means such-and-such'; for it is the placing of the article before them which gives them the characteristic of nouns.

Aristotle says that 'only' (*monon*) the name is common to homonyms.[284] Now, *monos* sometimes means 'one', as for example when we say 'the universe is one', and sometimes it denotes a contrast with something else, as when we say 'he has only (*monon*) a cloak', contrasting this with a tunic. This is the sense in which *monos* has been taken here, by way of contrast with the definition (*logos*) of substance. This also makes the means discovering homonyms clear: that is, the fact that one determinate thing – the name – is the only thing in common, and it is contrasted with one [other] determinate thing, namely the definition (*horismos*).

Again, 'common' (*koinon*) is also said in many senses:[285] 1. It designates either that which is divisible into parts, as land which is divided into allotments; or 2. that which is indivisibly available for common use, although not simultaneously, as with common slaves or horses; or 3. that which is made one's own by advance reservation,[286] but subsequently returned to common use, as a theatre;[287] and 4. that which is brought into the use of many both indivisibly and simultaneously, as a voice.[288] Thus the name, too, is common to the homonyms, belonging to all at once; and at the same time it can belong to other things, remaining indivisibly the same. This is why Andronicus, in his *Paraphrase of the Categories*, says that those things are called homonyms of which the name is identical.[289] After all, both the name and the account (*logos*), by virtue of their incorporeal nature, are present to many things indivisibly.

Nicostratus and his followers also raise problems about the fact that the name of homonyms is said to be common.[290] For he who says 'dog', thereby shows that he is not talking about an ox or a horse or any such thing, but he has not yet indicated what he does want to signify. For it is not yet clear which [kind of] dog he means: whether the dog-star, or the land-animal, or the sea-dog, or the kind of spasm that attacks people in the jaw.[291] If, then, [the word 'dog'] does not signify anything, it cannot be a name,[292] and consequently it cannot be a homonym either, for it was said that homonyms have their name in common. If it requires some kind of addition in order to specify which of those many kinds is meant – for instance, that he is talking about the dog-star or some other kind of dog – then the name no longer remains common, for by means of the addition, according to which it primarily signifies what is meant, it will be particularized.

Thus, if what is said in the case of those things which have been handed down as examples of homonyms does not signify anything, it is not a name. If, however, it signifies by virtue of the addition which makes the name particular to each thing, then homonyms are no longer such insofar as they participate in a common name, since that which is accompanied by an addition is no longer a name alone   27,1 (*monon*), but is rather a phrase (*logos*).

Thus, if it does not signify anything, it is not a name, for names must be significant. If it does signify, but only when accompanied by an addition, then once again it is not a name, but a phrase (*logos*), because of the addition of a differentia; but as a result of the differentia it is no longer common. At any rate, the name which is said of   5 homonyms could not be common according to any of the meanings of 'common'. It is not 'common' in the sense of being divisible, for something else which participated in another syllable of the name would no longer be a homonym. Nor [could it be said to be common] as a whole, but coming into the use of different people at different times, for names belong simultaneously to each of the things said homonymously. Nor [can it be said to be common] in the sense of being on reserve[293] and private property at the same time, and because each   10 one was to partake of different names at different times, like the places in a theatre, and once again they are not homonyms. Finally, [names cannot be said to be common] in the sense that the voice (*phônê*) is common. For the voice imparts the same disposition in all its listeners, whereas a homonym provides different people with different concepts (*ennoiai*) – if indeed it does signify something – while if it does not bring about different conceptions in different hearers, it remains non-significant, and is no longer a name.   15

Some solve this puzzle by saying that not every name is significant. 'Name', they say, has three meanings: (i) in accordance with its typical form (*kharaktêr*), even if it is not coordinated (*katatetagmenon*) with any significatum, as for instance 'blituri'; (ii) that which is coordinated [with some significatum], but does not have the typical form of a name, as for instance the conjunction 'nevertheless' (*alla mên*),[294] which Diodorus, making fun of grammatical definitions, and of those   20 who say names were established by nature, gave as a name to his slave; (iii) that which has both a nominal form *and* is co-ordinated, as 'Socrates', 'Plato', and the other so-called 'names'. What, then, [they continue], prevents homonyms from being non-coordinated (*akatatakton*) and yet having the form of a name? For it can be common when it is not taken in conjunction with any co-ordination (*katataxis*).[295]

'But', they would say, 'it is impossible that the name which is taken   25 up in the definition (*horos*) of homonyms should be such. For the "of which" [part of the definition] defines to which things they have been co-ordinated, but that which is a name by form alone is not co-ordinated. If, therefore, it is uncoordinated, it could not be brought under the definition (*horismos*);[296] or if it were coordinated, it would not be common, for neither can coordination be common.' But 'the definition

30 (*logos*) in accordance with the name is different'[297] is, at any rate, as if it belonged to something coordinated, for that which has [nominal] form alone does not have any definition (*logos*). For what would be the definition (*logos*) of 'blituri', which does not signify anything? If, however, it is coordinated, it is not common, as terms (*horoi*), which derive their difference from their different coordination (*katataxis*), are not common either.

28,1   Perhaps[298] the homonymous name, since it is a name and not a reality, can fit with many different things, and this is why it is unclear, once a name has been spoken, of *what* it is said, until it is defined. Once it has been defined, however, it is no longer merely a common name, but it has also taken on a differentia, so that it signifies one thing. 'Common' and 'indefinite' means being commonly and indivis-

5 ibly co-ordinated with all homonyms, which situation, when taken together with the definition (*diorismos*), presents the common as individualized and detached.[299] It is therefore incorrect for them to say that if a [name] is significant, then it is not common, for commons, too, have meaning, and there is such a thing as coordination [of a common] *qua* common.

It is worth noting that Aristotle carried out his entire description (*hupographê*) of homonyms by means of homonyms; after all, 'name',

10 'only' and 'common' belong to the class of things said in many senses, and which rather belong [*sc.* to their significata] homonymously.

Cat. 1a1-2 'The account (*logos*) of substance in accordance with the name is different.'[300]

The definitory account[301] must in any case be conjoined[302] to the name, in such a way that it neither exceeds the name nor falls short of it;

15 after all, the name and the definition (*horismos*) are of the same reality. Yet the definition unfolds and develops[303] the reality, and embraces it in so far as it consists of many parts. The name, by contrast, contracts it and folds it up,[304] representing it in its uniform aspect.

All definitions must therefore be conjoined (*suzugos*) to the name, neither exceeding it nor falling short of it. Exceeding and falling short occur if the definition does not take place 'in accordance with the

20 name'.[305] The definition is excessive when it is given in accordance with one of the things that are higher up [*sc.* on the scale of being]. For instance, if you want to define 'animal', but do not give the definition according to the name 'animal', but rather according to an attribute belonging to 'animal' in a more universal sense, such as 'animate', then you will give the following definition: 'Animal' is 'a

substance moved from within itself, or which feeds itself and grows from within itself, and generates things similar to itself', or however else one were to define 'animate'. Now, this will be true in the case of animals, but it will certainly not also be a definition (*horos*), for it is not equivalent.[306] For if something is an animal, then it nourishes itself, grows, and generates things similar to itself; but not *vice versa*, because plants are not animals.[307] The definition falls short of the name when it is taken as applying to a thing more partial (*merikôteron*) than the name, as when we define 'animal' as 'a rational, mortal substance', which is what man is. Now, such a thing is indeed an animal, but it is not the case that every animal is such.

    Thus, every definition (*horos*) comes about 'in accordance with the name', so that it may also be convertible with the name.[308]

    Homonyms, for their part, can have the same definition in accordance with some other aspect. For instance, the Ajaxes,[309] *qua* men, are rational, mortal animals; *qua* Ajaxes, however, one of them is the son of Oïleus, the other the son of Telamon. In both cases, 'Ajax' is the homonym, as substrate. They say that Speusippus was content with saying 'but the definition (*logos*) is different'.[310] Yet, if one were to give an account in this way, both synonyms would be homonyms and homonyms, synonyms. For there is a name which is common both to us and to horses, *viz.* 'animal', but the definitions (*logoi*) are different, in so far as we are men and horses [respectively]. Thus, the synonym will be a homonym.[311] Again, the sea-dog and the land-dwelling dog, with regard to 'animal', have the same definition (*logos*); and homonyms will be synonyms, since their definition (*horismos*) was given not according to 'dog', which is that by virtue of which they were homonyms, but according to 'animal'.[312] Thus, the addition of 'in accordance with the name' is necessary.[313]

    'Account' (*logos*)[314] means the calculation of votes, and it also means internal discourse in accordance with the concept (*ennoia*); it also means external discourse,[315] as well as spermatic reason,[316] and it also means the guiding and definitory formula[317] of each thing. He said 'account' (*logos*) rather than 'definition' (*horismos*), in order to include the descriptive account[318] as well, which fits both with the highest genera and with individuals; these cannot be included by a definition (*horismos*), since it is not possible to take either a genus of the highest genera, nor differentiae of individuals.[319] Descriptions (*hupographê*), by contrast, which give an account of the characteristic property (*idiotês*) of a substance,[320] extend to these[321] as well. This is why he did not simply say 'the definition (*logos*) in accordance with the name', but the definition (*logos*) 'of substance': since a descriptive definition (*logos*) defines the characteristic property of a substance, whereas a definitory (*horistikos*) one defines both the quiddity[322] of each thing, and the substance itself. Thus 'definition (*logos*) of substance' includes both the descriptive and the definitory definition (*logos*).[323] It is thus

    25

    30

    29,1

    5

    10

    15

    20

25   once again futile for[324] the followers of Nicostratus[325] to reproach
     Aristotle with appearing to say that homonymy is only to be found in
     substance, since he said that in the case of homonyms 'the definition
     (*logos*) of substance is different'. Yet, they say, homonymy is also in
     the Qualified (*en poiôi*), since we call 'white' both the colour and the
     noise;[326] as well as in Position, and in other categories. For it is in
     reply to this puzzle that Porphyry says, in the first place, that this[327]
30   is not written in all the manuscripts. Boethus, he says, did not know
     of it,[328] who says that Aristotle points out what homonyms are by
30,1 saying: 'Those things are called homonyms of which only the name is
     common, but the definition (*logos*) in accordance with the name is
     different.' Although Boethus was carrying out a word-by-word exege-
     sis, he omitted 'of the substance' as though it was not even written.
     Andronicus, moreover, in his paraphrase of the book, says 'of those
     things which are said without combination, those things are called
     homonyms of which only the name is identical (*tauton*), but the
5   definition (*logos*) in accordance with the name is different.[329] "Since,"
     says Porphyry, "Herminus and almost everyone else have read the
     name 'of the substance', as added to the definition (*horos*), we too say
     that the addition is necessary. For 'account' (*logos*) means 'induction',
     'syllogism', and every affirmation and negation; how then, if 'of the
     substance' was not present, could the other significata of 'account'
10   (*logos*) be separated from the definition (*horismos*) and the descrip-
     tion (*hupographê*)?[330] Thus, instead of saying "but the definition
     (*horos*) or the description is different", he included the explanation of
     the definition (*horos*) *and* the description, by saying "but the defini-
     tion (*logos*) of substance is different". After all, a definition (*horos*) is
     an account (*logos*) of substance, in the sense that it indicates (*dêloi*)
     the substance, while a description (*hupographê*) [is an account] in the
     sense that it signifies the characteristic property (*idiotês*) which is in
     conjunction with substance, as well as the existence (*huparxis*) which
15   is common both to substance in the proper sense, and to the rest of
     subsistence (*hupostasis*).'[331]
         Nicostratus[332] raises an additional puzzle about homonyms, and
     the puzzle was set forth even more clearly by Atticus:[333] 'For if
     synonyms are those things of which both the name is common and the
     definition (*horismos*) is common, but homonyms also have a name in
     common – since they are called 'homonyms' – and [they also have in
     common] the definition (*horismos*) of the homonym: for in the case of
20   each homonym, it is true to say that the name alone is common, but
     the definition (*logos*) in accordance with the name of substance is
     different. Therefore, homonyms are synonyms. But synonyms are
     also synonyms; therefore, everything that has the same name is a
     synonym.'
         Porphyry solves this puzzle, too, saying that there is nothing to
     prevent the same realities from being both homonymous and synony-

mous, in accordance with different appellations (*prosêgorias*). Take
for instance the Ajaxes, in so far as they are called 'Ajaxes' and 'men'. 25
Qua men, they are synonymous, but *qua* Ajaxes, they are homonymous; thus the homonymous Ajaxes, *qua* homonyms, are
synonymous, but *qua* Ajaxes they are homonymous.

But someone will easily object to this, and say that in so far as
homonyms are homonyms, they are not homonyms, but synonyms. In
so far, however, as they are not homonyms, but Ajaxes, then in this
respect they are homonyms. And perhaps it is not at all absurd that, 30
with regard to the very nature of the homonym, which is common, the
things which participate in this nature should be synonyms, in so far
as both are homonyms.[334] With regard to their name, however – that 31,1
is, in so far as the participants participate not in a common nature,
but only in a common name, for example that of 'Ajax' – then in this
respect they are homonyms.[335] Thus, just as 'two-syllable word' (*to
disullabon*), *qua* two-syllable word, is not a two- but a four-syllable
word;[336] but in so far as it is 'Dion' or 'Crates' – both of which are
something other than the nature of the two-syllabled, but they par- 5
ticipate in it – in this respect it is two-syllabled, and there is nothing
absurd about this. In the same way, homonyms, too, in so far as they
participate in the common nature of the homonym, are not homonyms, but synonyms; in so far, however, as they participate not in the
nature of the homonym, but only in a common name, then in this
respect they are homonyms.

If one were to say, however, that 'participating in the nature of the
homonym' is nothing other than 'participating only in a common 10
name' – this, after all, is the nature of the homonym, since such is its
definition (*horismos*) – and thereby prove again that a homonym, *qua*
homonym, is a synonym, then it should be said in response that
names, both individual (*idia*) and common (*koina*), are predicated
primarily of realities (*pragmata*). Being predicated homonymously or
synonymously, however, does not belong (*huparkhei*) primarily, but
rather through the various commonalities of names. For example, 15
when the name 'Ajax' is participated in such a way that the participants have only the name in common, then such participation is
homonymous. Again, when homonymy is participated in such a way
that its participants have in common not only their name, insofar as
they are called 'homonyms', but in addition they participate in the
very nature of Homonymy, then the form (*eidos*) of participation is
synonymous. 20

Such, then, are the puzzles (*aporiai*) against what is said about
homonyms, and their solutions.

Once arrived at this point, the commentators are accustomed to
enumerate the types (*tropoi*) of homonyms, and they say that with
regard to the highest types, homonyms come about in two ways.[337]
Some of them come about by chance,[338] as both Paris and the Mace-

25   donian are 'Alexanders'; and some are intentional.[339] The latter occur
        when someone thinks the matter over, and for a specific reason
        imposes the same names [on different things]. Chance homonyms,
        being contingent (*tukhaion*) and indefinite, admit of no divisions.[340]
        Intentional homonyms, by contrast, are divided into four: 1. by simi-
        larity (*kath'homoiotêta*): this is the kind Aristotle used in his example
        of homonyms, when he said 'both a man and a picture are animals'.[341]
30   These have this name in common, but their definition (*logos*) is
        different, since man is an 'animal' as an animate, sensitive substance,
        while an image or statue of a man is an 'animal' in the sense that it
        is a semblance (*homoiôma*) of an animate, sensitive substance. 2. The
        second kind of intentional homonymy[342] is that by analogy (*kata
        analogian*), as when the word 'principle' (*arkhê*) is said homony-
32,1   mously: for of numbers, [the *arkhê*] is the monad; of a line, it is a point
        (*stigmê*);[343] of rivers it is a spring, and of animals it is the heart. For
        as the monad is to number, so is it in the other cases, and this is the
        proprium of analogy.[344] 3. The third mode of intentional homonymy[345]
        is when a common predication comes about in several different reali-
5   ties by derivation from one thing. For example, a book is 'medical'
        (*iatrikon*) by derivation from 'medicine' (*apo tês iatrikês*), since it
        contains a transcription of medical doctrines; and a scalpel is 'medical'
        because it is the instrument of medical cutting; and a drug is 'medical'
        because it is useful for healing. Thus, [in these cases], the name is
        common, but the definition (*logos*) of each is different. A fourth
        mode[346] is when different things are referred to a single goal (*telos*),
10   and it is from the goal that they receive their appellation. For exam-
        ple, food is 'healthy' (*hugieinon*), and a drug is 'healthy', and so is a
        gymnasium, and whatever else is named after health as its goal.
        Some joined together these last two modes, and counted them as one,
        viz. 'deriving from one thing and relative to one thing'.[347] Others,
        however, did not place this mode either within [the class of] homo-
        nyms, or within that of synonyms, but between the two; for on the one
15   hand, it does participate in some kind of account (*logos*) – for 'medical'
        things derive from 'medicine', while 'healthy' things derive from
        'health', since not only the name is common – and it therefore resem-
        bles synonyms. In so far, however, as the participants do not
        participate to an equal degree – for a book containing medical science
        is not medical to the same degree as is a scalpel, and drugs and walks
        are not identically healthy – for this reason, then, they are not
        synonyms.
20   Other commentators, among whom is Atticus,[348] assimilate the
        metaphorical type of homonymy to the analogical, and say that the
        combination of the two constitutes one type of homonyms. This ac-
        count (*logos*) is worthy of scrutiny, for Porphyry says[349] that when a
        reality has a particular (*idion*) name, but someone uses another name
        in an extended sense to refer to it metaphorically, and uses this name

as if it applied to the original object, then there would be no homo- 25
nymy in such a case, for what is said figuratively would not be
homonymous with what is said in the proper sense. When, however,
it does not have another name, then homonymy comes about. For
instance, the lower parts of mountains are called 'foot' (*hupôreia*):

> But they dwelt in the foothills (*hupôreia*) of Ida with many
> springs.[350]

Now, the poets call these foothills (*hupôreia*) 'feet' (*podas*):

> And all the feet (*podes*) of many-springed Ida were shaken.[351] 30

And that which supports beds and tables is also called 'feet' (*podes*), 33,1
as is the rudder-oar (*pêdalion*) of a ship. For as the poet says,

> I was always handling the rudder (*poda*) myself.[352]

In these cases, says Porphyry, one would not say that the 'foot' of the
ship and the 'foot' of the mountain were said homonymously, since 5
both the foothills (*hupôreia*) and the rudder (*pêdalion*) have their own
names. In the case of the table and the bed, however, there is not
metaphor, but homonymy, for they do not have any other name, but
are called 'feet' because of their similarity to animals. Of these things,
therefore, only the name is common, while their definitions (*logoi*) are
different. In the case of the mountain and the ship, by contrast, the
names are other, but the appellation 'feet' has been transferred to 10
them metaphorically; unless there is some similarity after all, by
virtue of which they would be homonyms.

In his [commentary] *By Questions and Answers*, however, Porphyry says that the 'foot' of a ship is also said metaphorically, saying
that its proper name is called 'rudder' (*pêdalion*);[353] whereas in the *Ad
Gedalium*,[354] he says that the 'foot' of the mountain is so called
metaphorically, but that of the ship is so called homonymously, since 15
there is no other name said of it, although in the former work he had
stated it was called 'rudder'. Yet perhaps both statements were truth-
ful, if in the former case it was the rudder that was being called a
'foot', whereas in the latter it was the part of the sail, which does not
have any other name. He does seem, however, to be talking about the
rudder (*pêdalion*) in this latter passage as well, since the quote given
was:

> 'I was always handling the foot (*poda*)',[355] which is said of the 20
> rudder (*pêdalion*).

Cat. **1a6** 'Those things are called synonyms' to 'he will give the same account (*logos*).'[356]

Having first spoken about homonyms, since being seems to belong (*huparkhei*) homonymously to the ten categories, Aristotle goes on to
25   introduce the discussion (*logos*) of synonyms. There is a need for the knowledge of synonyms, because the predication of each of the remaining genera of what is beneath it comes about synonymously, and because things synonymous with each other are ranged under the same category. Now, synonyms have something in common with homonyms, inasmuch as the name is common in the case of synonyms, just as it is in the case of homonyms. They differ, however, in
30   that not only the name is common in the case of synonyms, but also the account (*logos*) in accordance with the name – both the definitory account and the descriptive one – is common in the case of synonyms,
34,1   even if 'in accordance with the name' is not present here.[357]

In his *Ad Gedalium*,[358] Porphyry wrote as follows: 'Those things are called synonyms of which the name is common and the account (*logos*) is the same.'[359] It[360] must be supplied in thought, for the definitory and descriptive account (*logos*) must be conjoined (*suzugon*) to the name.
5   Moreover, in the case of synonyms, one name is indicative of one reality, whereas in the case of homonyms one name is indicative of several realities, and sometimes it is one notion (*noêma*) that is predicated, but at other times many. Moreover, homonyms allow contradiction: a painted animal, for instance, both is and is not an animal, and a crow both is the bird 'crow', and is not a 'crow', for it is not the instrument used on doors.[361] Synonyms, by contrast, do not
10   admit of contradiction: man, for example, being an animal, cannot be called 'non-animal'.

'We must understand "the account (*logos*) of substance",' says Porphyry in his *Commentary by Questions and Answers*,[362] 'for that is the one which is definitory (*horistikos*).' In the *Ad Gedalium*,[363] however, he says: 'It is not, however, necessary also to supply in thought (*prosupakousteon*) "of substance (*ousia*)", for it is not in so far as each thing *is* in the case of the synonyms that its account (*logos*) is the
15   same, but rather in so far as they all participate in some common item.'[364] Here, moreover, he does not seem to have joined 'substance' (*ousia*) to 'account' (*logos*), so that the account (*logos*) of substance (*ousia*) would be the definition (*horismos*); rather, he seems to understand in accordance with the species (*eidos*), according to which each thing is. 'Man' and 'horse', for instance, are synonyms with regard to 'animal', and in this respect their account (*logos*) is the same; but they are not [the same] with regard to those things according to which they
20   are primarily substantiated (*ousiôntai*), *viz.* 'man' and 'horse'; for the account (*logos*) of each of these is different.[365]

A little further on, [Porphyry][366] himself says: 'Even if one were to supply (*prosupakouein*) "of substance (*ousia*)", it is clear that he will understand not that substance (*ousia*) which is so named in the proper sense of the term, but rather that "substance" which indicates the existence (*huparxis*) of each thing, as it were, in a more common way (*koinoteron*).'

It should be known, however, that here the following reading is current in the majority of manuscripts: 'Those things are called synonyms of which the name is common, and the account (*logos*) of substance (*ousia*) in accordance with the name is the same.' Now Porphyry, too, adopted this reading in his *By Questions and Answers*,[367] but Iamblichus omitted 'of substance (*ousia*)', and read as follows: 'Those things are called synonyms of which the name is common, and the account (*logos*) in accordance with the name is the same.' It has been remarked that 'and that which is in accordance with the name' is not current in some manuscripts, and that it must be supplied (*prosupakouein*). Syrianus followed Iamblichus' reading, but Alexander differed about the reading, and wrote as follows: 'Those things are called synonyms of which the name is common, and the account (*logos*) of substance (*ousia*) is the same.' He, too, says that 'the one in accordance with the name' must be supplied (*prosupakouein*).[368]

[Aristotle] took up the same example of 'animal' in the case of synonyms as he did in the case of homonyms,[369] not because he lacked other examples, but in order to point out that the same name is indicative of some realities homonymously – for instance, 'animal' indicates both a man and a statue – while it is indicative of others synonymously, as in the case of 'man' and 'ox'. Both of the latter are 'animal' by virtue of one and the same account (*logos*), for each is an animate substance capable of sensation. There is nothing surprising about this; but what would be more surprising is that the same thing can be both homonymous and synonymous with regard to the same thing.

It is worth noting that the same thing can be called 'homonymous' and 'synonymous' in four different senses, for sometimes (1) one and the same reality is both homonymous and synonymous to various other realities with regard to its various names. For instance, the bird crow (*korax*), in so far as it is called 'crow', is said homonymously with regard to the instrument on the door, but in so far as it is a bird, it is said synonymously with regard to other birds. (2) Sometimes, the same thing is found to be both homonymous and synonymous with regard to the same reality, by virtue of its different names. For instance, the philosopher Socrates, *qua* Socrates, is homonymous to Socrates the school-mate of Theaetetus, but the two are synonymous *qua* men.

There are, however, some things (3) which are homonymous and

25

30

35,1

5

10

15

synonymous with regard to one and the same name, but to various different things. The bird 'crow', for instance, is homonymous to the door-knocker, but synonymous to other crows.

20

Sometimes (4), the same thing is homonymous and synonymous in accordance with the same name and to the same reality, as for instance Melas in Homer:

Agrios and Melas.[370]

In so far as 'Black' (*Melas*) is a proper name, it would be homonymous to a person who is black in colour. If the man so called happened to be black in colour as well, however, he would be synonymous to a man who was likewise black. Thus, if the man whose proper name was 'Savage' (*Agrios*) happened also to be 'savage' (*agrios*) in character, he would be both homonymous and synonymous to someone who was savage in character.[371] There are many other such names; some derive from the virtues but are said as proper names, as for instance *Eleutherios* ('Free'), *Sôphrosunos* ('Temperate'), *Semnos* ('Venerable') and so forth. Some are derived from ethnic appellations, such as *Italos* ('Italian'), *Krêtikos* ('Cretan'), and *Eleusinios* ('Eleusinian'), when one person has [such a name] as a proper name, and another as a name denoting ethnic origin. If, however, both have the same proper name and the same disposition (*diathesis*), or both were called by the proper name 'Black' (*Melas*) and were black in colour, then they are homonyms with regard to their proper names, for the proper name denotes the individualizing quality of the thing so called.[372] With regard to their common blackish disposition, however, they would be synonyms; for the account (*logos*) of each of them is the same, with regard to their having the same colour, or psychological disposition, or same country of origin. In such cases, someone could even be homonymous with regard to himself, for if he was called 'Black' (*Melas*), and was also black in colour, 'black' would belong homonymously both to a proper name and to a black man.

25

30

35
36,1

5

'As for example animal',[373] the example given [by Aristotle], was not given with regard to synonymous realities, but rather with regard to the name of a synonymous thing. 'For man', he says, 'and ox are called by the common name "animal".'[374]

In calling 'synonyms'[375] those things which, together with their name, also have the same definition (*horismos*), Aristotle was more appropriate (*oikeioteron*) than the Stoics, who called synonyms those things which have many names at the same time – as Paris and Alexander are the same person – and, in general, the so-called polyonyms.[376] For the prefix *sun* ('with') does not fit with polyonyms, since it signifies sharing in the same thing, as in 'to walk with' (*sumperipatein*) or 'to fight alongside' (*sustrateuesthai*). Perhaps [the Stoics] were considering only the fact that the names are of the same

10

thing, for Aristotle, too, in his *On Poetry*[377] said that synonyms are
that of which the names are many, but the account (*logos*) is the same,
as is the case with polyonyms, such as 'robe' (*lôpion*), 'cloak' (*himation*) 15
and 'mantle' (*pharos*). 'There is nothing absurd,' says Porphyry, 'since
usage is twofold, in that Aristotle should have made use of both
aspects, especially since each of them makes some kind of sense. After
all, several names which are related to one thing, such as "column"
(*kiôn*) and "pillar" (*stulos*), since they have the same account (*logos*),
could be called synonyms. Moreover, when the account (*logos*) is the
same, and the name is named conjointly (*sunonomazetai*), they could 20
be called synonyms still more properly. Thus, one of them is synonymous because several names name one particular reality conjointly
(*sunonomazetai*), while another is synonymous because it names
conjointly both the name and the account (*logos*). This is why, wherever the subject of inquiry is genera or the words which signify
genera, what is needed is the second meaning, since it is according to
this meaning that the genera are predicated synonymously of their 25
species. Where, however, as in the *Poetics* and the third book of the
Rhetoric, the object of inquiry is the multiplicity of words (*phônai*),
and the multiform nomenclature of each thing, then we need the
other kind of synonym, which Speusippus used to call polyonyms.[378]
It is, moreover, unjust for Boethus to say that Aristotle has omitted
what recent authors[379] call synonyms, which are what Speusippus
used to call polyonyms.[380] For they were not omitted, but were taken 30
up in other treatises, in which the discussion (*logos*) of them was
appropriate.'

Cat. 1a12 'Those things are called paronyms' as far as 'and 37,1
brave from bravery.'[381]

Paronyms[382] are, in a sense, intermediary between homonyms and
synonyms: they participate in both, and yet they lack some of the
features of each one. Both the name and the account (*logos*) of
'grammar' (*grammatikê*) and 'grammatical person',[383] for instance, 5
are neither wholly the same, nor are they wholly different. The
account (*logos*) of grammar, for example, is 'the knowledge of writing
and reading'[384] ... say that three things are necessary[385] for that which
is formed paronymously (*tôi ... paronomazomenôi*) from something: 1.
the reality from which it was formed paronymously (*parônomastai*);
2. the name; and 3. in addition, the dissimilarity of the ending, which
Aristotle calls a 'case' (*ptôsis*). For by 'cases of names', the ancients 10
meant not only those five which are now so called, but also the
derivative inflections, whatever may be their formation (*skhêmatismos*). Thus, they also called 'cases' what are now called 'intermediaries'[386]: 'bravely' (*andreiôs*), for instance, would be the 'case' derived
from 'brave' (*andreios*); and 'beautifully' (*kalôs*) from 'beautiful'

(*kalos*). Thus, they also recognized a kind of 'masculine case',[387] deriving from a feminine noun, as 'literate person' (*grammatikos*)

15   derives from 'grammar' (*hê grammatikê*). There is also a feminine 'case', deriving from a masculine noun, as 'Alexandria' derives from 'Alexander'. They called these things, too, 'cases' because they underwent the same changes as cases in the proper sense of the term with regard to the transformation (*metaskhêmatismos*) of their endings.[388]

If any one of the three elements is lacking, paronyms do not occur. For example, a woman who shares in the art of music (*tês mousikês tekhnês metekhousa*), and who is called 'musical' (*mousikê*), although

20   she shares in the name and in the reality, is not called a paronym by derivation from 'music' (*mousikê*), but [is] rather its homonym, since she has the same ending.[389] Moreover, if a person participating in virtue (*aretê*) were called 'virtuous' (*spoudaios*)[390] by derivation from [virtue], he shares in the reality and differs in case, but since he does not share in the [same] name he is not said to be a paronym from 'virtue'. Neither, however, is the virtuous person (*spoudaios*) a paronym from 'seriousness' (*hê spoudê*); for a 'virtuous person'

25   (*spoudaios*) is one who has virtue (*aretê*), but anybody can 'be serious about' (*spoudazomen peri*) something.[391]

Aristotle, for his part, seems to attribute to paronyms only difference in case and appellation in accordance with the name. From his examples, however, he made it clear that participation in the reality is also to be found in paronyms; for the literate man (*grammatikos*)

30   does not participate only in the name of grammar (*grammatikê*), but also in the art (*tekhnê*) itself, and the brave man [participates] in virtue.[392]

When dealing with paronyms, we must investigate what is the primary element, and what has been named after it paronymously (*to parônomasmenon*). For example, that 'Alexander' is primary, 'Alexandria' is derived from him, and from 'Alexandria' is derived 'Alexandrian'; the order cannot be reversed. Now, what is prior by nature will be clear: a city-founder, for example, is prior to the city he

38,1   founds, and the city is prior to the citizen.

'Among paronyms,' says Porphyry,[393] 'would be patronymics and comparatives, superlatives and diminutives. Words such as "*passalophî*", "*hêiphi*" and "*biêiphi*",[394] which some people have called "derivatives" (*paragôga*), would not be paronyms, for paronyms must not signify the same thing without any change (*aparallaktôs*), whereas these words do not signify anything changed (*parêllag-*

5   *menon*) from "*hêi*" – that is, "to/by means of his own" – or from "*biêi*" ["by force"] and "*passalou*" ["from a peg"].'

Such, then, are the paronyms. Instruction about them is useful, so that we may know that paronyms, for the most part, fall under the same category as the principal things:[395] 'the qualified' (*to poion*), for instance, falls under 'Quality' (*hê poiotês*); 'to be standing' (*to hestanai*)

and 'to be lying down' (*to keklisthai*) fall under 'standing' (*hê stasis*).[396] and 'lying' (*hê klisis*), which in turn are under 'Position' (*to keisthai*).[397]   10

Now, whereas Aristotle has spoken of homonyms, synonyms, and paronyms, he omitted both heteronyms and polyonyms. Polyonyms were omitted because they do not present any difference or common feature with regard to realities (*pragmata*), but only multiply expressions (*lexeis*), while heteronyms were omitted because the present discussion does not carry out a division of expressions which are numerically infinite, but of those which signify something generically   15 (*kata genos*).[398] Moreover, as has been said, Aristotle omitted both of them because they pertain more to rhetorical and poetical punctiliousness than they do to philosophical speculation.[399] Nevertheless, it is as well to include these [two classes of words] as well into one single division, together with those that have been taken up.

Now Boethus reports[400] that Speusippus adopted a division which included all names. 'Of names', he says, 'Some are tautonyms, and   20 others are heteronyms. Of tautonyms, some are homonyms, and others are synonyms – and here we understand 'synonyms' according to the usage of the ancients. Of heteronyms', he says, 'some are heteronyms properly (*idiôs*), others polyonyms, and others paronyms.'

An account has already been given of these other types.[401] As for polyonyms, they are several different names for one reality, when   25 their account (*logos*) is one and the same, as in *aor, xiphos, makhaira,* and *phasganon*.[402] Heteronyms, by contrast, are things which differ   39,1 in names, accounts (*logoi*), and realities, such as 'grammar', 'man', and 'wood'. They differ from each other, then, in so far as polyonyms have in common both the same account (*logos*) and the same reality, whereas heteronyms differ in both respects.[403] With regard to the first,[404] polyonyms are convertible (*antistrephei*) with homonyms, in   5 so far as in the case of homonyms the name was common, while the definition (*horos*) of each thing was particular (*idios*). In the case of polyonyms the reverse is true: the reality (*pragma*) and the definition are common, but the names are different. Heteronyms, for their part, are the opposite of synonyms; for while the latter have something in common in both respects, the former have nothing in common in either respect.[405]

We must watch closely, in the case of polyonyms, lest we mistakenly consider that things which are not polyonyms are such. It is not   10 the case, for example, that if several names are predicated of one thing, they are *eo ipso* already polyonyms. Rather, [such names are polyonyms] only if, in addition, the same predicate is said *of one thing.* For instance, 'partless' (*ameres*) and 'smallest' (*elakhiston*) are two names, and are said of one reality, e.g. the letter 'A' or 'B'; and 'convex' and 'concave' are said of a circle, but that of which they are said is by no means a polyonym. For since the account (*logos*) of each one [*sc.* of   15 convex and concave] is different, each does not belong to it [*sc.* the circle] in the same respect.[406]

It is worth noting, however, that even in the case of polyonyms properly so called – as when, in the case of 'man', the same person is called both *merops* and *brotos* – each of the names is given in accordance with different aspects of man's nature. For instance, man is given one name in so far as he is analogical,[407] another in accordance with the ethnic differences in his dialect, and another according to his mortal condition;[408] and the account (*logos*) of each of these things is different.

What, then? Do polyonyms not exist at all? Rather, those things alone are polyonyms to which different names apply not with regard to their various natures, but as if with regard to the same nature, either because different people name them differently with regard to any random aspect, or because different names have been given out with regard to the same aspect, not etymologically, but in accordance with whatever licence the imposer of names may have had. This is shown by the fact that names which apply to one reality are often subsituted for the names of others, as 'however' (*alla mên*) was transferred to become the name of a slave;[409] for if we do not follow etymology, we can impose as many names, and of as many kinds, as we wish.[410]

It must also be a property of polyonyms that they are called by many names within the same ethnic group; otherwise *hêmera* and *hamera*[411] will be considered polyonyms. They also do well to note the following fact: whereas in the case of homonyms, 'homonymy' denotes both the homonymous name and the relation (*skhesis*) itself, in the case of polyonyms 'polyonymy' denotes only the reality (*pragma*), but not the name. Moreover, homonyms are at any rate said relative to something else: 'O homonym of the blessed Dardanids'[412] – whereas polyonyms do not have their being in any relation (*skhesis*).

Why, however, did Archytas omit this instruction about names in his *On the Universal Formulae*? The answer is that since the Pythagoreans say that names are by nature and not by imposition, they reject both homonyms and polyonyms, saying that by nature one name is said of one reality. It is therefore fitting that they should distinguish homonyms by ancestral or hopeful reference,[413] but that they should show that polyonyms, when they are genuinely words, are not said with reference to one thing, but are given according to different etymologies.[414] They will also appropriately explain the change in form (*paraskhêmatismos*) that takes place in the case of paronyms by means of the couplings (*suzugiai*) of realities.[415]

Cat. 1a16 'Of things which are said, some are said in combination' to ' "runs, conquers." '

After his teaching about homonyms, synonyms, and paronyms, Aristotle makes his approach to the discussion of the categories by means of the division proper to his subject-matter. Since the goal (*skopos*), as we saw, is about simple expressions (*lexeis*) in so far as they are significant, he makes a division of things said (*ta legomena*) into things which are said in combination – he does not propose to speak 20 about these here, but rather in his discussion of propositions[416] – and those without combination. The latter are then divided into the categories. That such is indeed the goal (*skopos*) of the division is shown by Aristotle himself a little further on, when he says, 'Of those said with no combination, each signifies either substance or a quantified or a qualified or a relative.'[417] The division is, moreover, not deficient, since it includes everything: both what is said (*ta legomena*) 25 and what exists (*ta onta*).

Aristotle named things in combination first because the first things we encounter are sensible, and these are composite (*suntheta*). Only later do we encounter the principles (*arkhai*) of these sensible things, which are simpler. Alternatively, he may have intended to indicate to us the simple things by the negation of those in combination; but a negation cannot be adequately known unless that of which it is the negation is known first. It is also true to say, however, that when, once 30 we have divided something, we neglect the prior section (*tmêma*) of the division, and subdivide the other, we range first the section we 41,1 have deferred, and the divided section after it. The divided section comes last, in order that we may not need to take up again those things we have omitted. Again, these postponed things are first, so that our division may proceed in serial fashion.[418]

Now, if the Ancients, too, used to say that 'the things said' (*legomena*), in the proper sense of the term, are what is signified by 5 discourse (*logos*), but in extended usage (*katakhrêstikôs*) they are also what is signified by a simple expression (*lexis*); and if discourse (*logos*) is uttered by means of a combination of expressions (*kata sumplokên lexeôn*), then it is reasonable that, when dividing 'things said', he should first mention ['what is said'] in the proper sense of the term.

It is to be noted[419] that 'what is said' is (1) the realities (*pragmata*), which is what discourse (*logos*) is about, and (2) the notions (*noêmata*) which are about (*peri*) the realities. This, indeed, is why, when we consider that someone is speaking without thinking, we say 'You're 10 saying nothing' (*ouden legeis*), even if he does utter some kind of discourse (*logos*) or expression (*lexis*).[420] According to a third meaning (3), 'what is said' is the significant expression itself, as well as the discourse (*logos*); for both expressions and discourses (*logoi*) are *said* by someone. According to a fourth meaning (4), even meaningless expressions like 'blituri' belong to the class of 'what is said', in so far as they are uttered at all.

Yet Boethus, although, as was said, he considers that 'what is said' must be understood in four ways in the case of non-compound expres- 15

sions, [thinks 'what is said' should be understood] in only three ways
15   in the case of those which have been combined. According to him,
combined realities,[421] such as 'It is daytime' (*hêmera estin*), are not
'what is said', not because the phrase (*logos*) does not signify anything, but because it is not the name of a reality (*pragma*), as 'day' is.
It is not *of* the reality, but is *about* (*peri*) the reality.

    Now that 'what is said' (*to legomenon*) and 'to be said' (*to legesthai*)
have been divided in this number of ways, it is worth investigating
20   which of these meanings [Aristotle] includes in the division. The
divine Iamblichus says that Alexander proposes that 'the things said'
are the simplest and most generic signified realities. For my part, I
find Alexander saying, and I quote: 'here he is not saying that "the
things said" are what is signified, but rather what signifies and is
uttered.'[422] How, indeed, could [Aristotle] be talking about realities
25   here, when further on[423] he says 'of those things which are said with
no combination, each signifies either substance or a quantified'? For
realities do not *signify* substance or the quantified, but they *are*
substance or the quantified, whereas what signifies are expressions,
which are *about* realities.[424]

    Boethus says that, among the Ancients, the only things said or
signified were intellections (*noêseis*), for truth and falsehood are not
30   in the realities, but in thoughts (*dianoiai*) and the developments
42,1   (*diexodoi*) of the intellect,[425] as Aristotle himself says in Book 3 of the
On the Soul.[426] But thought is also signified by discourse (*logos*); it is
therefore more appropriate to say that 'what is said' is significant
expressions in so far as they are significant, since, as has been
proved,[427] the categories are not realities (*pragmata*) either. As we
saw, what provides the categories is not notions (*noêmata*) nor mere
5   expressions (*lexeis*) in so far as they are words (*phônai*), but rather
expressions which are significant of realities by means of notions,
distinguished according to each genus.[428] Thus, 'the things said' is also
to be understood in terms of significant expressions.

    Of these [significant expressions], some are said 'in combination',
others 'without combination'. 'Combination' (*sumplokê*), therefore, is
10   also said in many ways, for they say things are combined (*sumplekes-
thai*) either by means of a conjunction, or by virtue of the kinship
among realities.[429] [Things are combined] by a conjunction, either
simply, as when we say '*If* it is daytime, it is light', or else by means
of a connective conjunction,[430] as when we say, 'It is daytime *and* it is
light.'[431]

    Combination is through kinship when accidents (*ta sumbebêkota*)
15   are said of substances, since accidents have the nature of existing
(*huparkhein*) in them, whether they accrue as qualifieds (*poia*) or as
things relatively disposed (*pôs ekhonta*),[432] such as 'on the right' (*to
dexion*) or 'to be shod' (*to hupodedesthai*). After all, substance is that
which exists by itself alone, while an accident is that which comes

about in something else. The combination of the accident with the substance, then, defines the underlying term (*horos*) in the proposition (*protasis*), and signifies how the accident is disposed towards it.[433] Since it would be possible to take the accident by itself, or to combine   20 it with its substrate, predications come about in both these ways. For instance, when I say 'white exists' (*to leukon einai*), I am taking up white (*to leukon*) by itself. When, however, I say, 'this object is white' (*tode leukon estin*), I am saying nothing other than 'this object possesses whiteness' (*tode leukotêta ekhei*). Being, then, and having have the powers of conjunctions.[434] When genera are predicated of sub-   25 strates, moreover, we also employ generic things as if they were accidents, since things which are combined by being or by having are woven together by means of these things [*sc.* being and having], as if by conjunctions.[435]

There is a third kind of combination (*sumplokê*): in general, every composition (*sunthesis*) of the elements of discourse (*logos*), of whatever kind it may be; whether it is names that we put together, as in 'mortal rational animal', or verbs, as in 'he is walking and conversing'; and whether it is deficient (*ellipê*) [things we put together], as in 'as   30 Socrates was going out', or complete (*autotelê*),[436] as in 'whither and   43,1 whence?',[437] or whether we carry out the initial linkage (*suzeuxis*) of the verb to the noun, as in 'Socrates is walking'. For what Plato said in the case of the genera of being – namely, that some are wont to commune with each other, while others do not mix together in any way[438] – is also true to say in the case of the parts of discourse (*logos*)   5 which are significant: those are woven together which are indicative of realities which are fitted together (*sunêrmosmena*), but those which are significant of separate (*kekhôrismena*) realities are not woven together.

Since, as we saw, there are also two kinds of community between beings:[439] connatural (*sumphutos*), and acquired (*epiktêtos*),[440] the highest species of combination will also be double: that of accidents *qua* inherent, and that of things ranged together (*suntattomena*) by a conjunction, which have their unity, as it were, from without.   10

That which is placed together [*sc.* with a subject] as an accident, being either a verb, as in 'runs', 'conquers', or predicated together with a verb, as in 'he is a man' (*anthrôpos estin*) – and indeed 'he runs' can also be analysed into 'he is running'.[441] Thus, wherever a verb is present, time is also co-indicated[442] – not that it co-signifies that both are in one time, or that one is prior to the other, but it presents only the relation (*skhesis*) of the accident both to the substrate and to time.   15 This is because accidents properly so called arrive and depart in accordance with time, since if [the accidents] were inseparable with regard to the substance and belonged to it everlastingly, time would not be co-signified. For although we do say that the intellect thinks (*nous noei*), we are [in so talking] adding the temporal element.[443]

As for things said in combination and without combination: we will
find them out by following the nature of the realities and the differ-
20   entiation of notions (*noêmata*). When the reality is one and the notion
is one, 'what is said' will be simple and without combination, even if
the expressions (*lexeis*) appear to be many, as in the case of 'Neapolis'[444] and 'Good Spirit';[445] for [in both cases] the significatum is one.
When, however, both the realities and the notions are many, we will
say that they are 'with combination', even if the expression is one.
Examples are *zô* ('[I] live'), for 'I' is conceived in addition,[446] and *huei*
25   ('it is raining'), for it is indicated that it is Zeus [who is raining].[447]

Archytas, however, at the beginning of his book of categories or of
universal formulae (*logoi*),[448] first instructs us about the account
(*logos*), and he encompassed thought (*dianoia*) and expression (*lexis*)
within the account; he said that the expression is significative, and
thought is what is signified. He also distinguished simple and com-
30   posite things, perfect and deficient, and he taught the criteria on the
basis of which things in combination and without combination must
be tested.

44,1   **Cat.** 1a20 'Of beings, some are said *of* some substrate' to 'for a
particular instance of grammatical knowledge is one of those
things *in* a substrate.'

It has seemed to some that this is not consistent with what was said
previously, and it was for this reason that the work seemed like a
mere collection of notes.[449] This is not so, however; rather, since the
5   goal (*skopos*), as we have seen, was about simple and generic expressions which signify simple and generic realities, [Aristotle] judged
that before carrying out the division of them into the maximum
number – that is to say, the division into ten, since it was not possible
to discover more than ten – he should first undertake their division
into the minimum number, to fewer than which it was impossible to
compress them. After all, this would be the scientific procedure),[450]
and the decad is contained within the tetrad, since when we add
10   together one, two, three, and four, we get the number ten; again, he
also compresses the tetrad into a dyad. These four things are substance, accident, the universal, and the particular (*to kata meros*); for
beings are divided into two: 1. Those which are capable of being *per
se* (*kath' heauta*), and need nothing else in order to subsist (*pros
hupostasin*). These are also called substance (*ousia*), since they are
sufficient unto themselves with regard to being (*pros to einai*).[451] 2.
15   Those which subsist (*huphestôta*) within other things. These are also
called accidents (*sumbebêkota*), since they occur (*sumbebêkenai*)
within other things.

Thus we have the division into two of the ten categories; nine of
them are gathered together under [the heading of] 'accident', while

substance has been enumerated before any of the others.[452] Moreover,
each of these gives itself either to several subordinate things, or to
only one, and for this reason there comes about another coupling
(*suzugia*), that which is generative, [*viz.*] of the universal and the
particular. When these are woven together, there comes about a total   20
of six combinations (*sumplokai*).[453] Among these, two are non-exis-
tent:[454] *viz.* those which bring together contradictories, such as the
combination of 'in a substrate' and 'not in a substrate';[455] and that of
'[said] of a substrate' and 'not [said] of a substrate'.[456] Aristotle does
set forth the remaining four combinations. Thus, it is either universal
substance, particular accident, universal accident, or particular sub-   25
stance.[457] Since, however, Aristotle has shown the aforementioned
things by means of rather uncommon names, we must translate them
into what the Philosopher says.[458]

He called accidents 'in a substrate' because, since they are not
autonomous (*autokrates*), they require something else in which to
exist, whereas substance was so called by negation of 'accident'. Since   30
it is true to say that beings are either autonomous, or else have their
being in other substrates which are autonomous – that is to say, they
are either substance or accidents – then whatever is not an accident,
is at any rate a substance, and everything other than the things in a   45,1
substrate is not in a substrate. Again, since some things are universal,
and others particular (*merika*); and none of the things that exist
escapes this division; and universals are what is predicated synonymously of several things, which are what Aristotle calls '[said] of a
substrate' (*kath' hupokeimenou*) (for what is predicated in this way is
predicated of what is essentially (*ousiôdôs*) the substrate); and what   5
is not such is particular (*merikon*); he was correct to signify the
particular (*to merikon*) by the negation of '[said] of a substrate'.
Elsewhere, however, he uses '[said] of a substrate' instead of 'accident'.[459]

Since we said that, from four combined things, there comes about
a total of six combinations, the common method should be known by
which it is possible, given any [specific] number of terms, to find out
how many two-by-two combinations arise from them. One must mul-   10
tiply the number of terms set out by this number minus one, then take
half of the product, and say that this is the number of combinations.[460]
The reason for this method is, moreover, clear: since each thing has a
relation (*skhesin ekhei*) to all the others, and the relations (*skheseis*)
are fewer than the terms by one, since they are between the terms,   15
this is the reason why we multiply the number of terms set forth by
this number minus one. In order that we not take the same relations
twice – for instance, the relation between substance and accident *and*
that between accident and substance – we take half of the product.

Why, however, did Aristotle not use meanings according to common
usage, and speak of universal substance, particular accident, and so   20

forth? The answer is that he has transmitted a description (*hupo-graphê*)[461] of each one by means of more emphatic[461] names: for 'being *in* a substrate' presents the substance (*ousia*) of accidents, as '[being said] *of* a substrate' presents [the substance of] universals. Moreover, he was right to indicate them by means of a description, for it was not possible to give the genera of the most generic things, and therefore it was also impossible to give their definitions (*horismous*).[462] It was

25   also appropriate to assign '[being] in a substrate' to the accident, and 'not being in a substrate' to substance. To the universal, however, he no longer assigned '*being* of a substrate', but rather 'being *said*'. For it is said of the substrate, whether or not it is in existence.[463] However, although he elsewhere speaks as though universals were non-exis-tent, here he divides them as beings, for he says 'of beings'.[464] This

30   division into four is not a division (*diairesis*) in the proper sense of the term, but rather an enumeration (*aparithmêsis*),[465] as if someone were to point at a group of people and say, 'of these, some are Lacedaemonians, and others Argives'.

46,1   ***Cat.* 1a24-1b3** 'By "in a substrate", I mean' to 'is neither in a substrate, nor is said of a substrate'.[466]

Since [Aristotle] himself came up with the name 'in a substrate', he was right to add 'I mean'. He took 'in something' as the genus of 'in a substrate', and in what follows he separates the differentiae of 'in

5   something' from the rest;[467] for 'in something' is said in many ways; eleven at the least;[468] for it is either as (1) 'in a place', as 'in the Lyceum'; or (2) as 'in a vessel', as wine is 'in' the amphora;[469] or (3) as 'in time', as in 'the Peloponnesian war [took place] in [the year of] such-and-such an Olympiad';[470] or (4) as the part is in a whole, as a hand is in the whole body;[471] or (5) as the whole is in its parts;[472] or (6)

10   as the species is in the genus, as 'man' is in 'animal', for the former is contained within the latter;[473] or (7) as the genus is in the species,[474] for the species participates in the genus, as 'man' [participates in] 'animal'; or (8) as in a goal (*en telei*), as all things are in their own good;[475] or (9) as form is in matter,[476] as in the bronze is the shape (*morphê*) of the statue; or (10) as in the moving cause;[477] or (11) as what belongs to those who are ruled is in the ruler.[478]

15   Which, then, of the meanings of 'in something' fits with 'in a substrate'? As the divine Iamblichus seems to say, 'as in matter'[479] is appropriate (*oikeion*) to 'in a substrate'. In saying this, Iamblichus believes he is following Aristotle, for the latter, when in Book 4 of the *Physics* he indicates the meanings of 'in something', joined together as one 'as in matter' and 'as in a substrate' by saying: 'Again, as health is in things which are hot and cold, and, in general, form is in

20   matter',[480] in accordance, it seems, with the unique shape-giving nature of that which is cast underneath; taking it as one.[481]

(12) 'In a substrate' is a twelfth meaning of 'in something', for there is a great difference between 'as in a substrate' and 'as in matter'.[482] For that which is in a substrate is in a substance, and as in a composite substance; for physical substance, at any rate, is composed of matter and form. The form which is in matter, by contrast, is as in what is formless (*hôs en aneideôi*) and [is] a part of substance.[483] And that which is in a substrate takes its being from the substrate, whereas form gives matter its being. And that which is in a substrate does not complete (*sumplêroi*) the substance of the composite, as is shown by its definition,[484] whereas that which is in matter[485] *does* complete it. Furthermore, I say that what is in a substrate is an accident, and ends up under some one of the nine categories, whereas form is referred under Substance and the substrate. Here, however,[486] since Aristotle has taken the sensible and the determinate something (*to ti*), he would not say that what is in matter is in a substrate, for he does not consider [the terms] 'a something' (*ti*) or 'this individual thing' (*tode*) to be appropriate, in general, to matter.[487] For although in the *Physics*, he does call matter, too, 'substance',[488] he does not say that it is such in the proper sense of the term. Here, however, he calls primary substance 'composite', and 'substrate'. Iamblichus himself, moreover, a little further on, objected that 'as in matter' is one thing, and 'as in a substrate' is another.[489]

We should note, however, that Aristotle, in Book 4 of the *Physics*, divided 'in something' into eight.[490] He did not make mention at all of [the meaning] 'in time', perhaps because he had not yet said anything about time.[491] Having joined 'in a substrate' to 'in matter', moreover, he also joined together 'vessel' and 'place', since at that point the difference between them had not yet been mentioned.[492] Now, of the other meanings of 'in something',[493] some exist as parts of that in which they are, as that which is properly a part [is a part] of the whole,[494] and the species (*eidos*) is a [part] of the genus[495] for this, too, is either a part, or like a part. In the case of 'in a substrate', Aristotle also eliminated 'like a part',[496] but not 'part' alone. The coordinated (*katatetagmenon*) genus, however, also completes (*sumplêroi*) the substance of the species (*eidos*), insofar as the latter is, as it were, composed of genus and differentiae; and the genus becomes a part of the species,[497] just as the species, taken together with matter, becomes a part of composite substance.

Others[498] are not parts, but can be separated from those things in which they are:[499] e.g. those which are 'in' a place, 'in' a vessel, 'in' time, and 'in' a goal (for when they fall out of the good in which they are, they do not have anything in which to subsist, but they nevertheless are somethings (*tina*); and when that which is moved is separated from its moving cause, or things which are ruled are separated from their ruler, they could subsist apart from the mover and the ruler.[500] Therefore, he separated it[501] from the first ones[502] by saying 'not as a

25

30
47,1

5

10

15

20

part', and from the second ones[503] by means of 'it is impossible for
them to exist apart from that in which they are'.

25   Perhaps, however, someone will say that the whole which is in its
parts does not exist *as* a part (*hôs meros*), nor can it be separated from
its parts, and it therefore would be in a substrate.[504] [The answer is]
that since he said 'in something' and not 'in some *things*', he thereby
separated it [*viz.* 'in a substrate'] from the whole in accordance with
this consideration; for the whole which is in its parts is not 'in
something', but in some *things*.[505]

48,1   Lucius and his circle, however, also raise the following objection
against the fact that what is in a substrate[506] is said to be 'not as a
part'. 'For if,' they say, 'we say that things which complete a substance
(*ta sumplêrôtika tês ousias*) are parts of that substance, and that
which simply completes the being of a sensible body is colour, figure,
magnitude, and simply quality and quantity (since there could be no
5   colourless or figureless body), and of this particular body, snow, for
instance, whiteness and coldness [*sc.* complete the substance], then
one of two things is necessary: either not to say that these things are
in a substrate, or [to say that] it was not correct to deny of things in
a substrate that they are like parts. How, moreover, is it possible for
completers (*ta sumplêrôtika*), in general, to be said to be in a substrate? For Socrates' shape (*morphê*) is not in Socrates as its
10   substrate; rather, if anything, it would be those things which enter
into already-complete things from outside[507] which would be in them
as their substrate'.

        Porphyry[508] solves this difficulty in the following way: 'There are,'
he says, 'two kinds of substrate,[509] not only according to those from
the Stoa,[510] but also according to the more ancient thinkers. Qualityless matter (*hê ... apoios hulê*), which Aristotle calls "potential
body",[511] is the first meaning of "substrate", and the second is that
15   which comes into existence as either a commonly qualified thing[512] or
as something individually qualified.[513] For both bronze and Socrates[514] are substrates for those things which supervene upon them or
are predicated of them. Therefore,' he says, 'many of the things which
inhere are in a substrate with regard to the first substrate; for
instance, all colour and all figure and all quality are in prime matter
as their substrate, not as parts of it and incapable of existing apart
20   from it. In the case of the second substrate, however, not all colour nor
all quality is in a substrate, but [they are so only] when they are not
completers (*sumplêrôtikai*) of substance. For white in the case of wool
is in a substrate, but in the case of snow it is not in a substrate, but
completes the substance as a part, and is rather a substrate as far as
substance is concerned. Similarly, heat is a part of the substance of
25   fire, but it comes to be in iron as its substrate, since it comes to be in
and departs from the iron without the destruction of the iron. Now
Aristotle here having taken up the second above-mentioned substrate

– that which is in accordance with the composite and with individual substance, which, he says, neither is in a substrate nor is said of any substrate – rightly says that everything which is not said of it essentially (*ousiôdôs*), but as an accident (*kata to sumbebêkenai*), is in this as its substrate, like heat in iron. Those things, however, which are completers (*sumplêrôtika*), like the heat of fire, he would say are a part of the fire, and in qualityless matter as their substrate.'   30

In response to this solution, however, I think it is reasonable to say   49,1 that if what is in a substrate is only that which comes to be [*sc.* in it] and goes away [*sc.* from it], then Aristotle no longer included all the categories within these two [classes; *viz.*] 'in a substrate' and 'not in a substrate'. For if 'not in a substrate' indicates substance, but 'in a substrate' denotes, not all qualities, but only adventitious ones, then not all the genera would be included.[515] Or perhaps we should say that   5 those qualities which are not adventitious, but rather are completers (*sumplêrôtikai*) of substance, being parts of substance, are themselves also substances and are included together with substance; for according to Aristotle, the parts of substance are themselves substances.[516] Perhaps, moreover, this was the reason why he called substance not 'substrate', but 'not in a substrate': so that he could also include such qualities.[517]

Some also raise difficulties about the fragrance of an apple and   10 vaporized incense.[518] For although fragrance is an accident, nevertheless it transfers from the apple and incense into the air and into clothing,[519] and the sweetness of honey passes into the whole of honey-water,[520] and when garlic and radishes are altered once they are within the belly, their bad odour becomes obvious to those who associate with him. But it must be noted that Aristotle did not say   15 that it is impossible for it [*sc.* that which is a substrate] to be separated from that in which it *was*, but 'from that in which it *is*'.[521] For even if it abandons its previous substrate, since as a whole it is continuous, either by contact or by unification, it is able to transfer over into other things without there being a void in between.[522] Moreover, how could a quality be transferred outside of substance? It would then be separable by nature, even if it comes to be within something else as it transfers.   20

Perhaps, then, it is better to say that all fragrances and all such accidents exist along with their proper substance, and are never detached from it, but that substance sometimes is unfolded as it becomes rarefied,[523] and is scattered among the other substances. At other times, the substance transforms into itself those things which are continuous [with it], and are naturally such as to undergo change. This is clearly seen in the case of fire: for it is not the initial spark which spreads over the entire matter, but rather the fire which,   25 starting out from the spark, gradually multiplies itself.

Perhaps it is clear from what has been said that the fragrance of

an apple or of incense, although they are completers (*sumplêrôtikai*)
of the form, could not be said to be in that which is completed (*en tôi
sumplêroumenôi*) as in their substrate. That some kind of substance
is dispersed together with such fragrances is clear from the phenom-
30   ena of apples shrivelling up and incense being consumed.[524]

'But why,' they say,[525] 'will not individual substances, such as
Socrates and Plato, be subsumed under the account (*logos*) of the
things "in a substrate", and be accidents, since Socrates is also "in
something" – for he is in time and space – and not as a part, and it is
impossible for him to exist apart from time and space? For even if he
50,1   were to change from this particular place, he will still be in some
other, as was said in the case of fragrance.'

Boethus thought he solved the difficulty based on place, when he
said that things in motion are, in general, never in the place in which
they *were*, for this was proved in the *On Motion*.[526] By the same
reasoning (*logos*), however, neither would they be in partial time. For
5   since time flows constantly, it is always other; so that if anything, they
are in universal time.

Boethus, however, provides a solution for this, too. In the first
place, he says, universals are not even in existence (*en hupostasei*)
according to Aristotle,[527] and even if they were, they are not a determinate thing (*ti*). Yet Aristotle said 'in some *thing*'.[528] Therefore, that
which is 'in something' cannot be in a universal.[529]

Such difficulties as these could, however, easily be resolved, if we
10   link together 'in' and 'existing' (*huparkhon*);[530] for accidents inhere
(*enuparkhein*) in a substrate, but neither things in space nor things
in time could be said to 'inhere'. If, however someone were to consider
that forms within matter are included by the definition (*logos*), since
this [kind of form] is also in matter, not as a part of it, and is
inseparable from it, it was said previously that Aristotle here says 'in
something' with the meaning of 'in a compound substance', of which
15   both 'substance' and 'something' (*ti*) can be said truly.[531]

It is worth inquiring why he placed the particular accident after
universal substance,[532] and not something universal, or some substance. For if you write down [all the possible combinations] in a
square schema,[533] placing 'universal' at the top and 'particular' at the
bottom, you will find that neither the vertical nor the horizontal are
ranged together (*suntetagmena*), but rather those on the diagonal.
20   The reason for this is that every division, if it is to be exhaustive, must
take place by contradiction. In this case, it is even more appropriate
to take the affirmative as opposed to the negative, i.e. '[said] of a
substrate' versus 'not [said] of a substrate', and the negative contradicting the affirmative, i.e. 'not in a substrate' contradicting 'in a
substrate'.

***Cat.* 1a29-1b1** 'Another thing is both said of a substrate and is
in a substrate.'[534]

25

It ought to be clear from what has been said that what Aristotle
names in this way is the universal accident. It is worth noting,
however, that throughout this passage Aristotle posits universal and
generic things as being in existence – 'universal knowledge', for
instance – and it is obvious that the latter is within the universal soul.
A little earlier on, however, he had divided beings into universal and
particular, and perhaps in this he was following the Pythagoreans,
from whom he took over his teaching about the ten genera.

51,1

***Cat.* 1b6-8** 'In general, things which are individual and numeri-
cally one' up to 'nothing prevents [some of them] from being [in
a substrate].'

5

Since [Aristotle] was the first to coin the terms 'in a substrate' and
'[said] of a substrate', it was necessary to clarify what these names
mean for him. Thus, having previously explained 'in a substrate', he
now presents what is indicated by '[said] of a substrate'. Or rather, he
first transmits what it does *not* signify, and then, in this way, what
power (*dunamis*) it has. He says, then, that it is 'individuals';[535] i.e.
those things which are not cut up by differentiae and are consequently not one in genus or in species, but only in number, since they
have their unity in being counted. These things, then, are not said of
any substrate, since they have nothing more partial than themselves,
of which they could be predicated as of a substrate. If, however,
Socrates' name is predicated of Socrates himself as its substrate, the
discussion (*logos*) is not about this kind of predication. Rather, it is
about the synonymous predication of one thing of another, and this
does not pertain (*huparkhei*) to individuals.

10

15

Having stated what is common to every individual, *viz.* that it is
not '[said] of a substrate', he also adds the differentia: it is possible for
a determinate thing (*to ti*) to be 'in a substrate' – that is, to be an
accident – but it is obvious that what is a substance is not in a
substrate. Perhaps, however, since [Aristotle] himself was the first to
impose these names, the reason he says 'nothing prevents' what is not
[said] of a substrate 'from being in a substrate', is so that no one, upon
hearing 'not [said] *of* a substrate', should immediately suppose it to
be also 'not *in* a substrate', considering the substrate to be identical
in both cases; for the substrate is different in each case. Now if
nothing prevents it from being *in* a substrate, clearly also nothing
prevents it from *not* being in a substrate. For nothing prevents what
is particular (*to merikon*) from being both an accident and a substance.

20

25

Cat. **1b10-15** 'When something is predicated of something else'
to 'for an individual man is both man and animal.'

30   Having stated what is *not* '[said] of a substrate', [Aristotle] now states
     what *is*: *viz.*, it is to be predicated synonymously and essentially (*en*
52,1 *tôi ti estin*). This takes place when, in giving the definitory account
     (*horistikos logos*) of a substrate, we give it by means of its predicate.
     For if one gave an account of what a human being is, he would say:
     'an animal'. When, therefore, predication takes place as 'of a substrate',
     as when 'man' is predicated of Socrates, and some other thing is predi-
5   cated of the predicate as well, not just at random, but as 'of a substrate',
     and synonymously, as 'animal' will be predicated of 'man', 'animal' will
     be predicated of Socrates too. For thus we will have [a syllogism of] the
     first mode of the first figure, in which the middle term is *in* the whole of
     the major term, but is *said of* the whole of the minor term.[536]
     Some people raise the following difficulty[537]: if 'animal' is said of
10   'man' as of a substrate, and 'genus' is said of 'animal', how is it that
     'genus' is not predicated of 'man'?[538] The solution to this is close to
     hand: 'genus', although predicated of 'animal', is not predicated of it
     as of a substrate;[539] if it were, it would be predicated of every animal.
     As things are, however, although Socrates, too, is an animal, yet he is
     not a genus, for 'genus' is not predicated essentially (*en tôi ti estin*) of
15   'animal'.[540] When asked what an animal is, at any rate, we do not say
     'a genus', but rather 'an animate substance'. For it is not the case that
     everything which is predicated, in any way whatsoever, is predicated
     as of a substrate. In [the phrase] 'Socrates is walking', at any rate,
     'walking' is predicated, but not as of a substrate. Thus, as I said,
     Aristotle shows by means of the present passage as well what it is to
20   be 'said of a substrate': it is to be predicated synonymously. He
     especially teaches the following point: of whatever something is said
     as of its substrate, the category under which the predicate is referred
     is said of that thing [*viz.* the subject] as well.[541] For if 'animal' is said
     of 'man' as of a substrate, but 'animal' is referred to Substance, then
     'man', too, will be referred to Substance. It is, moreover, by means of
     this theorem that individual things (*ta kath' hekasta*), which reason-
25   ing cannot grasp by means of their proper stages of ascent,[542] are
     concentrated into the ten categories. For it cannot be clearly known
     that Socrates is a substance unless one travels through many of the
     things predicated synonymously of what is beneath each of them; that
     is, things which are said of a substrate. For if Socrates is a man, then
     he is also what is predicated synonymously of 'man'; thus he is also
     an 'animal'; and he is also what is predicated synonymously of 'ani-
30   mal', so that he is also 'animate' and 'substance'. But if 'being said of
     a substrate' is the same as being predicated synonymously, since the
     definition (*horismos*) is also predicated synonymously of the definien-

dum (*kephalaiôdes*)[543] – for man is a rational, mortal animal – then the definition of man would also be said of man as of its substrate. But if this is so, then it is no longer the universal (*to katholou*) which is signified by '[said] of a substrate'. This was why Aristotle did not simply say 'when something is predicated as of a substrate', but rather 'when something other (*heteron*) is predicated of something other (*kath'heterou*) as of a substrate'.[544] But those things signified by a definitory account (*logos*) are not other than the definiendum (*horiston*).[545]

Some, however, take issue with this very point: that what is predicated of a substrate is said to be 'different' from that of which it is predicated; for 'animal' is predicated of 'man' as of an animal, and 'colour' of 'white' as of a colour. Porphyry says[546] that the concept (*epinoia*) of 'animal' is twofold: one is of the coordinated (*katatetagmenon*) animal, and the other of the uncoordinated (*akatatakton*). Thus, the uncoordinated is predicated of the coordinated, and thereby it is 'different'.[547]

Iamblichus,[548] however, says that 'it is not genera which are predicated of substrata, but other things by means of these. For when we say, "Socrates is a man", we are not saying he *is* the generic (*genikon*) Man, but rather that he *participates in* the generic Man, just as saying that "the vine is white" is the same as saying "it bears white grapes", since the vine is so called by reference to its fruit.[549] Aristotle made clear distinctions with regard to these matters in the *Metaphysics*.[550] Here, however, he has used meanings in a more common way, as we also do when we say that "definitions are from genus and differentiae": here we do not take "genus" in the proper sense, but are using it instead of "case",[551] which is explained by "participation in the generic".'

However, that [Aristotle] wants '[said] of a substrate' to be universal, he showed by saying that 'individual things are not said of a substrate';[552] while that it must be predicated synonymously, he indicated by the words 'and be predicated of the things below it',[553] for this characteristic pertains to things which are predicated essentially.[554] For that which is 'in a substrate' is *in* the substrate, yet it is not predicated synonymously *of* the substrate; for 'soul' is not called 'knowledge'.[555] Thus, when one and the same thing is both *in* a substrate and [said] *of* a substrate – that is, when it is a universal accident – there are two substrates to be considered: that in which it *is*, and that *of* which it is *said*. 'Is'[556] (*estin*) has been attributed to 'in a substrate', while 'is said' (*legetai*) has been allocated to '[said] of a substrate'; for whether universals 'are' (*estin*) or have their being merely in our concepts (*epinoia*), would have to be the subject of another investigation. That they are said *of* the substrate is clear. Here, however, Aristotle has also treated them as if they were beings (*onta*).[557] It is evident from what has been said how things which are

35
53,1

5

10

15

20

25

30

30   in a substrate differ from those which are [said] of a substrate. Let it
      now be said as well that there is [also] a difference between the
      universal and that which comes to be within something else. Indeed,
      of those things which are [said] of a substrate, both the name and the
      account (*logos*) are predicated of the substrate, whereas of that which
54,1 is in a substrate, the account (*logos*) is never predicated, but the name
      often is. Indeed, each of them is sometimes coupled with the other,
      and sometimes not; for that which is [said] *of* a substrate is sometimes
      in a substrate, sometimes not; and that which is *in* a substrate is
      sometimes [said] *of* a substrate, and sometimes not.
5   In general, however, both genera and species – whether in the case
      of substances or of accidents – will be said, in the proper sense of the
      term, of a substrate. [Aristotle] himself showed this by saying that
      'individuals (*ta atoma*) and things one in number are not [said] of a
      substrate'.[558]
          We should note, however, that Andronicus and some others[559] say
      that it is not only things predicated essentially (*en tôi ti estin*) which
10   are said to be predicated 'of a substrate', but other things as well, such
      as 'musical' of Aristoxenus,[560] and 'Athenian' of Socrates. And perhaps
      [this is true of] those things which, when we predicate them of
      something, we say that [the subject] is that very thing which we
      predicate, for when we say that Socrates is walking, we do not say
      that Socrates *is* 'to walk', but we do say he *is* 'Athenian' and 'a
      philosopher'.[561] Whatever is predicated of these,[562] moreover, when we
15   say the former are the latter, will also be said of the substrate.[563] For
      if Socrates is a philosopher and philosophers are knowledgeable, then
      Socrates will also be knowledgeable. Again, they say: 'if a body is
      white and white is a colour, then body will also be a colour'. But 'white'
      signifies two things: the quality and what is coloured,[564] and it is
      'coloured' which is predicated of 'body' – for whiteness is not a body –
      whereas <colour is predicated of quality, for it is not the coloured that
20   is a colour>, but rather whiteness.[565] Thus, it is not colour which will
      be predicated of the body, but the coloured.

      Cat. **1b16-24** 'Of genera which are different[566] and not placed
      beneath one another' to 'will also be of the substrate.'[567]

      Here it is necessary to state what a genus is, what a differentia is, and
      what relation (*skhesis*) they have to one another, with regard both to
25   otherness and to what they have in common.[568]
          Now, 'genus' has many meanings, as Porphyry indeed taught in his
      Isagoge.[569] The genus which has been taken up here is that which is
      predicated essentially (*en tôi ti esti*) of many things which differ in
      species;[570] whereas 'species' is 'that which is predicated essentially (*en
55,1 tôi ti esti*) of several things differing in number',[571] and the differentia
      is 'that which is predicated qualitatively (*en tôi poion einai*) of several

things which differ in species'.[572] Now, those things differ in species which have become distinguished from each other in the account (*logos*) of their substance. Those things differ in number, by contrast, which have determined the characteristic property (*idiotês*) of their own existence (*hupostasis*) by means of a concourse of accidents.[573] That is predicated essentially (*en tôi ti estin*) which is included in the account (*logos*) which states the essence (*to ti ên einai*), and indicates what is essential (*to ousiôdes*) and common in the reality (*pragma*). That is predicated qualitatively (*en tôi hopoion ti*), which takes what is essential (*to ousiôdes*) together with the quality: for 'rational' is not simply a quality, but it is an animal-like[574] quality. Moreover, the differentia must separate essentially (*ousiôdôs*) and in accordance with being, and not in accordance with some accident. For even if 'capable of swimming'[575] belongs to man, yet this is not an essential differentia; but the differentia must be a part of the substance, for it determines the separated characteristic property (*idiotês*) with regard to substance.[576]

Species and differentia differ from one another as whole and part,[577] for the differentia which is constitutive[578] of the species is contained by the entire species, as 'rational' is contained[579] by 'man'. Sometimes the differentia is even stated instead of the entire species,[580] as 'immortal' and 'mortal' are said instead of 'gods' and 'men'.

Of differentiae, some are of genera, and others of species.[581] Of the genus, some are constitutive (*sustatikai*) – viz., those which are said universally[582] – and others are divisive (*diairetikai*) – viz., those which, taken separately, are not said of it, but are all said of it simultaneously.[583] Proper to the species are only the specific (*eidopoioi*) differentiae, each of which is determined in relation to each species by counter-distinction,[584] albeit not all simultaneously.

Just as there are several species for every one genus, so many differentiae contribute to one species.[585] Herminus, however, does not consider it correct to call completive differentiae[586] 'differentiae'; but he reserves this appellation for the divisive (*diairetikai*) differentiae.[587]

In what sense, however, do we apply the term 'differentia' to things which differ in species, and how do we apply 'species' to things which differ in number? For behold, some differentiae are said of [only] one species, as 'light' is of fire (after all, other things are light because of their fieriness), and 'heavy' is said of earth,[588] and in general, the ultimate differentiae are said of each species – as 'capable of receiving intellect and knowledge' in the case of man[589] – and such differentiae are also convertible with regard to the definiendum (*horiston*).

But there are also some species which are monadic among sensible things, as well: for instance, all the perpetual (*aidia*) things, like the sun, the moon, and each of the others; whereas among generated

55,5

10

15

20

25

30

things, there is, it is reported, a bird called 'phoenix'.[590] How is it true, then, that species are said of several things which differ in number?

The answer is that this can be the case, if we take it that the species is predicated of many phoenixes,[591] even though the individuals do not
56,1   exist simultaneously, but successively. And in the case of the perpetual things: if it is not said of several things, then this is not the species we are now investigating; *viz.*, that which is uncoordinated (*akatatakton*) and observed within many things, but it is that which is monadic[592] and coordinated within matter (*en hulêi katatetagmenon*).[593] In the case of the former, even if there are many such things, yet they pertain to all. In fact, such species seem to be
5   intermediary between individuals (*atomôn*) and species/forms[594] in the proper sense of the term: they surpass individuals by virtue of their monadic nature, but are inferior to Forms properly so called by the fact that they have come to be within matter.

As for the differentia, Porphyry says that it usually is said of several species, but not always.[595] Iamblichus, however, says: 'even if some differentiae are not said of several species, nevertheless they too
10   are such that, in so far as it depends on them (*eph' heautais*), they *could* be said of many things. The differentia said determinately of one species,' says Iamblichus, 'is such in a more particular sense (*idikôtera*), and is more akin to nature engaged in matter. Nevertheless, despite the fact that it is disposed in this way, it possesses, in accordance with its own account (*logos*), the power of giving itself over to several species. If, however, some other conjunction of circumstances has prevented the expansion (*diastasis*) of the receiving
15   things into a multitude from taking place, yet this presents no obstacle to the proper account (*logos*) of the differentia.'[596]

Different genera,[597] species, and differentiae are those which differ in category, so that there are genera, species and differentiae in each category. 'Subordinate'[598] genera are those one of which is beneath the other, as 'winged' is beneath 'animal'. Those genera are not subordi-
20   nate of which neither is beneath the other; e.g. 'animal' and 'knowledge'. For of genera and species, some are genera alone, so that they have no genus above them, such as substance (*ousia*).[599] Some, on the other hand, are species alone, so that they have no species after them, such as the eagle.[600] Some, finally, are in between these two, such as 'animal' and 'bird'. These are both species and genera: species with regard to what precedes them, and genera to what comes after
25   them. 'Bird', for example, is a species of 'animal', but the genus of 'eagle'. They are called 'subordinate' not because each one is beneath the other – if this were the case, the same thing would be both species and genus of the same thing – but because only one is beneath the other.[601] When neither one is beneath the other, then they are not subordinate, as is the case with 'animal' and 'knowledge'. Both of
30   these is a genus, but neither is 'knowledge' a species of 'animal', nor

is 'animal' a species of 'knowledge'.[602] Since, then, there are different (*hetera*) genera between the highest genus and the lowest species, as well as the highest ones in each category, when [Aristotle says] 'of genera which are different',[603] we are to understand by this both the highest genera – insofar as they are *different* genera – and the intermediate ones, as long as, like 'animal' and 'knowledge', they are not subordinate one to the other.[604] After all, 'animal' has been placed after Substance, and 'knowledge' after Quality. It is, then, the differentiae of these genera which are different (*heterôn*) and not subordinate one to the other, that Aristotle says are 'different' (*heteras*); and he has in mind not only divisive differentiae, but also those which are constitutive. For the divisive differentiae of 'animal' are 'rational'/'irrational'; 'winged'/'footed'; while its constitutive differentiae are 'sensitive' <and 'moved by itself'>,[605] but these are not differentiae of 'knowledge'.

57,1

5

Those differentiae of subordinate genera which are constitutive of the higher genus necessarily belong also to the lower genera, for they are predicated synonymously.[606] Of those differentiae which are divisive of the higher, some are constitutive of the lower; for instance, 'winged', a differentia of 'animal', constitutes 'bird'; but 'footed' does not. There are also some differentiae which, although they are the same, are divisive of both [*sc.* higher and lower genera]. For of animals, some are herbivorous, others seed-eaters, others carnivorous, and these same differentiae could also be differentiae of 'bird'.[607]

10

Now, [Aristotle] did not simply say differentiae were 'different' (*heteras*), but 'different in species',[608] since it often seems that the same differentiae can characterize genera which are different, as in the case of 'animal' and 'furniture' (*skeuos*). After all, of animals, some have feet,[609] while others are footless; similarly, some kinds of furniture have feet, such as beds, tables, tripods, and the like, but most are footless. Yet these differentiae are no longer the same in species, but rather by homonymy, since the foot of an animal and of a bed are not identical in species. For one is said metaphorically after the other, since they share in common only the name, but not the reality (*pragma*).[610]

15

20

It must also be noted that the correct reading is 'of different genera' and not 'of heterogeneous things'.[611]

Herminus will have it that the reason that differentiae of genera which are not subordinate but different are different in species is 'because,' he says, 'there are some genera which are not subordinate, but are nevertheless both referred under one genus, as "winged" and "footed" are both under "animal". Of these, some of the differentiae are the same: for instance, one part of "winged" is "two-footed", the other "four-footed" (as is said of the griffin and the sphinx),[612] and the same is true of "footed". Yet these differentiae are not the same in species, but in *genus*, for they are primarily differentiae of 'animal'.

25

This is why,' he continues, 'Aristotle did not say that the differentiae of non-subordinate genera are simply "different" (*heteras*), but "different in species". After all, these are differentiae of non-subordinate genera, but even though they seem to be the same, they are not the same in species, but in genus.'[613]

30
58,1

If, however, Aristotle understands by 'different and non-subordinate genera' not only those which are not such that one is beneath the other, but also such genera as are not both referred (*anagomena*) under one thing – for being heterogeneous means just this: to have no genus in common, just as heterospecific things are those which have no species in common, as is clear from the examples given – then there is no need for such grasping after explanations.[614] After all, if those things are homogeneous which have the same genus, then heterogeneous things would be those whose genera are different.

5

Porphyry, by contrast,[615] says that the reason it has been said that the differentiae of different genera are different in species is that the differentiae of species which are under different genera are different.[616] 'Animal' and 'knowledge', for instance, are different genera; 'man' is a species of 'animal', and 'music' a species of 'knowledge', and the differentiae of these two genera are different. Thus, it is as if [Aristotle] were saying that 'of genera which are different and not placed under one another, the differentiae *according to the species* (*kata ta eidê*) are different'. Perhaps, however, it is better to understand Aristotle to mean *specific* (*eidopoiai*) differentiae, as Porphyry himself considers a little further on.

10

Nicostratus and his followers reproach Aristotle with indulging in useless verbiage[617] in this passage. 'For who,' he[618] says, 'is unaware that knowledge could never differ from another knowledge by being two-footed or four-footed, as is the case with "animal"?'

15

In the first place, even if this much is clear, it is not so obvious that 'there is nothing to prevent the differentiae of subordinate genera from being the same';[619] and it was necessary to discuss the two opposites at the same time. Moreover, we can see that Herminus and his followers misconstrued Aristotle's formula 'different and non-subordinate one to the other', since they thought it was possible even for things which are not subordinate one to the other to be referred under one and the same genus. Thus, Aristotle's statement was not self-evident (*prokheiros*), even though the examples, when correctly understood, do make the statement clear.

20

They also object to [Aristotle's] statement that, in subordinate genera, 'however many differentiae there are of the predicate, there will be just as many differentiae of the substrate'.[620] For example, 'animal' and 'rational animal' are subordinate one to the other; since 'rational' and 'irrational' are the differentiae of 'animal', how is it possible for one part of 'rational animal' to be rational, while other is irrational?[621]

25

Now Boethus gave in to this problem (*aporia*), and suggested emending the text as follows: 'so that however many differentiae there are of the subject, the predicate will have the same number.'[622] 'For the differentiae of the more particular shall also belong to the more universal, since the latter contains the more particular, even though the differentiae are not said as universally in the case of the predicate as they are in the case of the subject. "Rational", for example, is predicated of every man, but not of every animal; rather, of animals, some are rational and others irrational. If we were to retain the same reading', he continues, 'we should have to take into consideration Aristotle's remark that "there is nothing to prevent the differentiae from being the same".[623] For this does sometimes occur; "mortal", for example, is a differentia both of "animal" and of "man".'[624]

30

59,1

We must be grateful to Boethus for pointing the way towards the solution of this problem (*aporia*). Since of the differentiae of 'animal', some are divisive – for example, of 'animal', one part is rational, another irrational; one mortal, and another immortal – and others are constitutive: in the case of 'animal', for example, 'sensitive' and 'self-moved'.[625] This being the case, not all the divisive differentiae of the predicate will belong to the subject; not, at any rate, those which are opposite. For if 'rational' belongs to 'man', 'irrational' certainly does *not* belong to him as well. By contrast, the *constitutive* differentiae of the predicate *do* all belong to the subject as well. 'Sensitive', for example, and 'moved from within' belong both to man and to the other animals. 'There is nothing to prevent'[626] was therefore said because not *all* differentiae [*sc.* of the predicate] belong [*sc.* to the subject], but only the constitutive differentiae, and of divisive differentiae, [only] those which are proper to what is more particular.[627] For instance, 'rational' and 'mortal' are divisive of 'animal', and they belong to 'man'; but by no means do their contraries also belong to 'man'. As was said above, however, there are some differentiae which, while remaining the same, are divisive of both subordinate genera. For example, of animals, some are herbivorous, some seed-eaters, and some carnivorous, and 'bird', although it is beneath 'animal', has the same differentiae. Aristotle, however, when he states that the reason why the differentiae are the same is that 'the higher are predicated of the genera below them',[628] seems to be saying both that the constitutive differentiae of higher genera are the same as those of the lower, and that, as I said, of the divisive differentiae, those that are proper [are also the same].

5

10

15

20

It is worth noting, however, that when [Aristotle] says 'there is nothing to prevent the differentiae of subordinate genera from being the same',[629] he is talking about *some* differentiae, and not simply about all. When, however, he makes the further distinction that 'the higher are predicated of those below them',[630] and that 'there are just

25

as many differentiae of the subject as there are of the predicate as well',[631] he is talking about all of them universally, without excepting any of them.

As I have said, then, Aristotle solved this problem himself. If the reason that there will be just as many differentiae of the subject as there are of the predicate is that the higher are predicated of the lower, then it is clear that not *all* the differentiae of the higher will belong to the lower; rather, this will be true primarily of the constitutive differentiae, and of *some* of the divisive differentiae.

Iamblichus calls those differentiae which are constitutive of the genus 'generic' (*genikai*), and those which are divisive 'specific' (*eidikai*).[632]

Thus it is clear that if the differentiae of some genera were not at all the same, nor were the species identical, then such genera are different from one another and not subordinate. If, therefore, the differentiae of the ten categories are shown, by the division of each one, to be different, and the species were different, then it is clear that [the categories] are different genera and not subordinate. Thus, the preliminary clarification[633] of this theory is useful with a view to the account (*logos*) of the categories.

The objections which are customarily raised against the categories also indicate that Aristotle either divided things which are under the same genus – for example, 'doing' and 'being affected' are under 'being moved'[634] – or that some genera were omitted, such as 'being' (*to on*),[635] 'the one' (*to hen*), and the 'something' (*to ti*).[636] Nevertheless, if these genera were to turn out to have nothing in common with one another, it is clear that neither 'being' nor 'the one' nor the 'something' is predicated as a genus of the ten genera, since they are entirely different and have nothing in common with one another.[637]

Cat. **1b25** 'Of those things which are said without any combination, each one' to 'such as "man", "white", "runs", "is victorious".'

These things follow from the division transmitted previously, in which things said were divided into 'in combination' and 'without combination',[638] for after having divided the compound and simple parts of speech (*lexeôs*), the next thing was to teach us to how many genera, and of what kind, the simple things can be reduced. In another sense, these considerations follow from the division, which has just been carried out, of beings into the lowest number: for after the cut (*tomê*) into the smallest possible number, fewer than which it was not possible to grasp, it was necessary to juxtapose the division into the greatest possible number, into more than which no division could take place.[639] Thus, [the present discussion] follows upon the former, but precedes what is to be said later, since knowledge in outline-form (*en*

tupois) must always be taken up before that which is exact, and 20
knowledge grasped in summary form (*en kephalaiois*)⁶⁴⁰ must precede
that which is transmitted in an expository way;⁶⁴¹ for he who has
already obtained an overall notion⁶⁴² will easily be able to follow
expository developments.⁶⁴³

The signification of those [expressions] which are without combi-
nation⁶⁴⁴ comes about in three ways: 1. According to denomination⁶⁴⁵
alone, as when we say 'substance' (*ousia*); or 2. from illustrations
(*hupodeigmata*), as when we say 'like a man or a horse' (for this is 25
what indicates the description (*hupographê*) – like a kind of rough
draft (*hôs en tupois*) – which appears through the senses; and 3. in the
third place, according to the concepts which we have at hand,⁶⁴⁶ which
are not yet technical,⁶⁴⁷ but are already striving towards perfect
accuracy. Here, then, Aristotle indicated the genera by means both of
name and of illustration, saying 'substance, to speak roughly (*hôs* 30
tupôi eipein), is for example "man", "horse"; the quantified (*poson*) is
"two-cubit-long"; "three-cubit-long" '⁶⁴⁸ and similarly in the case of the
others. In his discussions (*logois*) of each genus, however, he also tries
to awaken our concept (*ennoia*) about them.⁶⁴⁹

Archytas, by contrast, having stated the name right in his very first
teaching, and then adding an illustration, also introduced in each
case the property (*idiotês*) in accordance with our concept (*ennoia*). In
the case of substance, for instance, once he had stated the name and
the illustration (*hupodeigma*), he added: 'in general, everything 61,1
which has come into existence by itself.'⁶⁵⁰ For the first concept
(*ennoia*) of substance strikes us thus: as being by itself (*kath'*
heautên). Again, having set forth the name and the illustrations of
Quality (the latter being twofold: those in conjunction with the soul,
and those in conjunction with the body), he does not omit the property
in accordance with the concept (*ennoia*), saying that it is 'simply, 5
whatever co-pertains (*sunuparkhei*) to some things.'⁶⁵¹ For this is the
concept which strikes us together with Quality, *viz.* that Quality
co-pertains to and perfects Substance. Having produced the names
and illustrations of Quantity in all its kinds – for instance, in accordance with magnitude,⁶⁵² with weight (*kata tên rhopên*), and with
discrete quantity (*kata to diôrismenon*) – he then added the proximate
concept (*tên prokheiran ennoian*): 'Whatever signifies something in 10
conjunction with number or in accordance with number.'⁶⁵³ To the
relative⁶⁵⁴ [he added] 'simply being said relatively to one another', and
'being of such a nature as not to be signified without one another'. To
doing (*tôi poiein*) [he added] 'that which simply signifies that an
activity has taken place in conjunction with something'.⁶⁵⁵ To 'being-
acted-upon' (*paskhein*), [he added] 'simply being of such a nature as
be transformed by something other'.⁶⁵⁶ To 'having' (*ekhein*) [he added]
'simply, those things which neither co-pertain nor grow together, but
are acquired',⁶⁵⁷ while to 'position' (*keisthai*) [he added] 'simply, signi- 15

fying the configuration (*skhêmatismos*) of a body in a certain state'.[658] To 'where' (*pou*) [he added] 'simply, determining place',[659] while to 'when' (*pote*) [he added], 'simply, signifying time'.[660]

It is thus clear that this man did not merely carry out a demonstration[661] in accordance with the senses, but also a description (*hupographê*) in accordance with our concepts (*ennoias*).

What shall we call this cut (*tomê*) which takes place as far as the generic genera?

20   A division (*diairesis*)?[662] But how could it be a division, if [it is so] neither as a genus is divided into species, nor as a whole is divided into parts?[663] For neither is there anything common to the ten categories,[664] such as some think is the case with 'being' (*to on*) or 'the something' (*to ti*), since they are not predicated equally of them all.[665] If there is no genus, however, it is not possible either for there to be differentiae, into which the genus could be divided. Nor, however, are they divided like a whole into parts, for there is no common compound

25   which undergoes such a partition. In general, since the parts are dissimilar, they could not be like the homoeomerous parts of something, nor could they be like anomoeomerous parts.[666] For whether one calls the whole 'being' (*to on*) or 'something' (*to ti*), each [part] is similarly called a 'being' (*on*) and a 'thing' (*ti*); however, it does not pertain to anomoeomerous things that their parts be called by the name of the whole.[667]

Does the division, then, resemble soldiers[668] drawn up according to companies (*lokhoi*), so that just as a captain (*lokhagos*)[669] leads a

30   company (*lokhos*), so substance is the leader of substances, and each
62,1   of the other [categories] leads the multitude assigned to it? Yet it would destroy the continuity and interconnection of the cosmic order,[670] if we did not leave any commonality between the primary genera. It is therefore better to determine the differentiae of the genera in accordance with some primary properties (*kata tinas prôtas*

5   *idiotêtas*); but accidents, insofar as they are in conjunction with substance and come into existence within substance, and are co-ordinated with relation to it, to the same extent they are to be assimilated to things which are co-ordinated 'from one thing and in relation to one thing'.[671]

This, at any rate, is the view of Iamblichus.[672] Herminus, however, says, 'it is thus neither a division (*diairesis*) nor a partition (*merismos*), but an enumeration (*aparithmêsis*), for there is no whole in their case, neither in the sense of a genus, nor is there any other kind of whole'.[673]

10   In response to the view of the divine Iamblichus, however, we may reply, using his own terms, that 'from one thing' (*to aph' henos*) is not to be understood as 'from substance' (*apo tês ousias*); for if this were the case, the enumeration we would carry out would not be of ten things, but of nine.[674] Rather, it is [to be understood as] 'from being'

(*apo tou ontos*), [and it is Being] which, here [considered] as something said in many senses,[675] Aristotle wishes to be divided into the
ten categories. Rightly so, moreover, since here the goal (*skopos*) is
about significant expressions. In the *Metaphysics*,[676] however, he says 15
that the ten [*sc.* categories] are produced in order as if from one thing
(*hôs aph'henos*), *viz.* from being, with substance holding the first rank
and the other [categories] being coordinated[677] around it.

Herminus, however, seems to be uncertain as to whether there is
[just] this number of genera; at any rate, he writes as follows: 'Therefore, if meanings (*sêmasiai*) are only of the things which are going to
be mentioned, however many primary genera there may be, there will
be [just] that many categories. If, however, there are others besides 20
them, then the line of reasoning (*logos*) does not reject them, either.'[678]
And yet Aristotle uses this same number of genera everywhere; he
neither adds to it nor subtracts from it, but always adopts the division
into ten, just as he had carried out their concentration into four.[679]

Many others disputed it, denouncing immediately the division into
such a multitude; as did Athenodorus in his book which, although it 25
was entitled *Against Aristotle's Categories*, only investigated the division into such a multitude.[680]

Both Cornutus, moreover, in the work he entitled *Against Athenodorus and Aristotle*,[681] and Lucius and Nicostratus and their followers
spoke out against the division, as they did against practically everything else. 30

We ought, however, to take up the opposing arguments in definite
terms, making a three-fold division of them.[682] For some reproach the
division with being excessive, others criticize it as being deficient, and
a third group is constituted by those who consider that some genera
have been introduced in the place of others. There have also been
some who raise several accusations at the same time: some [accuse
Aristotle of] deficiency and excess simultaneously, whereas others, in
addition to these, add [the accusation of] substituting[683] one genus in 63,1
place of another. In the case of each kind [of objection], let us now state
some problems (*aporiai*) as well as the solutions to them, through
which it is possible to grasp the general character of opposing arguments, so that we may not go to excessive length in setting them all
forth.

Those who accuse [Aristotle] of excess[684] say that he was wrong to
oppose 'acting' (*to poiein*) to 'being acted upon' (*to paskhein*). One 5
common genus, they say, should have been determined for them both:
that of 'being moved'.[685] In reply to them, it ought to be said that that
which acts (*to poioun*), insofar as it acts, is not moved, but rather
causes things to be moved while itself remaining unmoved.[686] Among
sensible things, however, some agents are moved accidentally,[687] because
the two principles – that of 'acting' and that of 'being-acted-upon' –
coincide.[688] Perhaps, however, in the case of 'acting' and 'being-acted-

10   upon' we should have raised the problem why they are not subsumed
     under the relatives (*ta pros ti*),[689] for that which acts (*to poioun*) acts
     upon something which is affected (*paskhon*), and what is affected (*to
     paskhon*) is affected by what acts (*hupo poiountos*). The answer is that
     if we link things up in this way, they will indeed be subsumed under
     the Relative; but in respect of activity (*energeia*) and affection (*pa-
     thos*), which have a different nature, they produce other genera. After
     all, in the case of the other relatives as well, like 'father' and 'son', the
15   same things, *qua* subsisting by themselves,[690] are subsumed under
     Substance, but in accordance with their relation (*skhesis*) [they are
     subsumed] under the relatives.[691] Yet how can 'being-in-a-position'
     (*keisthai*) fail to be 'being affected' (*paskhein*)? How can 'having'
     (*ekhein*) not be 'acting' (*poiein*)?[692] The answer is that 'being-in-a-po-
     sition' (*keisthai*) is no more an affection (*pathos*) than it is an activity
     (*energeia*), for 'being-in-a-position' is 'being seated' (*to kathêsthai*), or
     'standing' (*to hestanai*); they are received in the category not because
     they are affected (*kata to paskhein*) or because they act (*kata to
     poiein*), but because of their establishment (*hidrusis*) within some-
20   thing other.[693] Thus, 'having' (*ekhein*) is attributed not in accordance
     with 'doing' (*kata to poiein*) – for 'being armed' and 'being shod' are no
     less 'being affected' (*paskhein*) – but in respect of being positioned
     around (*alla kata to perikeisthai*).[694]

           Others raise the accusation of superfluity in another way.[695] Xeno-
     crates[696] and Andronicus[697] and their followers seem to include
     everything in [the opposition] 'by itself' (*kath' hauto*) and 'relative'
     (*pros ti*), so that, according to them, so large a multitude of genera is
     superfluous. Others make the division[698] into 'substance' and 'acci-
25   dent'; these people too seem somehow to be saying the same thing as
     those just mentioned, who say that accidents are 'relative' as [being]
     always of other things, and that substance is by itself (*kath' hauto*).[699]
     It should therefore be said to both groups at once that while striving
     after Aristotle's smallest cut, they have missed their mark, since they
     neglect the universal and the particular.[700] What is more, although
     accidents are many genera, they reduce them to one genus of acci-
30   dents, *viz*. the relatives.[701] 'Why, however,' they say, 'are accidents "of
     another"' (*allou*), although in the proper sense of the term, it is only
     relatives which are 'of another'? If it is because they are 'of any odd
     thing', then even things which exist by themselves (*kath' hauto*) are
     'of another', for Socrates is 'of Sophroniscus', and a field is 'of' its
     owner.[702] If we were thus to refer the accident, too, back to its
64,1 substrate, this is not surprising, since [an accident], taken by itself,
     is a particular nature (*phusis idia*).[703] According to this rationale,
     moreover, both matter and the substrate itself are relatives, but
     insofar as they are principles, they exist by themselves (*kath' hauto*).
     Such, then, is the classification made by Iamblichus and Porphyry[704]
     and their followers.

Perhaps, however, this being 'of another' and such a 'relative' as this belong to the accident insofar as it is opposed to substance, which 5 exists by itself (*kath' hauto*) and of itself (*heautês*); for 'relative' is opposed to 'by itself', and 'of another' (*allou*) is opposed to 'of itself' (*heautou*).

Aristotle also shows this; he who took up this cut (*tomê*) into two. It is, however, perhaps correct to say that Aristotle did well to divide the many properties (*idiotêtes*) of the accident, without neglecting to include the fact that it is comprehended under one single heading;[705] 10 so that he also divides things into substrate (*hupokeimenon*) and things in conjunction with the substrate (*ta peri to hupokeimenon*), as some have preferred, and thus sets against the definite (*hôrismenon*) substrate the indefinite (*aorista*) number of things pertaining to the substrate.[706]

Others, such as the followers of Nicostratus, declare that the division is deficient. 'Why,' they say, 'when Aristotle opposed "acting" (*poiein*) and "being acted upon" (*paskhein*), did he not set "being had" (*to ekhesthai*) against "having" (*to ekhein*)?'[707] But those who say these 15 things should have noticed that 'being had' fell into the category of 'being in a position' (*to keisthai*), which had already been determined.[708] For someone holds (*ekhei*) the shield, but the shield is being held (*ekhetai*) in its lying around in such-and-such a way.[709] Thus it is a position (*thesis*).[710]

'Why, however,' say Lucius and his followers,[711] 'did he omit conjunctions, if they are also significant expressions (*lexeis*)? For they are certainly not meaningless.'

[The answer is] that <…>[712] nor is their meaning primary, but they 20 co-signify (*sussêmainousin*),[713] just as we are accustomed to write angled marks and curved strokes in the margins.[714] These signs signify something when they accompany things which are written, but by themselves (*kath' heautas*) they signify nothing.[715] For conjunctions also co-signify when they are with the other parts of speech (*logou*); in this they are similar to glue.[716] In the third place, conjunctions are not even elements (*stoikheia*) of speech (*logos*), but at best 25 they are parts (*merê*) of the vocabulary (*lexis*),[717] just as glue is not a part of paper. Thus they are not even said (*legontai*), but at best are merely enunciated (*ekphônountai*).[718] Moreover, it should be said that even if conjunctions do signify, and are agreed to be lexically significant, it is by virtue of syntax and combination that they signify. Here, however, the discussion (*logos*) is about things without combination.

They also inquire about where articles (*arthra*) are to be placed,[719] but the same reasoning (*logos*) applies to them as well. After all, these 30 things [*sc.* articles] are like conjunctions, but they additionally signify 65,1 (*prossêmainontes*) gender – *viz.*, masculine or feminine – in an indefinite way. For they do not indicate what a thing is (*ti estin*), and are therefore called by some 'indefinite' (*aorista*).[720]

But what about negations,[721] privations,[722] and the various moods[723] of verbs? In which [category] will they be placed?[724]

Aristotle himself gave the answer to this in his *Notebooks* (*hupom-*
5 *nêmata*).[725] After all, in the *Methodicals*,[726] in the *Divisions*,[727] and in another *Notebook* (*hupomnêma*) entitled *On Lexical Matters*[728] – which, even if some hold that it is not a genuine work of Aristotle's, at any rate comes from some member of his school – in these he sets forth the categories, and adds 'I mean these together with their cases (*ptôseis*)', or moods; and he coordinated his teaching about them with
10 negations, privations, and indefinites. 'Going barefoot' is thus in the same category as 'to be shod'.[729] In general, then, since negations and privations have their existence in the elimination of beings (*en tôi ta onta anairein*), it is reasonable that they should be referred back to those things in which states (*hexeis*) and affirmations are found.[730]

'But what about the one,' they say, 'and the monad and the point? How can they not fall outside the categories?[731] They are not, as one
15 might think, quantified, for they are neither continuous – since they are without parts – nor are they discrete (*diôrismenon*).[732] But it is fitting that everything quantified should be either continuous or discrete, and if discrete, then either odd or even.' The answer is, as Alexander also holds, that they will be placed among the Relative, both as principle (*arkhê*) of numbers and as measure. If, however, number is twofold – one incorporeal, the other corporeal[733] – then, as
20 Boethus would say, the monad will also be twofold: one which is substance (*ousia*), and is in intelligible number – Aristotle also thinks that this one exists[734] – and one which is a relative or a quantified. Later, however, Boethus says that perhaps it is better to call it a quantified, for as whiteness (*leukotês*) is to white (*to leukon*), so is the dyad to two.[735] If, therefore, the former are both qualified, then the latter are also quantified.[736]

25 However, they contradict Alexander when he says that it is possible to posit the monad as a part of the quantified, and therefore counts it among the quantified: for number is a multiplicity (*plêthos*) composed of monads.[737] Thus, they say that [the monad] is the principle (*arkhê*) of number,[738] but not a part of number. But everywhere [they say], the principle is different from that of which it is the principle, as also the point (*sêmeion*), which is the principle of extensions (*diastêmatôn*),
30 would not be an extension.[739] But if these things are both principle *and* relative – since it is by having their own peculiar nature that all relatives also have 'being relative to something' (*to pros ti einai*), as a father, although a man and a substance, is a relative *qua* father[740] –
66,1 in the case of these things as well, it should have been said that although they are principles, they are also relatives, *qua* principles.[741]

Perhaps, then, since 'principle' (*arkhê*) is twofold, the coordinated and the transcendent,[742] the coordinated principle is in the same genus as the middle (*meson*) and the limit (*peras*).[743] It might be that

even the transcendent principle is in the same genus, for if the
transcendent monad of number is also a contracted (*sunêirêmenos*)   5
number,[744] then the contracted and the discrete would be in the same
genus.[745] After all, since the form is contracted and differentiated
(*diakekrimenos*), and the name indicates the contracted state, or as
the Stoics say,[746] the summary state (*kephalaiôdes*), while the definition (*horismos*) [indicates] the differentiated state, then the name and
the definition would be in the same genus. Matter and form, more-   10
over, which are the principles of composite substance, are themselves
substances, even if they were not taken up here.

It is possible, I think, both to raise the same problems about the
point as well, and to resolve them. The more distinguished exegetes,
however, say that it is better to leave the one as homonymous[747]
among the ten categories, as is also the case with being (*to on*); but of
homonymous things there is neither any determinate division, nor
can they be subsumed under one genus.[748]   15

For their part, finally, the third group,[749] those who accuse [Aris-
totle] of having made an substitution (*antallagê*), and say that some
genera were taken up in the place of others, say that movement
(*kinêsis*) should be taken up instead of 'acting' (*poiein*) and 'being-
acted-upon' (*paskhein*).[750] For neither is it possible to reduce
movement to any other genus, nor is any other genus predicated of it
essentially (*en tôi ti estin*). It cannot be reduced to 'acting', for many   20
movements are in [the category of] 'being-acted-upon'; [nor can it be
reduced] to 'being-acted-upon', for [in that case] where shall those
movements which are [in the category] of 'acting' be placed?

In answer to these objectors, it is to be said that the potential (*to
dunamei*) and the actual (*to energeiai*) are observed in all the categories, as pertaining to them homonymously, and that is why they have
not been placed determinately in any one of them. Movement, however, which is the path from the potential to actuality (*entelekheia*),[751]
is observed differently in Substance, where it is generation or corrup-   25
tion; differently in Quantity, where it is called 'increase' (*auxêsis*) and
'diminution' (*meiôsis*); differently in Quality, where we name it 'alteration'[752] (*alloiôsis*); differently in the 'Where' (*en tôi pou*); and
differently in each category. How, then, is it possible for movement to
be one category, when it, too, exists homonymously?[753] The same,
moreover, must be said of that rest (*stasis*) which is the opposite of
movement: for if there existed some rest in the true sense, then it   30
would be appropriate to search for it not among sensibles, but among
the intelligibles.[754]

For their part, the Stoics consider that the number of primary
genera should be reduced to a smaller one, and among these lesser
ones they take over some in altered form. For they carry out the cut
(*tomê*) into four: substrates (*hupokeimena*), qualifieds (*poia*), 'things   67,1
disposed in a certain way' (*pôs ekhonta*), and 'things relatively dis-

posed towards something' (*pros ti pôs ekhonta*).[755] It is obvious that
they leave out most of them – clearly the quantified (*to poson*), things
in time, and things in place[756] – for if they consider that things like
this are included by their 'things disposed in a certain way', because
that which is 'last year', or 'in the Lyceum'; or 'being seated', or 'being
5   shod' is disposed in a certain way in accordance with one of them, then
in the first place, there is a great deal of difference between these
things, so that the commonality of 'being disposed' is applied to it[757]
in an indistinct way. Next, this common 'being disposed' will fit with
the substrate as well, and above all with the Quantified, for these
things too are disposed in some way (*diakeitai pôs*).

This, then, is what it is possible to say in response to each of the
10   contrary arguments, taking each one individually. In general, however, [one could] say to them all that they should not have demanded
that introductory treatises be disposed towards exactness (*akribeia*),
for the ears of the inexperienced cannot endure exactness. Secondly,
the undertaking of dividing the most generic differentiae of beings, or
those expressions which are significant of them, is difficult, and it is
therefore necessary to join forces in combating the difficulty of this
15   undertaking, rather than frivolously to compete with it. In the third
place, we should say that everyone else who carried out the division
differently would be brought under more serious charges than the
Stoics, who seem to have been more exact with their four-fold cut into
substrates, qualifieds, disposed, and relatively disposed, what kinds
of things they omit has been stated above.[758] If, moreover, even more
20   recent thinkers, for whom it was easier to add what was missing,
nevertheless seem to be mistaken in many respects, how can we
refuse forgiveness to the first people to approach [this problem], if
they fall somewhat short of exactness? In any case, whoever speaks
against this division or enumeration should know that he is not, in
the first instance, attacking Aristotle, but the Pythagoreans and
25   Archytas, who had made the division into ten genera prior to Aristotle.

If, however, anyone desires to hear an inclusive division, which
includes these ten genera, perhaps it would run like this:[759] since all
beings are either existences (*huparxeis*) and potencies (*dunameis*), or
activities (*energeiai*),[760] but potencies, since they are intermediate,[761]
are rather observed together with existences, the first division must
30   be twofold: into existences themselves, which are what is active or
passive, and into activities. All activities are included by the category
of 'acting' (*tou poiein*), while all affections (*pathê*) [are included] by
[the category of] 'being-acted-upon'. Of existences (*huparxeis*) themselves, some have their being *per se* (*kath' heautas*), and these are all
included by Substance, whereas others come into existence
(*huphestêkasin*) within other things. Of these, some are to be seen as
in relation (*kata skhesin*), while others are without relation (*askhe-*

toi).[762] Of unrelated things, some are to be seen according to the
character and, as it were, the shape (*morphê*) of corporeal existences,   35
as all those which are determined with respect to Quality (*poion*),
while others [are observed] according to extension (*diastasis*) and   68,1
pluralisation (*plêthusmos*), as those in accordance with the Quantified (*poson*); for there are observed these two unrelated differentiae
of those genera which have come into being within other things in a
state of existence.[763] As for those which are in relation (*kata skhesin*),
some are said with regard to reciprocal correlatives,[764] and these are
all included by the category of the Relative (*pros ti*), while others are
not [said] with regard to reciprocal correlatives. Of the latter, some   5
are observed according to their relation to bodies, and others according to their [relation] to incorporeals.[765] Of the latter, one [branch] is
[observed] according to [its relation to] place, which things are included by the category Where (*pou*); while the other [is observed]
according to [its relation to] time, which things are included in [the
category of] When (*pote*).[766] Of those things which are in accordance
with the relation to bodies, one [branch] is in accordance with [the
relation] to those things in which we are established,[767] whether
standing, sitting, or lying down, all of which are subsumed under the   10
category of Position (*keisthai*). The other is [observed] according to [its
relation to] those things which lie around,[768] which are included by
the category of Having (*ekhein*); for the bodies to which there is such
a relation are such that either we are established in them, or they in
us.

Such, then, would be the kind of encouragement we would provide
to those who wish to accept the ten genera [on the basis of] a division
which is not lacking in any respect, and I am well aware that it will   15
be subject to many charges on the part of those who insist upon
niceties of terminology.

The divine Iamblichus himself,[769] however, also proves that the
enumeration (*diarithmêsis*) of the genera is complete (*aparaleipton*).
'In the first place,' [he says], 'there is something which underlies all
things; something pre-existent in which there come to inhere those
things which come into existence in it alone. Next, those things which
co-exist with the substrate are observed along with it; and these are
quality (*poiotês*) and quantity (*posotês*), one of which pluralises   20
(*plêthuousa*) the substrate, while the other specifies it (*eidopoiousa*).
Relations (*skheseis*) are observed in conjunction with the substrate,
and it is in accordance with these relations that the other categories
are observed.'

Archytas, arguing Pythagorically, reduces the cause of all beings to
the principles of the number ten.[770] He says that all art (*tekhnê*) and
science (*epistêmê*) is something ordered and a definite reality,[771] but
that such a thing is determined in number. Now, the overall number   25
(*ton sumpanta arithmon*) is the decade, and therefore it is reasonable

that all things should be divided into ten, and that all forms (*eidê*) should be ten, and that the ideal numbers should be ten;[772] and further that the extremities of the body should have ten parts. Thus, he says, the elements of the account (*logos*) of the All are also ten.

30   It is also possible to justify the same view by means of induction (*epagôgê*):[773] we can select any one of the things that exist, and see how it is referred back to at least one of these genera. However, since these matters have already received a fairly thorough articulation, it is now time to proceed to an examination of the letter (*lexis*) of Aristotle's text.

      As has already been stated many times, the goal (*skopos*) is about
69,1   significant sounds, insofar as they are significant. [Aristotle] showed this by saying, 'of those things which are said without any combination, each signifies either a substance or a quantity',[774] and so forth. For realities (*pragmata*) are neither spoken (*legomena*), nor do they signify; rather they are signified.

      If someone were to say that [Aristotle] was making a division or
5   enumeration of beings themselves, not *qua* beings, but insofar as they are signified by words of such-and such a kind; [we would reply that] they are only known by virtue of the mutual arrangement (*suntaxis*) of words and beings. If, moreover, he says that the signified things are ten in number, and that the signifiers are equal [in number] to these, then it is also clear that the division of concepts [*ennoiai*], which are
10   about realities themselves, is also included; for if one of the three is divided, the rest are divided along with it, because of the mutual interdependence (*sunartêsis*) between the three of them. For notions (*noêmata*) are dependent upon realities, and words (*phônai*) are dependent upon notions. Thus, if someone were to say that words are significant only of the notion in the case of universal genera and of all commons (*tôn koinôn*),[775] he has unwittingly declared commons to be
15   less worthy of honor than individuals (*tôn atomôn*). After all, he admits that Socrates is threefold: the philosopher himself; the concept (*ennoia*) in conjunction with him; and the trisyllabic name; but as far as genera are concerned, he judges that each should be considered in a twofold way: according to the name, and according to the notion (*noêma*) alone. And yet, the name would be in vain, and the notion would be empty, if what was signified or thought of was no being.

20   Others destroy the nature of commons, and consider that they subsist (*huphestanai*) only in individuals (*en tois kath'hekasta*), since they do not observe them anywhere *per se*. They are correct to talk this way about the coordinated (*katatetagmenê*) commonality, but they should have conceived of the transcendent (*exêirêmenên*) one as well,[776] from which the coordinated is derived; for the transcendent is prior to the coordinated,[777] and before that which belongs to another comes that which belongs to itself. If, then, that transcendent thing
25   is also the cause (*aition*) of all that comes after itself, it must not be

considered with respect to the commonality (*koinotês*) alone. For example, [let us take] the cause (*aition*) of all animals, by which I mean men, horses and the rest, whether they dwell in the heavens or the air or the water or the earth. If it were considered only with regard to the nature of 'animal', it would produce only the commonality of animals. Since, however, it also produces all the species of animals, it is obviously the union (*henôsis*), pre-existing in a concentrated state (*suneirêmenôs*), not of the commonality alone, but also of the various species, and it is all things prior to all things, producing both the commonality and the differentiae in accordance with its pre-eminence (*huperokhê*), which is transcendent of both.[778]

Perhaps, however, such a commonality is not to be found at all among that which is produced, in the undifferentiated state[779] in which we conceive of it; for when we say that both the soul and the body are substances, what common, undifferentiated thing could there indeed be in both soul and body? But it is obvious both that what is common is differentiated (*diaphoreitai*), since it is brought into existence (*huphistamenon*) provided with differentiae, in order that it may become commensurate (*summetron*) with the differentiae:[780] the substance of the soul, for instance, could never be moulded together with the differentiae of the body. That which is different (*to diaphoron*), however, has also been rendered common (*kekoinôtai*), in accordance with that unity (*henôsis*), which has been granted to all things by the One, so that all that is produced from the One might not be dispersed (*diespasmena*). We, however, who participate to a large extent in the 'mixed together'[781] and the dispersed, abstract in our conceptions (*ennoiai*) the commonality in and for itself, as something indifferent, which is not in individuals (*atomoi*) – for this one[782] is differentiated – nor is it in those things which come before individuals, since they have assumed in advance not only what is common, but also what is different, within some other nature which is truly unknown to us, but is the cause of this differentiated commonality and this differentness which has become common, for it produces both simultaneously.

Thus, when in dialogue Socrates seems to bring forth the beautiful which is in all things and the equal in all things,[783] it is not because the beautiful within the many is completely undifferentiated (*adiaphoron*), but because the dialectical method distinguishes our conception (*ennoia*) which was heretofore mixed up (*sumpephurmenên*), and incapable of separating the common from the particular, and then brings round (*periagei*) our henceforth distinguished conceptions to unity (*henôsis*), in the place of confusion (*sunkhusis*), for this is the goal (*telos*) of dialectic, as Socrates showed in the *Republic*.[784] Let us, then, not blame either Plato or his teacher Socrates for constantly pointing out, in a dialectical manner, the common forms (*ta koina eidê*) – both those which are in participation,[785] and those

prior to participation – for it was necessary thus to remind those who
conceive only of the differences between individuals (*atomoi*), both of
the commonality in individuals and of the common cause (*koinê aitia*).
25   Nor, however, should we mock Aristotle as if he did not know of the
existence of common natures and pre-existing causes; Aristotle, who
said there can be no demonstration at all without a universal prem-
ise.[786] Rather, let us praise him for having grasped, with astonishing
perspicacity, that these common and completely undifferentiated
things, in and of themselves, are not on the level of existence of
beings, but that it is we who, by abstracting them within our concep-
30   tions (*ennoiai*), have given them *per se* existence (*hupestêsamen*). But
71,1 let this be enough on this subject, lest we say more than is appropriate. It was said because of those who try to show, contentiously
but in vain, that the most eminent of philosophers differ from one
another.

The reason Aristotle said that 'of things said without any combination, each signifies a substance or the quantified or the qualified', is
that of simple words, there are some which, although they are simple,
do not signify anything unless they are combined with each other,
5   such as conjunctions and articles and prepositions. [Therefore Aristotle added his specification[787]] in order that the words significant of
generic things might be separated not only from that meaning of 'in
combination' which creates affirmations and negations, but also from
those which are simple, but signify only in combination, such as those
10   mentioned. Yet how ought we to consider that which is non-combined
(*asumplekton*): with regard to the word, or to power (*dunamei*) and
the significatum? If with regard to the word, it will turn out that not
every simple word indicates only one category. For, as we said before,[788] 'I live' (*zô*) additionally signifies 'I' (*egô*) as well, and
simultaneously indicates substance and an activity or an affection
(*pathos*); and 'it rains' (*huei*), since it also signifies that it is Zeus [who
15   is raining], will be subsumed under both 'substance' and 'acting'
(*poiein*).[789] If we were to assume that the non-combined is such with
regard to power, since one and the same expression (*lexis*) has different powers, we would subsume it under different categories, as
aikizomai[790] [would go] under 'acting' and 'being affected', and so
would all middle verbs. 'Boreas', moreover, since it indicates both the
wind and the climate,[791] will be subsumed under 'substance' and
under 'where'.
20   Perhaps, then, we should consider semantic powers, but once we
have divided them in this way, we should subsume each of them under
its own category, making no distinction even if it is the same expression. After all, expressions (*lexeis*), too, are taken up insofar as they
are significant. If these are what is 'without combination' (*aneu
sumplokês*), however, it is obvious that what is opposite to them is 'in
combination' (*kata sumplokên*): *viz.* those things which are made up

of two or more complete categories, and form a phrase (*logos*), such as
'a man is walking'.[792] Thus, neither homonyms, synonyms, nor 25
paronyms, although they touch upon several things,[793] are said in
combination; neither would the so-called quasi-compound (*hupo-
suntheta*) words,[794] such as *lithobolei* ('he/she throws a stone'), *pseudo-
doxei* ('he/she has a false opinion'), or *boukolei* ('he/she tends cattle')
be in combination, for they too consist of categories which are not
complete. Nor is that which consists of several expressions [said in
combination], when the significatum itself is one and the same, as is 30
the case with definitions (*horismoi*). For 'rational mortal animal' is a
phrase (*logos*), but it neither signifies several things – rather it
signifies only one thing, *viz.* 'man' – nor is it made up of several
categories; for both the genus and the substantial differentiae are 72,1
substances.

'In combination' must, therefore, be understood according to power,
and not according to lexical expression (*lexei*), so that simple words
should sometimes be said to be 'in combination'; *viz.* when they
contain a compound notion (*noêma*), as in the case of 'I live' (*zô*) and
'it is raining' (*huei*). [Conversely], sometimes composite words should
be said to be 'without combination', as has been said in the case of 5
definitions.

If these things are truthfully said, we must note why the philosopher Syrianus says that the previously made fourfold division of
beings – when [Aristotle] said 'some things are said of a substrate, but
are not in any substrate', and so forth[795] – is of things in combination,
whereas the one into ten is of things without combination. Syrianus
writes as follows: 'Having divided significant words (*phônai*) into 10
those which are said with combination and into those without combination, he carried out the cut (*tomê*) of beings in both branches
(*tmêmata*) of this division. For the fourfold one was in accordance with
complex words, for each of them was indicated in accordance with the
combination of words. The [division] into the overall number (*ton
sumpanta arithmon*),[796] by contrast, which [Aristotle] now transmits, 15
is in accordance with simple words.'

How, then, did he set this fourfold combination[797] against the
non-combined nature (*tôi ... asumplokôi*) of the genera, although, as
we shall see, Aristotle described substance in the proper sense of the
term, which is of non-combined things, by means of one of these four
combinations? For he says that 'substance, that which is so called in
the most proper sense, primarily, and most of all, is that which is
neither said of any substrate, nor exists within any substrate'.[798] For 20
in general, the universal and the particular, although they appear to
belong to the Quantified, are reduced to all the categories, as are the
singular and the plural. When I say 'man', therefore, no composition
(*sunthesis*) nor phrase (*logos*) comes about, even if I add 'one'.[799] Thus,
it is better to listen to what Aristotle himself says he means by 'in

25   combination': it is whatever creates an affirmation, so that 'without
combination' is not that which is 'of a substrate' or 'in a substrate' or
what is opposite to these, but whatever does not create an affirmation.
For after having transmitted the ten genera in paradigmatic outlines,
he adds: 'None of the above-mentioned things is said in any affirmation, but it is by their combination with each other that an affirmation
30   comes about.'[800] Neither particular substance, however, nor universal
accident – none, in short, of those four things – creates either an
affirmation or a negation *per se*; nor do they signify truth or falsehood.
Aristotle seized upon this as proof that simple things do not, by
themselves, produce a declaratory phrase (*apophantikos logos*), for he
73,1   concluded by syllogism that simple words are not a declaratory
phrase, which, he said, comes about through combination. He took as
a middle term the fact of being true and false, which pertains to the
declaratory phrase, but does not pertain to simple words.[801]

It is worth noting, however, that he separated simple words only
from the affirmation, but not from the negation as well, by saying:
5   'none of the aforementioned things occurs in any affirmation, but it is
by their combination with one another that an affirmation comes
about'. He did this because simple words, owing to the absence in
them of the negative (*to arnêtikon*), are more likely to produce the
impression (*phantasia*) of an affirmation than of a negation, since
they, like affirmations, signify an assertion (*thesis*), and not denial
(*arsis*)[802] or destruction (*anairesis*), as is the case with negations.
Thus, [Aristotle] distinguishes [simple words] from those things to-
10   gether with which, owing to their similarity, they could reasonably
have been placed.

By saying that simple words are not said 'in any affirmation',
[Aristotle] was alluding to the differentiae of affirmations; since of
affirmations and negations, some are universal, some partial, and
some indefinitely quantified.[803] Let this, then, be enough about the
letter (*lexis*) of the text.

15   If someone wonders[804] whether Aristotle here divided and enumerated sensible and generated things alone, or whether he did so with
all beings, whatever their mode of existence; and, in general, whether
the intelligible genera are different from the sensible; or whether
some are the same, and others different. After all, if they are different,
the intelligible genera have been completely omitted. If, however,
they are identical, sensible things will be synonymous with intelligible things.[805] But how could there be commonality (*koinônia*) in the
20   same substance among things in which there is something 'prior' and
'posterior',[806] and one of which is a model (*paradeigma*), the other an
image?[807] If the ten categories are said homonymously of the intelligibles, they will not be the same, since they will have in common only
the same name; but there will be more genera,[808] since the intelligible
things have not been included. Moreover,[809] how can it be other than

incredible that 'being-affected' (*to paskhein*) and the 'relatives' (*ta pros ti*) are in the intelligibles, when the latter are immutable (*atreptoi*); or that which resembles an offshoot (*paraphuadi*)[810] among things which stand primarily in self-identity? If, however, some are common to intelligibles and sensibles, and some are peculiar (*idia*), their articulation (*diarthrôsis*) has been omitted. Such, then, are the problems raised by the most divine Plotinus, as well as by the followers of Lucius and Nicostratus.

Those who raise such problems (*aporiai*) however, seem to have altered the presupposition (*hupothesis*), since they bring forward their problems as if the Philosopher had announced he was going to teach us primarily about beings.[811] We, however, say that he was not carrying out his account (*logos*) about beings *qua* beings; or, if at all, then only insofar as they are signified by words of such-and-such a kind. He is primarily discussing the things of this world, for these are what are immediately signified by words, since they were both the first things to be known, and the first to acquire names,[812] whereas the intelligibles are not to be seen (*atheata*). Those who have contemplated (*theasamenoi*), having taken their starting point in sensible things, have grasped that the intelligibles are ineffable (*arrhêta*); therefore, making a slight alteration, they spoke of 'humanness' (*anthrôpotês*) or of 'Man-in-himself' (*autoanthrôpos*) or of 'the primary Man' (*prôtôs anthrôpos*). Thus, the lover of the contemplation of beings (*philotheamôn*) could easily pass from these things over to the intelligibles, by making use of analogy.[813]

That he is speaking about sensible things, which are also what is investigated by the common man, is obvious first from the fact that he chose that substance which is so called by everybody. Secondly [it is obvious from] the fact that although he mentioned two substances, the sensible and that which is the object of discursive reason[814] – he did not rise up as far as that [substance] which is above these[815] – and says that in general, sensible substance is more properly so called than that which is the object of discursive reason, for it has the primary rank (*logos*) in the inquiry (*skemma*) concerning sensible things, within which even substance apprehensible by discursive reason is not considered in accordance with its own nature, but according to the relation (*skhesis*) it has with sensible substance. It is according to this relation that we, too, are able to rise up from the sensible to that which is apprehensible by discursive reason, whereas from discursive substance we encompass sensible substance, filled though it is with infinity and indefiniteness, within [the bounds of] a definition (*horos*). Not only in the case of substance, however, but also in that of the other categories, [Aristotle] ranks sensible and particular things before those which are universal or the object of discursive reason, and he is right to do so: for he seeks the difference in accordance with those meaningful words which were first and most properly assigned to sensible things, and which are familiar to the common man, and this, it would seem, is the reason why in other passages he says that substance is threefold:[816] there is substance according to matter, another according to form, and another according to the compound of the two (*kata to sunamphoteron*). In this passage

20   <...>[817] since he is pursuing his theoretical inquiry (*theôria*) in accordance with those meaningful expressions which are familiar to the common man, whereas matter (*hulê*) requires the mind of a philosopher, and form (*eidos*) of such a kind seems to the common man to be an accident (*sumbebêkos*). It is obvious that this transition (*metabasis*) by means of analogy from sensible things to these intelligible ones is appropriate for Aristotle, since, having previously posited matter and form as principles (*arkhas*) among sensible and

25   intelligible things, he again declares them to be the same by analogy and yet other, differing by their mode of subsistence (*tropôi hupostaseôs*). In the case of the ten genera as well, then, what is there to prevent identity by analogy from being preserved, along with otherness, in the case both of intelligibles and of sensibles?

        If, then, there are ten genera in this world, and ten identical ones in the intelligible as well, is the community (*koinônia*) between the things of this world and the intelligibles homonymous or synony-

30   mous? It is neither homonymous nor synonymous in the simple sense of the terms, but as deriving from one thing and relative to one thing.[818] For by means of the weaving together through intermediaries, there is brought about one continuity of the primary and the

75,1 ultimate genera, which neither confuses things engaged in matter with immaterial things – since each has been confined within the limits of its own proper definitions (*horoi*) – nor does it cleave them apart from each other, since they are held together by common bonds, and the more deficient things are always dependent upon the stronger ones. Rather, instead of this, it extends (*diateinei*) the same community and continuity of the genera, accomplishing (*sumperai-*

5   *nousa*) all things with the unbreakable bonds of similarity (*homoiotês*).

        This is why Plato, too, in the *Parmenides*, extends the One throughout all the hypotheses, whether the account (*logos*) is about God or the intellect, or the soul, or the body, in accordance with that differing commonality which proceeds as far as all things. But how can 'Being-affected' and the Relative and Position and such things be in the intelligible world? The answer is that it is possible to observe

10   these things there as well, by analogy, since in their case we say that there are participations of one another and establishments in one another, and we sing of some as causes, and others as effects. If someone were to understand 'Being-affected' and 'Relative' in some other way, and not consider that they can be observed in the intelligibles, it is not incredible to say that since there are ten overall genera,

all are in the compound ones, and in this one they display composition
(after all, in the more particular ones, existing things are always more   15
numerous, since they are plurified in accordance with particulariza-
tion. This is why Archytas demonstrates that the ten categories are
in Socrates as well). In the case of the intelligibles, however, not all
are present (*huparkhei*), but only the simplest genera, which are
appropriate for the simplest things. Nor would the division of the
genera be deficient for this reason, for the division is not shown to be
deficient because some things do not participate in the entire genera.   20
Only if some one of the things proposed falls outside of the reduction
(*anagôgê*) to the ten genera would the universal account of the categories be deficient.

Notes

1. The Neoplatonic *cursus* of study began with the study of Porphyry's *Isagoge*, before going on to Aristotle's logical treatises in the order *Categories, De Interpretatione, Prior* and *Posterior Analytics, Topics*.

2. See below, 8,15; 9,5ff. From its original meaning 'target', 'mark', the word *skopos* came to designate the goal or intention of a literary or philosophical writing. Among the Neoplatonists, each philosophical treatise studied as part of the Neoplatonic *cursus* was held to have a single, unifying goal or purpose, in the light of which each detail of the text was to be explained (cf. I. Hadot, 1987, 99-122). Cf. Ammonius *In Cat.* 7,17-20: 'Just as an archer ... has some definite target (*skopos*) at which he shoots and which he wishes to hit, so an author aims at some goal (*telos*), and endeavours to hit it'.

L.G. Westerink (1990, lxvi) thought the doctrine of the *skopos* was introduced by Iamblichus; yet it surfaces already in Porphyry and Alexander of Aphrodisias. Cicero quotes Plato's *Phaedrus* passage (237b7f.) with approval (*De Fin.* 2,2,4; *De Off.* 1,2,12), so that the search for the *skopos* may have already been an established methodological principle in Middle Platonism.

3. On Themistius, the rhetor and Peripatetic philosopher who flourished *c.* 337-384/5, cf. A. Cameron, 'Themistius I', in *PLRE* 1, 889-94; H.J. Blumenthal in R. Sorabji, ed. 1990, 113-23; O. Ballériaux 1989, 1994, 1996. Simplicius mentions Themistius only here in the present work, although he quotes him often elsewhere.

4. Porphyry of Tyre (*c.* AD 234-305/310), Neoplatonist philosopher, student and editor of Plotinus, and prolific polymath, was highly influential on all his successors. He composed between 68 (R. Beutler 1953, 278-301) and 77 works (J. Bidez 1913, 65*-73*); see the edition of his fragments by A. Smith (1993). The treatise here in question is his so-called 'minor' commentary *By Questions and Responses* ed. A. Busse (= *CAG* 4.1), Berlin 1887, 55-142; see now the translation in this series by S. Strange (London & Ithaca NY, 1992).

5. On the meaning of the technical term *zêtêma*, cf. H. Dörrie 1959, 1-6: a *zêtêma* is 'somewhere between the simple explanation of a text [e.g. of Plato *Timaeus* 27ff.], and a monograph-style excursus [e.g. Plutarch's *On the Creation of the World in the Timaeus*]'. Although taking its point of departure from a specific text, a *zêtêma* was not restricted to philology, but might include philosophical exegesis of the author's meaning, in the style of Plutarch's *Platonic Questions* (*Platônika zêtêmata*). A *zêtêma*, then, is the examination of a philosophical problem, together with its solution, on a level accessible to non-specialists. *Zêtêmata* were often proposed as the subject for discussion in symposia; cf. Porphyry's description of a *zêtêma* on the topic of plagiarism in the school of Longinus (*ap.* Eusebium *Praeparatio Evangelica* IX,3,1ff. = fr. 408 Smith).

6. Several works by Alexander (born *c.* 158-171; fl. *c.* 200), have already

appeared in this series. On the life and times of the Alexander, head of the Peripatetic school and known in Antiquity as the 'Second Aristotle', see R. Goulet and M. Aouad, 'Alexandre d'Aphrodise', *DPhA* I (1989), 125-39; R.W. Sharples 1987; P. Thillet, *introduction* to his Budé edition of Alexander's *De Fato* (Paris 1984), vii-clviii. Alexander's *Commentary on the Cat.*, now lost in Greek, was still available to Porphyry; it was translated into Arabic, as we know from Ibn Abî Usaybî'a (P. Thillet, *op. cit.*, liv & n. 3).

7. On Herminus of Pergamon (*c.* AD 120-180/190), student of Aspasius and teacher of Alexander of Aphrodisias, see J.-P. Schneider, 'Herminus', *DPhA* III (2000), 652-4; P. Moraux 1984, 361-98; K. Prantl 1855/1955, vol. I, 545-6; 548-50; 552-3; 555-7; Zeller 3, 1^5, 812-13; H. von Arnim, 'Herminos 2', *RE* VIII 1 (1913), 835.

8. This probably refers to Maximus of Ephesus (*c.* 320-372). After having studied logic under Iamblichus' student Hierios (Ammonius *In Anal. Pr.* 31,16), he initiated the future emperor Julian into the mysteries of philosophy; then, after Julian's accession, retained considerable influence at his court until the latter's death. After Julian's death, however, Maximus was accused of necromancy, initially fined, then tortured and finally beheaded. For a discussion of his commentaries on the *Prior Analytics* as well as the *Categories*, cf. K. Praechter, 'Maximus 40', *RE* XIV (1930), col. 2567; Zeller III, 2^5, 789 & n. 2. None of M.'s works have come down to us.

9. Aidesius of Cappadocia (*c.* 280/290 – *c.* 355). According to Eunapius, Aidesius studied under Iamblichus after the latter had left Porphyry's school in Rome to establish himself at Apamea in Syria. He later established a school in Mysian Pergamum, where, together with Sosipatra, widow of Aidesius' former classmate Eustathius, he taught Maximus of Ephesus, and, briefly and near the end of his life, the young Julian. Cf. R. Goulet, 'Aidésius de Cappadoce', *DPhA* I (1989), 75-7.

10. This strikes Simplicius as odd, since Alexander had defended a Peripatetic interpretation of the *Cat.*, while Iamblichus applied to it his 'intellective theory' (see below, p. 2,13ff. & n. 20). We know from elsewhere that Maximus sided with Boethus and Porphyry on a technical point of Aristotelian syllogistic (Ammonius *In Anal. Pr.* 31,15ff., quoted by Zeller *loc. cit.*).

11. Boethus of Sidon, student of Andronicus and his successor at the head of the Peripatetic school at Athens, flourished probably *c.* 50 BC. Although a nominalist Aristotelian, he was respected by the Neoplatonists for his critical acumen; indeed, Simplicius' wording here allows the interpretation that he admired B. more than any other pre-Porphyrian exegete. On Boethus, cf. J.-P. Schneider, 'Boéthos de Sidon', *DPhA* II (1994), 126-30.

12. An *aporia*, unlike an *enstasis*, is a *constructive* criticism. In Antiquity as in the Middle Ages, the discussion of a philosophical point often took place by *quaestio et solutio*; thus the *quaestiones/aporiai* are not mere quibbling fault-finding, but an essential part of the philosophical process. In Plotinus' school, a certain Thaumasius once objected that Plotinus spent too much time (three days!) allowing Porphyry to question him about a specific philosophical point; why did he not just write a book on the subject? Plotinus replied: 'But if we cannot solve the *aporias* Porphyry raises with his questions, we'll have nothing whatsoever to say in a book' (Porphyry *Life of Plotinus* 13). On the usefulness for philosophical progress of raising *aporiai*, cf. Proclus *In Alc. I* §236,3-4.

13. For J. Dillon (1977, 344-5) Lucius was a Pythagorean 'of the strict observance', a contemporary of Plutarch; for S. Strange (1987, 956 n. 8) he was a Stoic; for H.B. Gottschalk a Platonist (1987, 1104). P. Moraux (1984, 528-63) maintains that his thought cannot usefully be distinguished from that of

Nicostratus, in conjunction with whom Simplicius usually mentions him. Cf. also W. Capelle, 'Lukios 1', *RE* XIII 2 (1927), 1791-7; K. Praechter 1922, 481-517 (= 1973, 101-37), 502 n. 1; L. Deitz, *ANRW* II.36,1, p. 154.

14. On Nicostratus cf. K. Praechter, 1922, 481-517 = 1973, 101-37; K. von Fritz, 'Nikostratos 26', *RE* XVII 1 (1936), cols 547-51; J. Dillon 1977, 233-6; P. Moraux 1984, 528-63.

15. Thus, although Simplicius considers Lucius and Nicostratus to have been personally rather antipathetic, he recognizes that they furthered the progress of philosophy by providing fertile and appropriate *aporiai*, with which their successors had to come to grips. For Simplicius the mere fact that a thinker is wrong – or even wrong-headed – is no justification for ignoring him; philosophy progresses by considering the views of one's predecessors, and correcting them where necessary.

16. That is, Plotinus *Ennead* VI,1-3. On the life and times of Plotinus see P. Hadot 1993; and the bibliographical surveys of H.J. Blumenthal, *ANRW* II.36,1, pp. 528-70; K. Corrigan and P. O'Cleirigh, *ANWR* II.36,1, pp. 571-623. On *Ennead* VI,1-3, cf. Prantl (I, 1855, 613-14); Zeller (III, 2⁴, 575 & n. 1); Chr. Rutten 1961; K. Wurm 1973. Porphyry wrote an important *Life* of his master Plotinus; cf. L. Brisson *et al.* 1982; 1993.

17. Gedalios is mentioned only by Simplicius; he may have been Porphyry's student at Rome. The best study of Porphyry's thought – and of Neoplatonism in general – is Pierre Hadot's *Porphyre et Victorinus*, 2 vols, Paris 1968. On Porphyry's life, the presentations of J. Bidez (1913) and R. Beutler (1953) should be supplemented by J. Bouffartigue and M. Patillon, *Porphyre, De l'abstinence*, vol. 1, Paris 1977, xi-lxviii.

18. *kata tên koinônian tou logou*. Among the features which distinguished Porphyry's *Commentary Ad Gedalium* (cf. below, n. 24) was the fact that he included in it concepts of Stoic origin, a peculiarity for which Iamblichus and Dexippus frequently took him to task. Porphyry held that many Stoic doctrines were true, if freed of their materialism and transposed from the plane of logic and physics to that of metaphysics; cf. H. Dörrie 1959; P. Hadot 1968.

19. cf. B. Dalsgaard Larsen 1972, vol. 2, 9; cf. vol. 1, 232f. On Iamblichus (*c.* 245 – *c.* 325), first the student and then the doctrinal adversary of Porphyry, see J.M. Dillon 1973; a revised version of the preface to this work appeared in *ANRW* II.36,2, pp. 862-909. Iamblichus' thought as a whole is illuminatingly placed in its context by D. O'Meara 1989.

20. *noera theôria*. Iamblichus discusses his Intellective theory most notably at *De Myst.* I,2 ; VI,9. John Dillon (1997) describes this theory as a kind of 'higher criticism', both more holistic and more transcendental than that of Porphyry.

21. As P. Moraux remarks (1984, 608), this is a quite exact description of the Pseudo-Pythagorean treatise *Peri tô katholou logô étoi deka katêgoriôn*, edited by H. Thesleff (1965, 21-32) and studied by T.A. Szlezák 1972. Although Iamblichus and Simplicius thought this text had been written by Archytas of Tarentum, a Pythagorean companion of Plato, and had served as Aristotle's model for the *Cat.*, modern scholarship now considers it a forgery dating from the first or second century AD.

22. *ekeina te noerôs sunespeiramena eksêplôse. eksaplôsis* here means the process of explaining something clearly; cf. Sextus *M* 7,51 (explanation of a poem by Xenophanes), 7,233 (clarification of a Stoic definition). Simplicius himself uses different expressions elsewhere to designate the same concept; cf. below, 17,3: 'Porphyry gives a simpler explanation (*haploïkôteron exêgoumenos*)'; significantly said of a passage from Porph.'s 'more elementary' *Commentary by Questions and Answers*.

23. Such instances as there are of disagreement are due to Aristotle's failure correctly to understand Archytas; cf. Iamblichus *ap.* Simplicium *In Cat.* 351,4-8.

24. Just as Plato was traditionally considered to have continued the Orphico-Pythagorean tradition (cf. D. O'Meara 1989), so legitimacy was sought for Aristotle's *Cat.* by inventing a Pythagorean antecedent for them. The transmission of the fragments of Archytas seems to have been the work of Iamblichus; Porphyry, although he reports Archytas' views on musical questions in his *Commentary on Ptolemy's Harmonics* (ed. I Düring, Göteborg 1932) seems not to have mentioned him in his works on the *Cat.* Did Porphyry, like Themistius (*ap.* Boethium *In Cat.* col. 162A) later on, suspect Archytas' authenticity?

From Simplicius' account, we can deduce the following characteristics by which Iamblichus' *Commentary on the Cat.* may have differed from Porphyry's *Ad Gedalium*: (1) It was more brief; that is, it probably did not contain, as did Porphyry's commentary, extensive citations from previous commentators, nor set forth their objections raised against points raised by Aristotle, as well as Porphyry's attempt at a resolution of them; (2) It contained extensive reference to and quotation of the pseudo-Archytas; (3) It was more 'metaphysical'; in the majority of the subdivisions (*kephalaia*) of the *Cat.*, Iamblichus discerned a reference to the doctrine of ultimate principles.

25. Dexippus' only known work, the *Commentary on Aristotle's Cat.*, was edited by A. Busse (= *CAG* 4.2), Berlin 1888; cf. J. Dillon's translation in this series (London & Ithaca NY, 1989). D. was probably a fourth-century student of Iamblichus, but we know little about his life; cf. M. Chase, 'Dexippos [4]', *Der Neue Pauly* III (1997), col. 496. With Simplicius D. is one of our two main sources for Porphyry's lost *Ad Gedalium*; cf. P. Hadot in R. Sorabji, ed. 1990, 125-40.

26. *enetukhon.* The verb *entunkhanein* in this context often means 'to read silently to oneself' (as opposed to *anaginôskein*, 'to read out loud or in public'). Cf. A.-J. Festugière 1971, 536 n. 16, citing Plato *Symposium* 177B5.

27. From this offhand remark, we may conclude: (1) that, by Simplicius' time, not all the writings of the authors he cites were readily available, and (2) that Simplicius himself does not claim to have read them all himself. It is, however, probably impossible to make an exact demarcation, in the case of each ancient authority, between what Simplicius himself read and what he gleaned from compendia.

28. For Simplicius the mere act of transcribing Iamblichus' writings is a spiritual exercise, intended to impress more firmly in his mind the wisdom contained in the work he is copying; cf. P. Hadot 1995; Simplicius *In Ench. Epict.* 2,26-7 Dübner: 'For he who writes will become more and more attuned to [these sayings] and will obtain a better comprehension of their truth (*tês alêtheias autôn katanoêtikôteros*)'. On the spiritual significance of composing commentaries on the writings of the Ancients, cf. Ph. Hoffmann in R. Sorabji, ed. 1987, 57ff.

29. Not only was Iamblichus considered too difficult for the average reader, but Simplicius himself was forced to write down his commentary before he himself was able to understand it. Cf. below, n. 481 and text thereto, where Simplicius admits he is not sure he has understood Iamblichus.

30. Syrianus (died *c.* 437), successor in 431 to Plutarch of Athens at the head of the Neoplatonic School of Athens and teacher of Proclus, composed commentaries on Homer and the rhetor Hermogenes; on Plato and on Aristotle. His only philosophical work to have been preserved in his *Commentary on Aristotle's Metaphysics* (ed. W. Kroll [= *CAG* 6.1], Berlin 1902). On his life and work, see K. Praechter, 'Syrianos', *RE* II.8, cols 1728-75; Saffrey/Westerink, Introduction to *Proclus, Theol. Plat.* vol. 3, pp. xl-li; vol. 4, pp. xxix-xxxvii; D.J. O'Meara 1989, ch. 6, with bibliography; R.L. Cardullo 1995.

31. *kheiragôgoumenos*, literally 'led by the hand'; a technical term used of spiritual exercises carried out under the guidance of a master. For parallels in Plato, Seneca and Augustine, cf. I. Hadot 1986, 428 n. 27.

32. Some of the meanings of *logos* include: 'statement', 'discourse, 'word', 'treatise', and 'reason', 'definition', as well as more technical philosophical uses (the *spermatikos logos* of the Stoics, for example, comes close to having the same meaning as 'genetic blueprint' in the sense of DNA). Porphyry (*In Cat.* 64,28-30) enumerates several of these meanings, while Theon of Smyrna (p. 75,24ff. Hiller) enumerates some twenty, *kai alloi pleistoi* 'and many others'.

33. *gumnasia*. Another technical term used in the context of spiritual exercises.

34. From here on, Simplicius goes through what I. Hadot has termed the 'first introductory schema' to the philosophy of Aristotle, which recurs, with differences in detail, emphasis, and order, in all Neoplatonic Commentaries on the *Cat*. It consists of ten points, the order of which in Simplicius is as follows: (1) Reasons for the names of the various philosophical schools. (2) Classification of Aristotle's writings. (3) Determination of the proper starting-point for the study of Aristotle. (4) Goal (*telos*) of the study of Aristotle. (5) Means leading to this goal. (6) Aristotle's type of expression (*eidos tês hermêneias*), i.e. his style. (7) Reasons for Aristotle's obscurity. (8) Qualities necessary for the good exegete of Aristotle. (9) Qualities necessary for the good student of Aristotle. (10) These points must be examined prior to the study of any individual Aristotelian treatise.

The divergences between the five commentators are so random that no conclusions can be drawn as to their possible dependencies on or derivations from one another. All that can be said is that all five are drawing – some more extensively than others – on a copious mass of common scholastic material, which probably goes back at least as far as the lost work of Proclus entitled *Sunanagnôsis*. With what follows, cf. Ammon. *In Cat.* 1,13-3,19; Philop. *In Cat.* 1,19-3,7; Olympiodorus *Proleg.* 3,8-5,6; David (Elias) *In Cat.* 108,15-110,30.

35. *eidos*. This Greek word can mean either 'form' or 'species'; cf. below, nn. 365, 594.

36. With the following passage (Simplicius 3,30-4,9), cf. Ammon. 1,13-3,19; Philop. 1,19-3,7; Olympiodorus 3,8-5,6; David (Elias) 108,15-110,30). The first traces of this classification can be found in Cicero (*Orator* 3,28,109; *Acad.* I,4,17), and it appears in fully developed form by the time of Diogenes Laertius (*Lives* 1,17).

37. David (Elias) 108,18 adds the Aristotelians as an example of this first type of denomination, while Ammonius (1,14-16) and Olympiodorus (3,12-14) add 'Epicureans and Democriteans'. Nowhere else is a school of 'Democriteans' attested.

38. To the examples adduced by Simplicius Olympiodorus (*Proleg.* 3,15-18) and David (Elias) (*In Cat.* 108,36-106,4) add that of the Elians, named after Socrates' companion Phaedo of Elis, and the Eretrians, who took their name from Menedemus (*c.* 352-276 BC), who transferred the Elian school to his native city of Eretria.

39. Aristippus (*c.* 435-355 BC), of North African Cyrene, student of Socrates; he subsequently founded the Cyrenaic or Hedonist school. See the collections of his fragments by G. Giannantoni, *I Cirenaici*, Florence 1958; *idem*, *Socratorum Reliquiae*, Rome/Naples 1982-1985, vol. 1, 185-285; and on his life and works R. Goulet-F. Caujolle-Zaslawsky, 'Aristippe de Cyrène', *DPhA* I (1989), 370-5.

40. Not, of course, the famous geometer, but Euclides of Megara, one of the earliest of Socrates' disciples (cf. Plato *Phaedo* 59c; *Theaetetus* 143c). Zeller characterizes his thought as 'Eleaticism ethicised under Socratic influence'.

41. The literature on Xenophanes of Colophon (*c.* 570-475) and Parmenides of Elea (= modern Velia) in southern Italy (*c.* 540-470 BC) is immense: cf. KRS. The Eleatics are usually presented as extreme monists reacting to the Heraclitean doctrine of eternal flux.

42. Ammon. 1,18; Olympiodorus 3,19; and David (Elias) 109,6 add the information that the Stoics were so called because their founder, Zeno of Citium (*c.* 334-262 BC), used to teach in the *Stoa poikilê* ('painted portico') in Athens.

43. *apo sumbebêkuias energeias*; cf. Diogenes Laertius *apo sumptômatôn*. The Peripatetics were said to have received their name from the fact the Aristotle and his followers gave their instruction while walking (*peripatein*) in the garden of the Lyceum. Cf. Cicero, *Acad. Post.* 1,4,17; Ptolemy al-Garîb *ap.* Ibn Abî 'Usaybi'â, *'Uyûn al-anbâ' fî tabaqât al-atibbâ'*, translated in I. Düring 1957, 214,4: 'On Plato's return from Sicily Aristotle moved to the Lyceum and there founded the school that was named after the walking philosophers.'

44. *apo tês en tôi philosophein kriseôs*. Olympiodorus (*Proleg.* 3,29-34) explains as follows: 'Philosophical schools are also named after their type of knowledge, that is, after their philosophical criterion (*apo tês en tôi philosophein kriseôs*). This is how we call the *Ephektikoi*, who, when they concerned themselves with the nature of reality and sought after it, were not able to get it straight and thought up the idea of the impossibility of perception (*akatalêpsia*).' The other Neoplatonist commentators subject the Ephectics to lengthy criticism and refutations, mostly purporting to stem from Plato; cf. Ammon. 2,15ff. (for whom the Sceptics are not worthy of the name of 'philosophers'); Philop. 2,3-4; 2,7ff.; David (Elias) 109,24ff. The reason may be that the view was still current in the Commentators' period – or rather, in that of their indeterminable source – that Plato himself had held Ephectic views, as was argued by the Middle Academics; our Commentators are anxious to destroy this view by showing Plato's opposition to their tenets. On the technical term *krisis*, cf. Alcinous, *Didask.* 4, 154,12ff. Hermann: 'In the proper sense one would call *krisis* the criterion (*kritêrion*), but more generally, it can also designate the faculty of judging.'

45. The word *ephektikos* derives from *epekhomai*, 'to withhold (*sc.* one's judgment)'; cf. D.L. 1,16. For the Sceptics, the way to a life free of worry and disturbance was to *withhold* judgement on the existence and value of exterior objects. The fragments of Pyrrho of Elis (*c.* 360-270 BC) have been collected, with commentary, by F. Decleva Caizzi, *Pirrone testimonianze*, Naples 1981. On Scepticism in general see the bibliography in LS, vol. 2, 478-80; 510-12.

46. The Epicureans considered pleasure (*hêdonê*) the only good and hence the supreme goal of philosophy; not, as S is quick to point out, crass physical pleasures, but especially those of intellectual achievement and friendship. On Epicureanism cf. the bibliography in LS vol. 2, 480-90. Our commentators are remarkably well-disposed towards the Epicureans, when one considers the ferocious polemic of other schools against them in the Hellenistic age; this is perhaps because, having long since disappeared by Late Antiquity, they were no longer considered as posing a threat.

47. The other *Cat.* commentators go into more detail on the Cynics; cf. Ammon. 2,2-8; Olympiodorus 3,20-30; Philop. 2,4-5; 24-9; David (Elias) 111,1-32. Their explanation of the name 'Cynics (*Kunikoi*)' is thus summarized by I. Hadot (1990): 'Because they lived in a random way (*hôs etukhen*), like dogs, eating whatever food they could find in the marketplace, going barefoot, making love in full view of everybody, and sleeping any odd place, for example in wine-vats (*pithoi*) ....' They were also named after dogs, we are told, because of their uninhibited speech (*dia to parrêsiastikon*), and argumentative nature (*dia to elenktikon*). Finally, all the Commentators cite with approval Plato's remarks on the philosophical nature of dogs (*Republic* 375e). On the Cynics cf. M.-O. Goulet-Cazé 1986; for the later period, *eadem* 1990.

48. The following is a fine example of the Neoplatonic passion for systematization, in which all Aristotle's writings are discussed, divided and classified, with a view to justifying the Neoplatonists' choice of those Aristotelian treatises they considered worthy of being commented upon. On the division – identical in our five Commentators, with some variations in detail – see P. Moraux 1951, 145ff.; 1973, 67ff. (for whom the classification is ancient); I. Düring 1957, 444ff.; O. Regenbogen, 'Pinax', *RE* 20 (1950), col. 1443 (for whom it was a Neoplatonic invention); and above all I. Hadot 1987c.

49. For a Neoplatonist, the more *merikos* ('particular') something is, the farther removed it is ontologically from the first principles; hence things which are *merika* are less real, since they have less being in the true sense, and are therefore less worthy of being studied.

50. Other commentators (David [Elias] 113,14-16; Olympiodorus) add that the collection of Aristotle's letters was made either by Artemon or Andronicus, and included one 'To Alexander on Royalty', and another 'To Alexander on Colonies' (Philop. 3,22-4).

51. Ammonius (3,25) glosses *ta katholou* ('universals') as follows: '*ta katholou* are those writings in which [Aristotle] inquires after the nature of realities (*en hois peri tês tôn pragmatôn phuseôs zêtei*)'. As things which are *merika* are lacking in ontological significance, so the more *katholou* a thing is, the greater its ontological worth. Ammonius (3,25-6) lists Aristotle's 'general' works as *De An.*; *De Gen. et Corr.*; *De Cael.*; Philoponus (3,10.24-5) as *Phys.*; *De An.*; *De Gen. et Corr.*; David (Elias) (113,26-9) as *Phys.*; *De Cael.*; *De Gen. et Corr.*; *Meteor.*

52. For Simplicius intermediary (*metaxu*) works are thus investigations (*historiai*) dealing with plants and animals. Since an *historia* is an investigation based upon observation, by 'investigations on plants and animals' Simplicius probably means all Aristotle's treatises on natural history, e.g. *History of Animals, Generation of Animals*, and *Parts of Animals*. Cf. Aristotle *Meteor.* 1, 339a5-10; Olympiodorus *In Meteor.* 4,4-5; David (Elias) *In Cat.* 113,33-4.

53. For similar dismissals of the class of intermediary writings cf. Ammon. 4,3-4; Olympiodorus 6,21-2.

54. A *hupomnêma*, as its name implies (*mnêmê* being the Greek word for 'memory'), is something written as an *aide-mémoire*; it can vary in extent from notes to extensive commentaries. David (Elias) (114,8-14) is the only Commentator to give an example of these uninteresting hupomnematic works: he cites seventy books of mixed investigations (*summikta zêtêmata*), addressed to a certain Eukairius. Interestingly, David informs us that the *De interpretatione* was previously classed as an hupomnematic writing, until Ammonius proved it belonged among the syntagmatic writings, 'by showing that it possessed an introduction and an epilogue, and that it was written in a style appropriate for publication'.

55. For a discussion of the meanings of *poikilos*, see M. Detienne and J.-P. Vernant, *Les ruses de l'intelligence: la Mètis des Grecs*, Paris 1974, 25-8, who settle on the translation *bigarré*, 'motley, variegated'.

56. *suntagmatika*; cf. Ammon. *In Cat.* 4,4; Philop. *In Cat.* 3,12; etc. A *suntagma* (from the verb *suntattein* 'to arrange, draw up in order') was a book or treatise; thus the adjective *suntagmatikos* means 'having the nature of a (publishable) treatise'.

57. Apparently, Alexander argued that Aristotle was not exposing his own views in the dialogues, but rather those of other people. This view is combated by Ammon. (4,20-2); Olympiodorus (7,8-10), and David (Elias) (115,3ff.), who explain Alexander's view by the fact that he disagreed with the doctrine of the immortality of the soul which Aristotle defended in his *Dialogues*. Yet the Commentators did not consider the *Dialogues* worthy of study (whether or not they still had access to them). They were held to be exoteric: that is to say, Aristotle had composed them for an audience of non-philosophers, and consequently expressed himself clearly in them, relying not on scientific demonstration, but on persuasion. For the Neoplatonists, excessive clarity automatically excluded an Aristotelian treatise from serious study; cf. 23,19 and n. 58 below.

58. Aristotle's autoprosopic writings were also termed *akroamatic*, because they were to be listened to (*akroaomai*) by students who had already attained, thanks to preliminary ethical preparation, a certain stage of progress in virtue, and were authentic initiates into philosophy (Olympiodorus 7,22-3; Ammon. 4,25-7; Philop. 4,11-13; David [Elias] 114,18ff.). Autoprosopic/akroamatic writings were, it was held, identifiable by two characteristics: they dealt with subjects of universal significance, and they were composed in an obscure style.

59. The other commentators enumerate the 'physical' treatises as follows: Ammon. 3,25-6: *De An.*; *De Gen. et Corr.*; *De Cael.*; Philop. 5,3-4: *Phys.*; *De Gen. et Corr.*; Olympiodorus *Proleg.* 7,31-3: *Phys.*; *De Gen. et Corr.*; *De Cael.*; *Meteor.*; *De An.* A different enumeration, probably of Peripatetic origin, accounted for *all* of Aristotle's physical treatises; cf. David (Elias) 115,21ff.; Simplicius *In Phys* 2,8-3,12.

60. David (Elias) *In Cat.* 116,15-19 explains that there were two *Nicomachean Ethics*, one, the 'Larger' or 'Greater', addressed to Nicomachus the elder; the other – the 'Smaller' or 'Lesser' – addressed to the latter's son, also named Nicomachus.

61. cf. David (Elias) *In Cat.* 166,29; Olympiodorus *Proleg.* 8,1 (where I. Hadot [1990] suggests the reading 'The Politics' instead of 'The Politician').

62. cf. Philop. *In Cat.* 5,8-14; David (Elias) *In Cat.* 116,29-117,14; Ammon. *In Cat.* 5,6-29 ≈ Olympiodorus *Proleg.* 8,4-28.

63. *ta de peri tôn tên apodeixin hupoduomenôn.* Cf. David (Elias) *In Cat.* 115,14-22: Aristotle's *autoprosôpa* are divided into theoretical, practical and logical works, each of these three divisions being further subdivided into three. The third and final subdivision of the logical writings is made up of 'those which assume the appearance of method' (*ta hupoduomena tên methodon*). The origin of the idea is probably Aristotle *Metaphysics* 4.2, 1004b17-26, where it is said that dialecticians and sophists 'assume the same appearance (*to auto ... hupoduontai skhêma*) as the philosopher, although they are intrinsically different.

64. With Simplicius' discussion (5,3-6,5) of point 3, cf. Ammon. 5,31-6,8; Philop. 5,15-39; Olympiodorus 8,29-9,13; David (Elias) 117,25-119,25.

65. cf. David (Elias) *In Cat.* 118,20ff. This was the view, for example, of Andronicus of Rhodes; but the necessity of preliminary training in logic could also, of course, be supported by texts from Aristotle himself; cf. *Metaph.* 1.3, 995a12-14; 3.3, 1005b2-5; etc.

66. The *môlu* was the plant given to Odysseus by Hermes to ward off the evil spells of Circe, who had turned his companions into pigs; cf. Homer *Odyssey* 10.275-308. For a rich study of ancient and medieval attempts to identify this plant and allegorize the episode, see H. Rahner 1945. David (Elias) expresses the same idea as Simplicius albeit in somewhat blunter language: those who are armed with the Hermetic *môlu*, he writes (*In Cat.* 119,21-4), 'are not enchanted by the Sirens of heterodox schools of philosophy', while a student not armed with the method of demonstration 'becomes a Boeotian pig'. For Olympiodorus *In Phaed.* 6,2 (p. 97,5ff. Westerink), the *môlu* of Hermes is reason, needed to protect Odysseus from the deleterious effects of Calypso [*sic*], who signifies imagination.

67. cf. Philop. *In Cat.* 5,24ff.: we must first of all set our characters in order (*katakosmein to êthos*), and then proceed to other studies, so that our logical faculties may not be muddied by passions to the extent that our judgment is impaired. Cf. David 119,13-15: '... we must begin with logic, having previously set our character in order (*prokosmêsantas ta êthê*), so that we may be pure when we approach pure philosophy.'

68. That is to say, logic.

69. *ta mesa.* For the Stoics, this class included all things which were not intrinsically either good nor bad, but indifferent.

70. *tês apo tôn êthikôn katartuseôs.* The verb *katartuô* originally designated the breaking in of horses (Sophocles *Antig.* 484), and then came to mean training, especially of children, by means of laws, institutions and education (Plato *Laws* 7, 808d). By the time of the Neoplatonists, it had come to mean the ethical training upon which students were required to enter before embarking on the study of philosophy; cf. Iamblichus *Life of Pythagoras* 94, 15ff. The term is characteristically Iamblichean; cf. A.-J. Festugière, 'La doctrine des "viri novi" sur l'origine et le sort des âmes', in *Hermétisme et mystique païenne* (Paris 1967), 309 n. 92.

71. *ouk apodeiktikôs, all' orthodoxastikôs.* For Synesius (*Dion* 10,39-40), the first stage for the beginning philosopher consists in holding fast to first principles, 'honouring right opinion, apart from argument and demonstration' (*doxan orthên presbeuontes dikha logou kai apodeixeôs*). Synesius likens the beginner at this stage to Plato's definition of a philosopher at *Symposium* 202a: 'no longer ignorant but not yet sages (*sophoi*).' Finally, this stage is linked, in Synesius as in Simplicius with the idea of moderation. Those who are satisfied with having reached this stage, says Synesius, *metriôs an eiête pepragotes* (not, as in FitzGerald's translation, 'would have been treated with moderation,' but 'would behave in a moderate way'). All this probably derives from Porphyry, and we can perhaps assume that the parallel passage in Philop. *In Cat.* 5,29ff. (... *prôton men orthodoxastikôs ... husteron kai apodeiktikôs ...*) goes back, through Ammonius, to Porphyry as well. Cf. also Olympiodorus *In Gorgiam* 9,6f. Westerink.

72. *kata tas autophueis peri tôn ontôn ennoias.* The *ennoiai* are innate ideas, traces of the direct vision of the intelligibles which, according to Plato, we enjoyed in our pre-incarnate state. Cf. Ph. Hoffmann 1992-3; A. de Libera 1996.

73. *katêkhêseis ... parainetikai.* The noun *katêkhêsis* derives from the verb *katêkheô*, 'to instruct orally'. Before taking on its Christian meaning of 'catechism', 'elementary religious instruction', *katêkhêsis* simply meant 'oral instruction', or, more loosely, education picked up in casual social intercourse (Chrysippus *ap.* D.L. 7,89; cf. Cicero *Letters to Atticus* 15,12,2). Syrianus uses the term of the Aristotle's oral instruction, as opposed to his writings (*In Metaph.* 84,24 Kroll; 106,6 [quoting Boethus]).

74. I. Hadot 1978, 192 suggests that the writings Simplicius is referring to are the so-called *Sentences of Sextus* (ed. H. Chadwick, Cambridge 1959) and/or the Pythagorean *Carmen Aureum*. The fifth-century Neoplatonist Hierocles had composed a *Commentary on the Carmen Aureum*, which is frequently cited in Neoplatonic commentaries on the *Gorgias* and *First Alcibiades*, the Platonic dialogues which were the first ones read, according to the Neoplatonic school curriculum, by beginning philosophy students. Simplicius himself chose to comment the *Manual* of Epictetus. What the Neoplatonic spiritual directors found in such writings were maxims which formulated ethical doctrines in short, pithy sentences, such as the student could memorize, meditate upon, and thus always have 'at hand' (*prokheiron*), ready to be applied to every moment of the day. Cf. P. Hadot 1995; I. Hadot 1986.

75. *prokatartuein di'autôn ta êthê.* Commenting on Homer *Odyssey* 16.274-7, Plutarch writes (*Quomodo adolescens poetas audire debeat* 31D): 'Just as horses are not bridled *during* the race, but *before* the race, thus they anticipate with calculations those who incline impetuously to bad things and are high-spirited, and give them preliminary training (*prokatartuontes*) by taking them to athletic contests.'

76. The reason being that the many 'divisions and demonstrations' contained in Aristotle's ethical works presuppose the logical training which does not come until later in the curriculum. Cf. I. Hadot 1978, 161-2; Ph. Hoffmann 1985, 63 n. 13.

77. *di'agraphou sunethismou.*

78. *paraineseôn agraphôs te kai engraphôs to êthos hêmôn apeuthunontôn.* In the parallel passage of his commentary (118,30), David (Elias) gives the writings of Isocrates, in particular his addresses to Demonicus and Nicocles, as examples of such written and non-written exhortations.

79. cf. Ammon. 6,3-8; Olympiodorus 9,9-11: The student should begin with logic, and then progress to ethics, mathematics, and theology in that order.

80. cf. Ammon. 6,9-16; Philop. 5,34-6,2; Olympiodorus 9,14-30; David (Elias) 119,32-121,4.

81. *epi tên mian tôn pantôn arkhên*: the typical designation of the Neoplatonic First Principle, commonly identified as the One, the Good, or God, but strictly speaking beyond all denomination.

82. *esephthê.* A probable allusion to Sophocles, fr. 164 Radt. Porphyry was fond of this rare form of the verb *sebomai*: he uses it at *Life of Plotinus* 12,1; *On Abstinence* 4,9; 10; 18; *In Tim.* Book 2, fr. 28 Sodano.

83. Homer *Iliad* 2.204. Aristotle cites this passage twice, at *Politics* 1292a,13ff., and at *Metaphysics* 12, 1076a. It is the latter citation that Simplicius probably has in mind: 'The rule of many is not good; *let there be one ruler.*' Aristotle insists there must be only one ultimate principle, a view obviously pleasing to a Neoplatonist like Simplicius. The quotation also appears in Olympiodorus 9, 22-6, and David (Elias) 119, 32ff., but they both indicate the location of Aristotle's citation, while Olympiodorus gives the end of the Homeric verse truncated by Simplicius. The Christian David cannot resist a shot at pagan Homer: 'What has been said,' he writes (*loc. cit.* 119,32-3) 'ought rather to be demonstrated about God than about a king'.

84. 10.7, 1177a26ff.

85. On this, the fifth introductory point, cf. Ammon. 6,17-21.

86. *to eidos tês hermêneias.*

87. *gorgos.* A technical term of rhetoric. *gorgotês*, we learn from Hermogenes of Tarsus (*Peri Ideôn* Book 2, B, pp. 132ff. Rabe) is the opposite of 'flatness' (*huptiotês*). It is characterized by 'the use of short clauses that develop the thought quickly'; 'passing quickly from one topic to another' (p. 318), and by certain 'figures and rhythms': the use of parentheses, asyndeton, frequent and slight variations in a list (*exallagê*), anaphora, antistrophê, and interweavings (*sumplokai*). In forensic oratory, we learn, this effect can be obtained by frequently shifting one's attention from the jurors to one's opponent (p. 314); while in tragedy it is produced by the use of trochaic metre (p. 319). Cf. *Hermogenes: On Types of Style*, translated by C.W. Wooten (Chapel Hill & London 1987). *On Types of Style* was a second-century rhetorical handbook highly valued by the Neoplatonists: Syrianus commented upon it, and Simplicius may have as well.

88. By rendering *hê enargeia* as 'vividness', I am following Wooten in his translation of Hermogenes *On Styles*; cf. Hermogenes 1,12,68 Rabe; 1,12,194; 212; 2,5,98; 2,9,166.

89. cf. David (Elias) 120,31-121, 3: 'Know that Aristotle does natural history when he discusses theology ... just as, in reverse, Plato always does theology when he discusses natural history; he is always bringing in the theory of Ideas.'

90. *oude muthois oude sumbolikois ainigmasin.* Aristotle's 'predecessors' are the Pythagoreans (who used symbolic riddles, or *akousmata*) and Plato (myths). Cf. Proclus *In Euclid* 22,9-16 Friedlein.

91. On the seventh *kephalaion*, cf. Ammon. 7,7-14; Philop. 6,22-8; Olympiodorus 11,21-12,17; David 124,25-127,2. These commentators see two main reasons for Aristotle's use of obscurity: it frightens off the lazy, the stupid and the frivolous, i.e. precisely those who are unfit for philosophy; and it incites the interest and quickens the wits of those who are truly interested in, and capable of, piercing surface obscurity to arrive at the truths lying hidden beneath. The commentators' doctrine is nicely summed up by Olympiodorus (*Proleg.* 12,14-17): 'What ambiguity (*to loxon*) is for Apollo, curtains are for priests, myths are for poets (cf. Proclus *In Remp.* 1,74,16ff. Kroll), dreams are for Pythagoras, intoxication (*methai*) are for Plato (cf. *Phaedrus* 244ff.): this is what obscurity tends to be for Aristotle.'

92. cf. Plato *Theaetetus* 180d; Proclus, *In Tim.* I, 130,4ff. Diehl; Damascius *De Princ.* 7,19ff. Ruelle: after having risen to the One, Plato kept silent after the fashion of the Ancients, 'For indeed, such discourse was extremely dangerous (*parakinduneutikôtatos*) if it fell into the ears of the common herd.'

93. According to A. Pelletier (1984, 404-5; cited by I. Hadot 1990) the use of curtains in Greek temples, first attested in the mid-fourth century AD in the temple of Hera at Samos, was inspired by their use in the Temple of Jerusalem. On the curtain installed before Pheidias' chryselephantine statue of Zeus in Olympia, cf. Pausanias 5,12,4; for curtains in the temple of Hecate in Lagina, and in the temple of Artemis at Didyma, cf. L. Robert 1937, 552; *idem, Hellenica* 11-12, pp. 470ff.

94. *ankhinoia.* Aristotle gives a clear definition of this quality at *An. Post.* 89b10-16; for him, it is the ability to draw quick conclusions. Among Greek philosophers, Simplicius singles out both Boethus (*In Cat.* 1,17-18; 11,23 K) and Aristotle himself (*ibid.* 348,24-5; 351,8-9) as remarkable for their *ankhinoia*.

95. cf. Simplicius *In Phys.* 8,18-20 Diels: 'In his akroamatic writings [Aristotle] practised obscurity, using it to repel frivolous readers, to the point that it seems to them that nothing has been written at all.'

96. On the eighth *kephalaion* (Simplicius 7,23-32), cf. Ammon. 8,11-19; Philop. 6,30-5; Olympiodorus 10,24-33; David (Elias) 122,25-123,11.

97. This declaration alerts us to an important aspect of Simplicius' activity as a commentator: presupposing accord between Aristotle and Plato, he will attempt to minimize divergences between the two. The view that differences between Plato and Aristotle were only surface-deep, and/or resulted from their different methods of approach and expression, dates back at least to Antiochus of Ascalon, and was forcefully expressed by Porphyry, who had written at least one work 'On the Unity of the schools of Plato and Aristotle' (*Souda* s.v.

'Porphurios', vol. 4, 178, 21-2 Adler). This work was known in Arabic translation; cf. R.R.K. Sorabji 1990, 2 & n. 7.

98. On the ninth *kephalaion* (Simplicius 7,33-8,8), cf. Philop. 6,29-30; Olymp. 10,3-23; David (Elias) 121,20-122, 64; Ammon. 6,21-4.

99. *spoudaios* might also be rendered as 'serious'; but, as I. Hadot points out (1990), it is also a technical term for a person having attained the first stage in the Neoplatonic scale of values: that of the political/practical virtues based on Aristotelian *metriopatheia*. Cf. Simplicius below 37,21-16.

100. The reference here is probably to exercises of memorization of and meditation upon the fundamental dogmas of philosophy, such as had been an essential part of philosophical education since Epicurus and the Stoics. On the importance of friendship for spiritual progress in Antiquity, cf. I. Hadot 1969a; 1969b; 1986, 445-9.

101. *phulattesthai ... tên eristikên phluarian.* Again, the student is urged to stick to the rules of what P. Moraux has called the 'dialectical joust'; the student must not love controversy for controversy's sake, and he must not sink to using invalid arguments. Cf. David (Elias) 122,22-3: '[The student] must not be quarrelsome nor a lover of fights (*dei auton mê einai duserin kai philoneikon)'*.

102. *hoi perittôs sophoi.* Moerbeke renders this as 'superflue sapientes'. The phrase is probably a reminiscence of Euripides *Medea* 294-5: 'A person ought never to have children/Brought up to be more clever then the average (*paidas perissôs ekdidaskesthai sophous*; trans. R. Warner). This passage was famous already in Antiquity; Aristotle cites it as his first example of a moral maxim (*gnômê*); cf. *Rhetoric* 2.21, 1394a29-30.

103. The reference to 'the eye of the soul' (*to omma tês psykhês*) derives from Plato *Republic* 7, 533d2ff. [and cf. *Sophist* 254a], where the goal of dialectic is said to be to draw up the soul's eye from the 'barbaric slough' in which, for the non-philosopher, it lies wallowing.

104. Arist. *Top.* 1.11, 105a3ff. Aristotle's examples of a questioner needing punishment are people in doubt as to whether or not they ought to honour the gods or love their parents; people who need perception are those unsure of whether or not snow is white. The passage is also quoted by David (Elias) 122,22-4; Julian *To the Cynic Heracleios* 237D.

105. On the tenth *kephalaion* (Simplicius 8,9-9,3), cf. Ammon. 7,15-8,10; Philop. 7,1-8, 6; Olympiodorus 12,18-14,11; David (Elias) 127,3-129,3.

106. Unlike many of the other Commentators, Simplicius is faithful to this programme (8,13-31); with the one exception that he, like Ammonius, omits this point concerning the order of reading. Olympiodorus (12,31-37), David (Elias) (128,25-7) do discuss it, however, and Philoponus (7,31-8,1) states that the importance of this point is that it enables us to start with the less difficult Aristotelian treatises and work our way to the more complex.

107. cf. below, 20,8-12. This point, omitted by the other commentators and mentioned somewhat tentatively by Simplicius may have belonged to an earlier form of the schema, which we also find in Boethius *In Porph Isag.*[1] 5,6-8 Schepss/Brandt. I. Hadot (1990) assumes the point was first eliminated by Proclus, then re-introduced by Ammonius; she cites Ammon. *In Anal. Pr.* 5,3-5; Philop. *In Anal. Pr.* 1,9-10.

108. On the *skopos*, see above, 1,7 & n. 2. Olympiodorus (12,22-3) makes the interesting remark that the *skopos* of Aristotle's writings is always easy to discover, but that this is *not* the case with the writings of Plato.

109. 'He who does not know the *skopos*', writes Philoponus in the parallel passage of his commentary (7,7), 'resembles a blind man, who doesn't know where he is going.' Simplicius probably has the same image in mind here; cf. David (Elias) 119,24-5.

110. David (Elias) adds that discovering the usefulness is necessary in two cases: (1.) When the work in question seems to have been written in vain, like the *Topics*, which sets up arguments only to destroy them; and (2.) When the work seems to have been written with an evil intention; as the *Sophistical Refutations* to teach people how to deceive others. Neither objection, of course, is true, David hastens to add; the *Topics* and *Sophistical Refutations* were not written to teach us how to deceive others, but in order that we may not be deceived and led astray ourselves (127,15ff.; cf. Olympiodorus 12,25-32). In general on the *kephalaion* of usefulness, cf. Dexippus *In Cat.* 5,26-8; Olympiodorus 22,3-12; David (Elias) 132,5-21; Ammon. 13,3-6; Philop. 12,12-14.

111. *suntonôterous kai prothumoterous ergazetai*. Cf. Philop. 7,9-11: the knowledge of a work's usefulness inspires in the reader zeal and enthusiasm (*spoudên kai prothumian*). David (Elias) uses an erotic metaphor (127,13-15): 'The usefulness should be sought out because the audience becomes more zealous (*suntonôterous*) when they see the profit from it being added on like a charm (*delear*) for erotic dispositions.'

112. The other Commentators provide examples of works whose title are obvious: *On the Heavens, On the Soul, On Generation and Corruption* (Philop. 7,14-15; Ammon. 7,23-8,1); and of titles which are *not* immediately obvious: *Cat.* and *De Interpretatione* (Philop. 7,12-14).

113. *prosaphênistheisa*. Apparently another coinage by Simplicius.

114. See below, 18,16-21.

115. Simplicius does not, in fact, actually take up the question of authenticity beforehand.

116. cf. Arist. *Top.* 1.14, 105b1: 'When drawing up lists of philosophical opinions, we should write in the margin the names of the holders of each doctrine, since 'any one might assent to the saying of some reputable authority'. Again, Simplicius reminds us that his audience is made up of beginners, who must be persuaded at the level of emotions and common sense, and not convinced by rationally binding demonstrations. At this level, the Pythagorean *autos ephê* will, in some cases at least, have to suffice as a reason for believing the basic doctrines of philosophy; only later on, when the students are more advanced, will the rational proofs for the truth of such doctrines be adduced.

117. See below, 18,16-21. Olympiodorus specifies the kings in question: there was a certain 'Iobates King of Libya' (= Iuba of Mauretania, reigned *c.* 25 BC – 23 AD?), who collected Pythagorean writings; Ptolemy Philadelphus, who collected Aristotelica, and Peisistratus, who collected Homeric writings. As all these 'kings' paid good money for the books they wanted, people were inspired either to forge new writings or to attribute already-existing works to popular ancient authors. Cf. C.W. Müller 1969.

118. The analogy of the division into chapters with dissection-both allow us to perceive the function of each part and its contribution to the whole-appears in Ammon. 8,6-11; Philop. 8,1-6; and David (Elias) 128,27-129,1. Olympiodorus (14,6-9) prefers to liken Aristotle's method to geometry, in which lemmata and axioms are first laid down before one proceeds to the construction of theorems.

119. cf. Ammon. 7,20-1; Olympiodorus 13,2-3. Philop. 8,7-21 adds *On the Heavens* as an example of a writing whose usefulness becomes apparent simultaneously with its title, and adduces the *Topics* as an example of a work in which neither the *skopos*, the usefulness, nor the title is *prima facie* clear.

120. With the following passage on the *skopos*, cf. Ammon. 8,20-13,2; Philop. 8,27-12,11; Olympiodorus 18,14-22,2; David (Elias) 129,4-132,4.

121. i.e. Aristotle's *De Interpretatione*.

122. That is to say, terms: words are to be studied not in their function as grammatical entities, but *qua* logical terms.

123. Arist. *Cat.* 2, 1a16-17.

124. *ibid.* 4, 1b25-6.

125. *ibid.* 4, 2a4-6.

126. cf. Porph. *In Cat.* 57,6-8.

127. On the 'ontological' interpretation of the *skopos*, cf. Ammon. 9,5; Philop. 8,33-9,4 (who attributes it to Eustathius); Olympiodorus 18,30-19,13; David (Elias) 129,11-130,8 (who attribute it to Herminus).

128. *pathê*. In ancient grammar, the *pathê* of a word were those changes in form which did not affect its meaning.

129. *skhêmatismoi; paraskhêmatismoi*. On the latter term, cf. below, 11,34; 40,12; 209,26f.; Apollonius Dyscolus *On Syntax* 70,1; 276,25 Uhlig; *On Adverbs* 142,20; 143,27; *On Pronouns* 27,5; *On Conjunctions* 237,27; Ammonius *In De Interp.* 52,24f.; 65,7-9. See also J. Lallot, *La grammaire de Denys le Thrace*, Paris 1989, 132; 139-40.

130. *ideai*. In rhetorical usage, the word *idea* comes close to meaning 'style', but Ph. Hoffmann is probably right to translate the term here by 'class' or 'part of speech'; he cites Apollonius Dyscolus, *Syntax* 63,13; 65,6; 321,2 Uhlig.

131. Arist. *Cat.* 2, 1a20-1. Cf. Ammon. 9,5-7; Philop. 9,2-3; Herminus *ap.* Olympiodorum 19,9-12 (inexact quotation).

132. Arist. *Cat.* 5, 2a11-12.

133. This was the view of Porphyry, according to Ammonius (9,9), Philoponus (9,5-6) and David (Elias) (129,10-11); of Alexander of Aphrodisias, according to Olympiodorus (18,31; 19,17ff.).

134. *ennoêmatikos*. This word does not seem to occur before Galen; it here refers to the abstracted universal or common, the third of the three varieties of common item discussed by Simplicius at 82,35-84,26. A good account of the meaning of the term is given by Ammonius *In Porphyrii Isagogen* 69,5-9 Busse.

135. Arist. *Cat.* 2, 1a16; 4, 1b25; see above, 9,12-14.

136. On the Stoic *lekta* or 'sayables', cf. LS §33; bibliography vol. 2, 497-8.

137. cf. with P. Hadot 1980, p. 316, Clement of Alexandria *Stromata* 8,4,13,1.

138. cf. with Ph. Hoffmann, Arist. *De Interp.* 16a8-9.

139. This is one possible translation of this awkward Greek phrase, but it might also be interpreted 'speech is significant because its parts signify the primary things'.

140. It was normally held that a *diairesis* could not result in innumerable members; cf. P. Moraux I (1973) 130ff.

141. Alexander of Aigai (fl. mid-first century AD) was, along with Chairemon, the tutor of Nero. Although Simplicius omits his name from his initial list of commentators on the *Cat.*, he cites him twice, here and at 13,11-18, both times in connection with Alexander of Aphrodisias, from whom he probably has his information about the Aigaian. Cf. A. Gercke, 'Alexandros 92', *RE* I 2 (1894), col. 1452; P. Moraux 1984, 222-5.

142. Porphyry fr. 46, 35-6 Smith.

143. *en tôi Peri tôn tou logou stoikheiôn*. Kalbfleisch assumed this was the title of a lost work by Theophrastus (c. 370-288 BC), the student and successor of Aristotle, while other scholars interpret it as a reference to Theophrastus' elsewhere attested work *Peri lexeôs* ('On Expression'). Philo, *De congressu* *quaerendae eruditionis gratia*, §147, argues that the study of such grammatical questions *does* pertain to philosophy; but at *De Agricultura* 140-1, he argues the exact opposite.

144. cf. Boethius *Introductio in syllogismos categoricos*, PL 64, 766A-B; *In Perihermeneias²*, 14,25ff. Meiser; *De syllogismo categorico*, PL 64, 796Df.; cited by G. Nuchelmans, *Theories of the Proposition*, Amsterdam & London 1973, 124.

145. Apocope is the loss of a short vowel before a following consonant (*kat* for *kata*; *kabbale* for *katebale*), etc.

146. Aphairesis is the loss of a short vowel at the beginning of a word after a long vowel or a diphthong. Examples: *mê 'gô* for *mê egô*; *pou 'stin* for *pou estin*.

147. *huposunthetoi*. This is a rare word; Simplicius uses it twice, here and at 71,27, while the only other occurrence in Greek seems to be Dexippus *In Cat.* 12,7 (cf. Dillon's n. 26 at p. 36 of his translation). The common source of both Simplicius and Dexippus is thus likely to be either Porphyry or, less probably, Iamblichus. Did this entire passage, with its grammatico-rhetorical technical terms, and quotations from Theophrastus, originally stand in Porphyry's *Ad Gedalium*?

148. On these rhetorical styles, cf. Hermogenes, *On Types of Style*, with the translation by Wooten; G.L. Kustas 1973.

149. cf. Porph. *In Cat.* 56,8-9. The entire following passage on the constitution of the table of categories (Simplicius 11,2-22), absent from Porphyry's smaller commentary but paralleled in Boethius (*In Cat.* col. 160b12-161a12), probably derives from Porphyry's lost commentary *Ad Gedalium*; cf. S. Ebbesen 1987, 303. *kata* + *agoreuô* is obviously an attempt at an etymological explanation of the verb *katêgoreuein*, 'to predicate'.

150. cf. Porph. *Isag.* 6,13ff. Busse: 'Individuals ... are infinite; this is why Plato recommends, when we are descending from the most generic to the most specific, that we stop ... "Leave the infinite alone," he says, since there can never be any knowledge of them ....' The probable Platonic references are *Philebus* 16c-18d; *Sophist* 266a-b; *Politicus* 262a-c. See also Alexander, quoted above, 10,14.

151. Note this addition, absent from Aristotle's own examples, but added by the Neoplatonists as early as Plotinus, so as not to leave Plato out of the picture; cf. M. Tardieu 1991, 158.

152. B. was apparently replying to the objection that the *Cat.* is incomplete, because it leaves out conjunctions and thus does not deal with all *lexeis*; cf. Athenodorus and Cornutus (below, 18,24-19,1); Lucius, below, 64,18-65,3.

153. cf. above, 1,4-6; 9,9; Ammon. *In Cat.* 10,9-10.

154. *paraskhêmatizontai*.

155. *suskhêmatizontai*. Cf., with Ph. Hoffmann, Ammon. *In De Interp.* 65,7-9; Apollonius Dyscolus, *On Pronouns*, 15,24; *On Adverbs*, 128,25; 131,3.

156. On grammatical *pathê* and *ideai*, see above, nn. 128, 130.

157. cf. Arist. *Metaph.* 4.7, 1017a24-30; 28, 1024b12-15; 6.2, 1026a33-b1; 7.1, 1028a10-b7.

158. cf. Arist. *Topics* I, 9, 103b20-39; 15, 107a3-12.

159. cf. Arist. *Nicomachean Ethics* A.4, 1096a24ff.

160. In the following passage (12,13-13,11), Simplicius gives a metaphysical foundation for the linkage between words, notions, and realities which is absent from all other extant commentaries on the *Cat.* Ph. Hoffmann thinks the doctrine exposed here may be an echo of the oral instruction of Simplicius' teacher Damascius.

161. cf. with Ph. Hoffmann, Aristotle *On the Soul* 3.4, 430a3ff.

162. *dia tên adiakriton henôsin*. A favourite expression of Damascius'. At *De*

Princ. I, 233,4ff. Ruelle, when explaining the possibility of the birth of the Many from the One, Damascius describes the various ways different levels of reality have of being the All. The One, he writes, is all things 'alone, according to the one'; according to the unified (*kata to hênômenon*) all things are in an undifferentiated unity (*kath' henôsin adiakriton*), and the differentiated (*to diakekrimenon*) is all things 'in a certain distinction' (*en tini diorismôi*).

163. A commonplace of Neoplatonic thought, at least since Plotinus (*Ennead* IV,3 [27] 18). Cf. Ammon. *In Cat.* 15,4-10; Philop. *In Cat.* 9,31-4; Anon. (= Sophonias?), *Paraphr. In Cat.* 4,29ff. Hayduck; Gregory of Nyssa *Contra Eunomium* II, 1, 390, 1ff., quoted *c.* AD 1300 by Nicephoras Gregoras, *Historia Romana*, vol. 3, 286-7 Schopen/Bekker, etc.

164. The theme of forgetfulness goes back ultimately to Book 10 of Plato's *Republic* (621a-c), with its myth of the plain of *Lêthê*.

165. *pros anamnêsin.* The reference is to the Platonic doctrine of *anamnêsis*, the recollection of the knowledge we had when, prior to our incarnation, we accompanied the chariots of the gods and enjoyed direct communion with the intelligible Forms. Cf. Plato *Phaedrus* 248c, *Republic* 10, 621a-c; Ammonius *In De Interp.* 38,8-17.

166. That is, according to Ph. Hoffmann (1987, 83ff.), the philosophy teacher. Cf. Proclus *Commentary on the First Alcibiades* §235, 8-10 Westerink = vol. 2, 285 Segonds.

167. On the *logoi* in the soul-portions of the *nous* which is the substances of the intelligible Forms – as a spark buried in ashes, the rekindling of which constitutes the process of learning, cf. Philoponus *Commentary on Aristotle's De Anima* 4,30ff. Hayduck.

168. In other words, learning/recollection takes place when the notions of the teacher stimulate, through their similarity, the corresponding notions in the student, which had hitherto lain dormant in the latter's mind.

169. *sc.* those of the teacher.

170. On the soul's innate *erôs* for knowledge – derived ultimately from Plato's *Symposium* – cf. Proclus *Theol. Plat.* I,25, vol. I, 109,10-110,8 Saffrey/Westerink; *In Tim.* vol. I, 212,21-2 Diehl; Damascius *Life of Isidore*, ed. Cl. Zinzten, *passim.*

171. With this definition of the *skopos* of the *Cat.*, cf. Herminus *ap.* Porph. *In Cat.* 59,20-30; Porph. *In Cat.* 57,20-58,20. It became the canonical definition; cf. Ammon. *In Cat.* 11,19-12,1; Philop. 9,34-10,8; 12,10-11; Olympiodorus 21,17-22,1; David (Elias) 131,15-132,4.

172. Alexander of Aigai, that is, and Alexander of Aphrodisias; cf. above, 10,8-20.

173. Simplicius was taught by both Ammonius (in Alexandria) and Damascius (in Athens); but whether both, or only Ammonius, are referred to here seems unclear.

174. cf. Philop. 9,34-10,8; Olympiodorus 21,14-20; David (Elias) 131,15-19.

175. For Aristotle (*De Interp.* 2, 16a20ff) names have meaning by convention (*kata sunthêkên*), and not by nature.

176. *artioperisson* and *perissartion.* In his *Introduction to Arithmetic* I, chs 9-10, Nicomachus of Gerasa defines these terms as follows: the *artioperissoi* are even numbers, the halves of which are odd: e.g. 6, 10, 14, 18, etc.; while the *perissartioi* are those even numbers which are products of odd numbers and of powers of 2 above 1: e.g. 24 (= $3x2^3$), 28 (= $7x2^2$), 40 (= $5x2^3$), etc. Cf. Theon Smyrnaeus 25,19ff.; 26,5 Hiller; Euclid *Elements* 7, Def. 9-10.

177. *phthora.* The destruction caused by natural disasters is ephemeral and merely physical, and therefore lacks importance; the 'destruction' caused by faulty reasoning, which can lead to the holding of incorrect views, is destruction only in a metaphorical sense. Evil deeds, however, constitute moral evil: they lead to destruction in the only sense of the term that truly matters, in that they destroy the soul of whoever commits them.

178. *to gumnoun panta kai basanizon.* Literally, 'which strips everything naked and submits it to the torture'.

179. *huparkhei.* A technical term of logic. Strictly speaking, to say 'X *huparkhei* [to] Y' is to say 'X is a property/logical predicate of Y'.

180. This example of the syllogism comes from Plato *Phaedrus* 245c, and was highly popular among the Neoplatonists. Cf. Ammonius *In Porph. Isag.* 35,19-22; Philoponus *In De An.* 1,21-22,6.

181. With what follows – the six-point second half of the standard Neoplatonic introduction to the study of Aristotle – cf. Ammon. 13,6-11; Philop. 10,24-11,33; Olympiodorus 24,21-25,4; David (Elias) 132,5-21. All our Neoplatonic commentators are agreed on the proper reading order of the *Organon*: starting with the *Cat.*, the student must proceed to read *On Interpretation*, then the *Prior Analytics*, and then the *Posterior Analytics*; as usual, the progression is from the more simple to the more complex.

182. *hê prôtê thesis.* The Neoplatonic theory of the two-stage imposition of names is probably of Porphyrian origin; cf. Porph. *In Cat.* 57,18-35; Ammon. 11,7-12,1; Dexippus 11,4-17.

183. The Aristotelian definition of the verb; cf. Arist. *De Interp.* 3, 16b6-18; *Poetics* 20, 1457a14-18.

184. Adrastus; cf. Porphyry *In Cat.* 56,18ff.

185. Plotinus.

186. On Adrastus, a second-century AD Peripatetic philosopher, cf. R. Goulet, 'Adraste d'Aphrodise', in *DPhA* I, 56-7: P. Moraux 1984, 294-332; H.B. Gottschalk in *ANRW* II 36.2 (1987), 1155-6.

187. On this work, see P. Moraux 1984, 314-17.

188. That is to say, the Aristotelian dialectic, as formalized in the *Topics*.

189. Plotinus *Enneads* VI,1-3, treatises 42-4 in the chronological order.

190. According to Simplicius, Plotinus has misunderstood the *Cat.*, because he has failed to take into account the fact that it is a work on logic, directed towards beginners, and that the consideration of *pragmata* consequently has no place therein. On the need to keep the discussion 'appropriate to the study of logic', cf. above, 12,11; 13,12.

191. Arist. *Cat.* 4, 2a4-6.

192. cf. above, 9,14.

193. On the reason for the title cf. David (Elias) 127,24-5; Olympiodorus 22,13f.; Philop. 12,17f. Olympiodorus and Philop. also include at this point long passages taken from Porphyry's *Isagoge*.

194. This is not quite correct, if we are to trust the text of Porphyry's minor Commentary as edited by Busse (Porph. *In Cat.* 56,8-9), which varies slightly from Simplicius' formulation. I am not sure, as S. Strange claims (1992, 31 n. 10) that this passage proves Simplicius had direct knowledge of Porph.'s smaller Commentary, nor, as Ph. Hoffmann believes, that it represents a quote from a parallel passage in Porphyry's *Ad Gedalium*: Simplicius *may* have found this quotation, in more or less corrupt form, in Iamblichus.

195. Proper names like 'Socrates' may – at least in Porphyrian logic – be predicates, but only in what the Alexandrian commentators call 'counter-natural' predication: e.g. 'the man now approaching is Socrates'. The categories, by contrast, may be predicated no matter what their position in the phrase.

196. *apophantikos logos.* The assertoric or declaratory *logos* is the genus of which affirmations and negations are the species. Aristotle discusses it in his *De Interp.* 5, 17a8ff.

197. Thus, the predicate must always have a wider extension than the subject.

198. And, for that matter, in Aristotle's *Prior Analytics* 43a25ff. But whereas Simplicius' students have already read the *Isagoge*, they have not yet tackled the *Analytics*, which come after the *Cat.* and the *De Interpretatione* in the Neoplatonic *cursus*.

199. *ta genikôtata genê.* Cf. Porphyry *Isagoge* 5,17-18 Busse: 'They define "the most generic" (*to genikôtaton*) as follows: that which, while it is a genus, is not a species; or else as that above and beyond which there could be no higher genus.' The latter definition is Stoic; cf. Diogenes Laertius 7,61.

200. *hupokeitai*: literally, 'lie beneath them'. In the logical schema derived from the Porphyrian tree, less universal classes of beings are pictured as 'beneath' more universal classes: 'man', for example, is 'situated beneath' (*hupokeitai*) 'animal' in schematic representations of the Tree, and 'man' also 'serves as a substrate' (*hupokeitai*) for 'animal' in the sense of being the subject of which 'animal' is predicated.

201. *holikôtera.* Cf. Proclus *Elements of Theology* prop. 60, p. 58,11-12; prop. 70, p. 66,11-13 Dodds, etc.

202. cf. Porph. *In Cat.* 55,10-14.

203. i.e. Aristotle's work is entitled *Katêgoriai* – nominative plural – and not *Peri Katêgoriôn*, the noun being in the genitive plural because governed by the preposition *peri* ('about', 'on'). David (Elias) here inserts some interesting – albeit jejune – remarks about the philosophical significance of the nominative case.

204. The reference would seem to be to the work of the second century AD Roman orator Aelius Aristides; cf. Arethas *In Cat.* 136,21-2 Share. Cf. *Oratio* III, 'Against Plato on the Four', §§209ff., ed. F.W. Lenz and C.A. Behr (Leiden: Brill, 1976-1980), and for an English translation *P. Aelius Aristides, The Complete Works, Volume I, Orations I-XVI*, translated into English by Charles A. Behr, (Leiden: Brill, 1986), 189ff.

205. i.e. Plato's *Republic*.

206. On the *kephalaion* of authenticity, cf. Ammon. 13,25-14,2; David (Elias) *In Cat.* 133,9-14; Olympiodorus *Proleg.* 24,6-9; Philop. *In Cat.* 12,34-13,5; Arethas *In Cat.* 137,10-138,20 Share. The commentators enumerate some or all of the same criteria of genuineness, albeit in varying order: (1) Aristotle's style/phraseology (*phrasis*); sometimes referred to as the work's 'matter' (*hulê*; cf. David *In Porph. Isag.* 82,20ff.); (2) density/cleverness of concepts/ideas (*deinotês tôn enthumêmatôn*), sometimes called the work's 'form' (*eidos*; cf. David *loc. cit*); (3) the fact that Arist. mentions the work elsewhere; (4) the fact that the study of logic would be 'headless' (*akephalos*) without it; and (5) the fact that Aristotle's students also wrote treatises 'On the Categories', in emulation (*kata zêlon*) of their Master.

207. *sunestrammenos.* Cf. Plato *Protagoras* 42e.

208. *hetairoi*; that is to say, the early Peripatetics. Other Commentators mention the names of Theophrastus and Eudemus of Rhodes.

209. cf. Philop. *In Cat.* 7,26-8; 13,1-5; *In Anal. Pr.* 6,7-9; David (Elias) *In Cat.* 133,15-17; Ammon. *In Cat.* 13,20-5; Boethius *In Cat.* 161d-162a; Arethas *In Cat.* 138,16-18. Most of these authors add that, besides the two books of the *Cat.* which could be found in ancient libraries, there were no less than forty of the *Analytics*! On Adrastus and his work cf. Simplicius *In Phys.* 6,4ff. Diels; P. Moraux 1973, 83-4; 1985, 314-17.

210. Whereas Aristotle's 'authentic' *Cat.* begins with the words 'Those things *are said* (*legetai*) to be homonyms, of which ...', the pseudepigraphic version began 'Of *beings*, some are (*estin*) ....' Moraux assumes that the second *Cat.* mentioned by Adrastus was a paraphrase after the manner of Andronicus, composed by some first-century BC scholar who – like many moderns – had been displeased at the abruptness of the discussion of synonyms, homonyms, etc. at the very beginning of Aristotle's *Cat.*. The goal of this paraphrase would have been to provide a more satisfactory introduction to the discussion of homonyms. By substituting the verb 'to be' for Aristotle's 'to be said or called', the paraphrase came down hard on the 'ontological' side in the debate over the *skopos* of the *Cat.*: the work was now unequivocally about *beings*, not words.

211. On the *kephalaion* of the division into chapters, cf. Ammon. 14,3-15,2; Philop. 13,6-33; Olympiodorus *Proleg.* 25,5-24; David (Elias) 134,29; Arethas 138,21-139,12. These 'Alexandrian' commentators, however, tend to speak only of a tripartite division of the *Cat.*, into (1) preliminary material (discussion of homonyms, synonyms, etc.); (2) discussion of the doctrine of the categories; and (3) the so-called *Post-praedicamenta*.

212. The image here is of a butcher, cutting up a carcass according to its joints; cf. Plato *Phaedrus* 265e. One must not, like a bad butcher, chop up one's subject-matter just any old way, but according to the pre-existing natural articulations. It is the skill in finding these articulations that, for Plato, distinguishes the good dialectician, and for the Neoplatonists, distinguishes the good commentator.

213. *stoibêdon.* Apparently a *hapax legomenon.* In explaining the word *stoibê*, the Suda explains that the metaphor derives from a heap of merchandise (*apo tês stoibês tôn phortiôn*). Something lying *stoibêdon*, then, would be lying in a disorderly, unconnected pile.

214. We have seen (above, 4,15ff.) that hypomnematic writings are works which an author composes for his own use as an *aide-mémoire*; since they are not normally intended for publication, they may lack a polished literary structure.

215. On the Stoic Athenodorus of Cana in Cilicia (*c.* 85 – *c.* 3 BC), teacher of Octavian, the future Augustus, R. Goulet, 'Athénodore', in *DPhA* I (1989), 652.

216. Lucius Annaeus Cornutus, Stoic philosopher, teacher of Persius and Lucan, was born *c.* AD 20 in Leptis Magna, North Africa. He was well known as a literary critic and theologian until his banishment by Nero in 65, cf. P.P. Fuentes González, 'Cornutus', in *DPhA* II (1994) 460-73; P. Moraux 1984, 592-601.

217. cf. Porph. *In Cat.* 59,6-14; 86,20-4; Dexippus *In Cat.* 11,1-12,32; Simplicius below, 62,24-7; 359,3. Although this is the first formulation within Simplicius' commentary of the objection that Aristotle did not include a discussion of all kinds of words in the *Cat.* (cf. a similar point raised by Lucius at 64,18-65,3), certain remarks by Boethus imply that it had already been formulated in the first generation of *Cat.* commentators, perhaps by Andronicus himself. Cf. below, 11,25ff.; 24,6-7; 25,10-14; P. Moraux 1973, 150.

218. *sc.* the *Post-praedicamenta.*

219. 'Theological' presumably means 'metaphysical' here, as it does in Aristotle *Metaphysics* 1026a19, where the three branches of theoretical philosophy are listed as mathematical, physical, and theoretical.

220. On the Speusippian concepts 'heteronym' and 'polyonym', see below, 23,4ff.; 38,12ff.

221. cf. Arist. *Cat.* 5, 3a7ff.

222. cf. *Cat.* ch. 8.

223. cf. Porph. *In Cat.* 60,1-8; Boethius *In Cat.* col. 163B8-C7.
224. That is, the central section of the *Cat.* is devoted to the discussion of the ten categories.
225. i.e. the so-called *Post-praedicamenta*; *Cat.* chs 11-15. For the Neoplatonists, the whole educative process has as its goal the re-awakening of our innate ideas (*ennoiai*), muddled traces of that true knowledge of Reality we enjoyed prior to incarnation in the physical body. Aristotle carries this out, says Simplicius first by giving us a general, descriptive sketch (*hupographê*) of the categories, and then by returning to clarify and sharpen this sketch, leaving us with an *ennoia* which, in its clarity, resembles ever more closely the perfection of our pre-incarnate knowledge. Simplicius is following Porphyry here.
226. Arist. *Cat.* 7, 6a36ff.
227. *Cat.* ch. 13.
228. An allusion to the fact – notoriously problematic, for a Neoplatonist – that in the *Cat.* Aristotle accords the title of 'primary substance' to individual, sensible entities, whereas elsewhere in the Corpus (primarily the *Metaphysics*), he accords this primacy to intelligible entities.
229. cf. Arist. *Cat.* 12, 14a25ff.
230. cf. Olympiodorus *Proleg.* 23,28ff.; Arethas *In Cat.* 137,18ff.
231. For the *Cat.* discussion of kinds of motion, cf. 15a13ff. The mention of motion in the context of doing and being-affected, may refer to 5b1-3, where practice (*praxis*) is said to be lengthy when there is much movement.
232. *Cat.* chs 10-11, 11b21; 33ff.; 12b25ff.; 13b36ff.
233. *Cat.* ch. 7, 6b15-1.
234. *Cat.* ch. 8, 10b12-24.
235. Porphyry's *aporia*, present *in nuce* in his lesser extant commentary (59,34-60,11 Busse), is taken from his commentary *Ad Gedalium* (fr. 49 Smith), whence it was taken up by Ammon. Philop.; Olympiodorus; and David (Elias). Its gist is as follows: as the *Cat.* stand now, we have the discussion of the ten categories preceded by
(a) a discussion of synonyms, homonyms, and paronyms; followed by
(b) a discussion of the meaning of 'simultaneous' and 'prior', of motion and of contraries (i. e. the so-called 'post-praedicamenta'). Why, asks Porphyry, did not Aristotle either
(i) place (b), along with (a), before the discussion of the categories (since a) was intended to clear up concepts necessary for understanding the rest of the *Cat.*); or else
(ii) relegate (a), like (b) to an appendix at the end of the exposition of the categories themselves. The *lusis* of this *aporia* is that (a) contains technical terms completely unfamiliar to the student, such as 'homonym'; these had to be explained beforehand, or else the student, upon first encountering them, would have been confused and/or frightened away from the *Cat.* The material contained in (b), by contrast, (*sc.* the *Post-praedicamenta*) is more familiar. Dealing as it does with such concepts as motion, simultaneity and contrariety, it does not deal with subject-matter so strange it is likely to throw the student for a loop. All humans have innate concepts (*ennoiai* or *prolêpseis*) of such terms, which we use all the time in daily speech. As we are not yet philosophers, however, these vague, dim notions of ours require clarification, and this is the goal of the *Post-praedicamenta*.
As for the question why Aristotle did not discuss all the accessory and clarificatory matter at once, before proceeding to the discussion of the categories themselves, Porphyry's answer seems to have been twofold: (1) The result would have been aesthetically displeasing: to have a prologue longer than the discus-

sion of the subject-matter itself would fly in the face of the rules of literary composition; and (2) It would have entailed too long a postponement of the discussion of the categories themselves; one may assume that students would have got bored and lost interest before even beginning the study of what was important.

236. *sc.* the meaning of 'simultaneous' and 'prior', of motion, and of contraries.

237. The concept of legislators of names (*onomathetai*) goes back to Plato's *Cratylus*, but the insistence that names must be in accord with the nature of things is characteristic of the Pythagoreans and the Stoics: see Alcinous *Didaskalikos* 6, 160ff. Hermann with the references given by Whittaker in the notes *ad loc.* to his Budé edition. See also Proclus *In Cratylum* 49, 17,18ff. Pasquali.

238. For this comparison, cf. Philop. 4,31-5; David (Elias) 117,9-13.

239. Arist. *Cat.* 1, 1a1.

240. The same objection – minus the information that its originator was Nicostratus – is raised by the anonymous questioner in Porph. *In Cat.* 59,34-6 (cf. following note); and cf. Dexippus *In Cat.* 16,14-17; Ammon. 16,19-24; Olympiodorus 27,36-9; Philop. 14,24-8; David (Elias) 135,3-6; Boethius col. 163B.

241. Throughout this section, Simplicius is following Porphyry very closely; cf. Porph. *In Cat.* 60,1ff.; Dexippus *In Cat.* 16,18-32 (possibly from P.'s lost *Ad Gedalium*). On Porphyrian semantics cf. S. Strange 1987; S. Ebbesen 1990; P. Hadot 1974; A.C. Lloyd 1990, ch. 2.

242. For the Neoplatonist tradition probably inaugurated by Porphyry, Aristotle's categories were interpreted as dealing with the primary words or expressions (*prôtai lexeis/phônai*), i.e. those words which had been invented by a group of ancient sages to designate the ten highest (that is, most fundamental and all-encompassing) genera or kinds of being. Cf. Ph. Hoffmann 1984-85; 1987a.

243. cf. Dexippus *In Cat.* 16,18ff.

244. Andronicus of Rhodes, head of the Peripatetic school *c.* 50-5 BC, rekindled interest in Aristotle, after centuries of eclipse, by his edition of the Stagirite's school-treatises. Cf. P. Moraux 1973, 58ff.

245. Apparently Andronicus, in his capacity as first editor of the Aristotelian corpus, had transposed the sentence currently printed as *Cat.* 1a16-17 to the beginning of the *Cat.* There followed a combination of 1a17 to *fin.* and 1a1.

246. It was Aristotle's view that 'being' (*to einai*) was *not* a genus; cf. *Post. An.* 2.7, 92b12-19; *Metaph.* 3.3, 998b17-28, etc.; H. Happ 1971, 327-8 & n. 80. Aristotle's view was seconded by Porphyry in his *Isagoge* 6,6-9 Busse.

247. Fr. 10 Dalsgaard Larsen (1972), vol. 2, 12; for a useful general survey of Neoplatonic commentaries on the *Cat.* cf. *ibid.*, vol. 1, 223-301.

248. cf. Porph. *In Cat.* 61,10; Dexippus *In Cat.* 17,25-30; Boeth. *In Cat.* 166C; Arethas *In Cat.* 140,14-15.

249. As Porphyry points out (*In Cat.* 55,5ff.), the original meaning of *katêgorein* is 'to make an accusation before a court of law'.

250. cf. Aristotle *Sophistical Refutations* 4, 165b26-8: six kinds of fallacy have their origin in *lexis* (diction), of which homonymy is the first to be mentioned; *Rhetoric* 1404b37-9: 'Of words, it is homonyms which are the most useful to sophists ....'

251. Plato *Euthydemus* 277e; 295d. On the links between the *Euthydemus* and Aristotle's *SE*, see L.-A. Dorion, *Aristote, Les réfutations sophistiques* (Paris/Québec 1995), 91-104.

252. cf. Porph. *In Cat.* 60,15-21; Ammon. 15,10-16; Philop. 14,2-11; Olympiodorus 26,11-13; Boeth. col 163D; Anon. <Sophonias> *In Cat.* 1,5-7.

253. *dia logou hupographikou ê horistikou*; cf. Porph. *In Cat.* 60,15f.; 63,6ff. A *logos hupographikos* (description) gives a sketch of the accidental properties of realities, including the highest genera themselves and individuals, which cannot be defined (cf. Simplicius below, 29,19-20, and especially Porphyry *To Gedalius ap.* Simplicium below, 30,13-15). A *logos horistikos*, by contrast, is one which proceeds *per genus et differentiam*; it is therefore impossible to give a definition of the highest genera (i.e. the ten categories), since there is no higher genus under which these could be subsumed. Cf. P. Hadot 1968, I, 251-2.

254. i.e. from its original *significatum*. See following note.

255. i.e. the word 'man' stands for/becomes the symbol of a picture of a man, as well as of the man.

256. *ton ... exêgêtikon logon tês ousias*. The *logos* of substance is the same as a definitory *logos* (*logos horistikos*); it applies to one species or genus alone, and gives a complete, sufficient and exclusive account of it.

257. cf. Porph. 60,21-33; Ammon. 15,16-16,6; Philop. 14,11-16; Olympiodorus 26,13-22; 27,10-20; <Sophonias> 1,8-17; Boeth. 163D-164A.

258. On polyonyms cf. Alexander of Aphrodisias *In Top.* 577,16-578,14.

259. cf. Alexander *In Top.* 578,7f. *Merops* and *brotos* both mean 'man', and were first used in epic poetry (*Iliad* 2.285; 5.304; Hesiod *Works and Days* 109 etc.). *Brotos* seems to mean 'mortal'; the meaning and etymology of *merops* are disputed by modern scholars. Ammonius *In De Interp.* 38,9-14 gives far-fetched etymologies of both terms.

260. cf. Boethius *In Cat.* 165B-D.

261. cf. Alexander *In Top.* 398,1-5 Wallies; *In Metaph.* 247,22-4 Hayduck (who adds to his examples of *heteronyms* 'partless' (*ameres*) and 'least' (*elakhiston*); 'seed' (*sperma*) and 'fruit' (*karpos*); Ammon. *In Cat.* 16,24-17,3; *In De Interp.* 10,4; Anon. <Sophonias> 1,13; Philop. 14,17-23; Olympiodorus 126,22-7,10. The example of the ladder as common substrate of ascent and descent is found already in Clement of Alexandria's *Stromata* (8,8,24,3,1f.), which probably means it was current school doctrine by the early second century BC; cf. J. Pépin 1980.

262. As Porphyry puts it (*In Cat.* 60-1): every reality has (a) a name and (b) an account (*logos*). We thus wind up with the following schema:

    (1) Things having in common (a) but not (b): are homonyms.
    (2) Things having in common (b) but not (a): polyonyms.
    (3) Things having in common both (a) and (b): synonyms.
    (4) Things having in common neither (a) nor (b): heteronyms.
    (5) Things having in common (a) and (b) *in a sense only*: paronyms.

263. So Porph. *In Cat.* 61,2-3.

264. Boethius, too, remarks on the rejection of polyonyms and heteronyms (col. 168C); but unlike Syrianus he does not say why.

265. Simplicius has already underlined that concern for clarity in expression is quite distinct from the practice of philosophy; cf. above 10,30.

266. cf. Ammon. 16,19-23; Philop. 15,11-13; Olympiodorus 28,8-13; David (Elias) 135,3-9.

267. cf. Porph. *In Cat.* 61,10-12. This is one of several instances in which Simplicius quotes as Iamblichean a passage taken more or less verbatim from Porphyry's *Commentary by Questions and Responses*, leading one to doubt that Simplicius was at all familiar with it other than *via* Iamblichus.

268. cf. Porph. *In Cat.* 61,13-27; Dexippus *In Cat.* 17,30-18,12; Boethius *In Cat.* 166C-D.

269. P. Moraux 1973, 150, assumes that this objection goes back to the Stoics Athenodorus and Cornutus, who have already been mentioned (above, 18,26-19,1), as representatives of the belief that the *Cat.* were about words (*peri lexeôn*). Moraux later (1984, 532; 544) revised his view, and declared it most probable that the source of this *aporia* was Lucius and Nicostratus.

270. cf. Dexippus *In Cat.* 10,9-10. Interestingly, the explanation by means of our concepts/*ennoiai* is absent from Porphyry's 'minor' commentary: did he think it too complex for his beginning students, so that the present passage in Simplicius derives from Porphyry's philosophically more sophisticated *Ad Gedalium*?

271. cf. Dexippus *In Cat.* 19,20ff; Boethius *De Divisione*, PL 64, 877D, p. 8 Magee = Porphyry *Commentary on the Sophist* fr. 169, p. 167 Smith. The sea-dog (*thalattios kuôn*; Latin *canicula*, *canis marinus*, or *caeruleus*) may have been a member of the shark family. Athenaeus (*Deipnosophistae* 4,56,4 Kaibel) preserves a poem by Timon in praise of its flavour; yet for Boethius and Isidore of Seville (*Etymologies* XII,6,10) it seems more like a whale. According to Pliny (IX,11) and Procopius (*De Bell. Pers.* I,4), it stood guard over the pearls in deep-sea oyster beds. 'They are snouted like dogges', writes Pliny (in Philemon Holland's 1601 translation), 'when they snarle, grin, and are readie to do a shrewd turne'.

272. In modern terminology, until he agrees to disambiguate; cf. Aristotle in ch. 17 of the *Sophistici Elenchi* 175b40-176a18; cf. 30, 181a36ff. Does Simplicius' reference to 'the dialecticians' instead of to Aristotle, indicate that he was not familiar with the *SE*?

273. If we follow the reading of MS A., and emend the *epi* of line 21 into *apo*, the text would read: 'This is why Aristotle, too, <begins> his teaching with synonyms: since, at any rate, the discussion on homonymy is immediately consequent [upon the discussion of homonyms].'

274. Plato *Sophist* 218c1-3.

275. Moraux once held the originators of this *aporia* to be Athenodorus and Cornutus (P. Moraux 1973, 150), but he later decided for Lucius and Nicostratus (1984, 533).

276. This *aporia* is based on an ambiguity of the Greek word *onoma*. It can mean either 'name' – this is the normal translation in the passage from the *Cat.* to which Simplicius is here referring – or it can mean 'noun' in contexts such as the present one, where it is opposed to *rhêma*, 'verb'. The originator(s) of this *aporia* appear to have understood Aristotle's expression in the *Cat.* as though the meaning were the second. of these two. Cf. Porph. *In Cat.* 61,31-5; Ammon. 18,18-20; Olympiodorus 30,4-9; Philop. 18,4-6; David (Elias) 137,23-5; Boethius 164B-C.

277. 'He has been enslaved', perfect passive/middle, third person singular of the verb *andrapodizô*. As Sophonias explains (*Paraphrasis of the Cat.* 2,29 Hayduck), *êndrapodistai* is ambiguous because it can mean either 'he has been enslaved' – if we take the verb to be in the passive – or 'he has enslaved someone else' if we take it to be in the middle. Simplicius' immediate source for this example will have been Porph. *In Cat.* 61,32-4.

278. 'Having been enslaved', masculine perfect participle of the same verb, or 'having enslaved [someone else]', if taken as the middle voice.

279. *ê* and *êtoi*. Modern grammarians have followed suit: for example Denniston in *The Greek Particles*, devotes nine pages to the various meanings of *ê*, and another three to *êtoi*.

280. On the division of names/nouns into *kurion* and *prosêgorikon*, cf. Dionysius Thrax *Grammar* ch. 12, 33,52ff. Uhlig. D.'s examples of an *onoma* *kurion* are 'Socrates'; 'Homer'; of an *onoma prosêgorikon* 'man', 'horse'. This grammatical doctrine is Stoic in origin; cf. D.L. 7,58.

281. *to kuôn, to êndrapodistai.* Boethus' point is simply that the neuter definite article *to* is placed both before nouns (*to kuôn* = 'dog') and before verbal infinitives (*to êndrapodistai*). The presence of the definite article in a phrase thus cannot be a criterion for determining the kind of 'name' it contains.

282. cf. Porph. *In Cat.* 62,1-6 (who does not mention he is following Boethus); Boethius *In Cat.* 164B; P. Moraux 1973, 150.

283. By 'indeclinable names' Simplicius here means verbal infinitives, which do not alter in declension, although the article modifying them does. In Boethus' examples, the article is given in the nominative, genitive and dative cases respectively.

284. cf. Porph. *In Cat.* 62,7-16; Dexippus 18,12-24; Ammon. 19,1-8; Philop. 18,17-24; David (Elias) 138,1-11; Olympiodorus 30,18-27; Arethas 141,8-12. For analysis and comparison with a passage from Boethius' second commentary on Porphyry's *Isagoge*, see now A. de Libera 1999, 211ff.

285. cf. Porph. *In Cat.* 62,18ff.; Dexippus 18,34-19,16; Boethius 164CD; Ammon. 9,9-14; Philop. 18,25-19,5; Olympiodorus 30,27-31,3; John of Damascus, *Dialectica sive Capita philosophica* (recensio fusior) 65,67-74 Kotter = *Fragmenta philosophica* (e cod. Oxon. Bodl. Auct. T.1.6) §15, 2-10; Arethas *In Cat.* 141,12-16 Souda s.v. *koinon*. The origin of this canonical four-fold division of the common may have been Andronicus' *Paraphrase of the Cat.*; Moraux thinks its originator was Porphyry.

286. *en prokatalêpsei.* This rare phrase appears in all the commentators, starting from Porphyry (*In Cat.* 62,24). Cf. Dexippus 19,1; Philop. 18,29-30; Olympiodorus 30,32-3.

287. cf. Cicero *De Finibus* III,20,67.

288. *phônê.* I have usually translated this by 'word', but the parallel passages listed above speak of the *phônê* of a herald, in which context the word must mean 'voice'.

289. Thus, Andronicus altered Aristotle's formulation, according to which homonyms were those things the name of which is *common* (*koinon*), to '... the name of which is *the same* (*tauton*)'.

290. On this *aporia*, cf. Dexippus *In Cat.* 19,17-20,4; who does not mention its Nicostratian origin.

291. cf. Galen *On the Difference between Pulses* vol. VIII, 573,11ff. Kühn. K. Praechter (1922, 50 n. 1) deduced from the fact that the facial spasm called 'dog' seems only to be mentioned in these two instances, that Nicostratus had taken this example from Galen's *Commentary on the Cat.*. This seems unwarranted, for the dog had been a frequent example in school-discussions of homonymy since the time of the early Empire.

292. A Stoic view. Although a Platonist, Nicostratus often uses Stoic arguments; cf. K. von Fritz, 'Nikostratos 26', *RE* XVII 1 (1936), 547-51.

293. *kata to en prokatalêpsei.*

294. 'Nevertheless' is, of course, only one of many meanings of *alla mên*; for a full enumeration cf. Denniston, *Greek Particles*, 341-9. The Diodorus in question is the Megarian philosopher Diodorus Cronus (died *c.* 307 BC), teacher of the Stoic Zeno. The same anecdote, interpreted differently, is recounted by Ammonius *In De Interp.* 38,17-22.

295. Thus, on this view, a homonym could be a name in sense (i) above: like the meaningless noun 'blituri', it could have a nominal form and yet not be coordinated with any particular significatum. On the technical terms *akatataktos/katatetagmenos*, see below, 53,8; 56,2f. and notes.

296. Aristotle has defined homonyms as 'those things *of which* the name alone is common'. But if the name is *of* a thing, then that name has been assigned to that thing. Thus the name is not unallocated/meaningless, as suggested in hypothesis (i); cf. A.C. Lloyd 1990, 58ff.

297. Arist. *Cat.* 1a4.

298. On Simplicius' suggested solution, cf. A.C. Lloyd, 1990, 60-1.

299. *idiôthen kai apomeristhen.* The passive form of the verb *idiôomai* seems to appear only here (cf. above, 26,30: *idiothêsetai*) and in Damascius *De Princ.* I, 205,8 Ruelle.

300. Arist. *Cat.* 1, 1a1-2.

301. *horistikos logos.*

302. *suzugos einai.* Cf. Porph. *In Cat.* 63,4; David (Elias) 138,8; Boethius 165A. Saying that the *logos* must be 'in accordance with the name' (*kata tounoma*) is the same as saying it must be *suzugos.*

303. *anaploi kai diexodeuei.*

304. *sunairei kai sunptussei.* Cf. Proclus *De sacrificio et magia* (ed. J. Bidez, *Catalogue des manuscrits alchimiques grecs*, vol. 6, Brussels 1928), 149,12-17: '... in what respect do men raising and lowering their jaws and lips and singing hymns to the sun, differ from the lotus folding (*sumptussonta*) and unfolding (*anaplounta*) its leaves?'

305. cf. Porph. *In Cat.* 63,6-7; Boethius 165A.

306. On the importance of the equivalence or convertibility of definitions, cf. Porph. *In Cat.* 63,20ff.; Boethius *In Cat.* 165A-D.

307. Thus it is true to say that 'if something is an animal, then it nourishes itself, grows, and generates things similar to itself'. It is not, however, true to say that 'if something nourishes itself, grows, and generates things similar to itself, then it is an animal', for plants fulfil these conditions, but are not animals.

308. In other words, subject and predicate must be co-extensive; in Stoic terminology, the definition must be *kat' apartismon.* If A is defined as B, everything said of A must be able to be said of B. But the relationship must be convertible: everything said of B must also be said of A. For the Stoic Antipater, such convertibility was the mark of a genuine definition; cf. *Scholia Vaticani in Dionysium Thracensem, Grammatici Graeci* 3, 107,5ff. Hilgard (= *SVF* II.226) with O. Rieth 1933, 24; 42f., cf. also *Schol. Vat. in Dion. Thrac.* 188,4 Hilgard; Cicero *On Oratory* 2,108.

309. For the example of the Ajaxes, cf. Porph. *In Cat.* 64,10-21; Porph. *Ad Gedalium ap.* Simplicium *In Cat.* 30,25ff. below; Dexippus 20,20-7; Ammon. 15,29-16,4; Philop. 19,11-20; David (Elias) 138,28-139,6; Arethas 142,2-5. Boethius (165D) replaces the Ajaxes with Pyrrhus son of Achilles and Pyrrhus of Epirus.

310. Fr. 68b Tarán = 32b Lang. In other words, at *Cat.* 1, 1a1-2, instead of 'the definition *of substance in accordance with the name* is different' (*ho de kata tounoma logos tês ousias heteros*), Speusippus preferred to read simply 'but the definition is different' (*ho de logos heteros*). Simplicius probably has his information on Speusippus from Boethus of Sidon, *via* Porphyry's commentary *Ad Gedalium*; cf. L. Tarán in *Hermes* 106 (1978), 73-99.

311. cf. Dexippus *In Cat.* 20,32-21,4; Boethius *In Cat.* 165C. In so far as both a person and a horse are called 'animal', they are synonymous; that is to say, they have both the same name ('animal'), and the same definition. As individuals, however, horses and people have different definitions (one is rational, the other not), and therefore they are homonyms.

312. If the sea-dog and the land-dwelling dog are defined *qua* animals, then they are synonyms, since they share both the same *logos* (of animal) and the same name ('animal'). Individually, however, land- and sea-dogs have different *logoi* (one is a furry canine that barks, for example, and the other a mischievous sharp-toothed fish), and so they are homonyms. Thus homonyms have here become synonyms.

313. On the necessity of definitions being 'in accordance with the name', cf. Porph. *In Cat.* 63,1-64,25.

314. With this enumeration of the meanings of *logos*, cf. Porph. *In Cat.* 64,27-65,1; Boethius *In Cat.* 166A; Porph. *On Interpretation, ap.* Boethium *In De Interp.* ed. 2ᵃ, I, c. 1, p. 36 Meiser.

315. *logos endiathetos* and *logos prophorikos.* Originally Stoic terms (*SVF* II.135ff.), meaning respectively 'thought' and 'vocal expressions'. The distinction between interior and uttered *logos* goes back to Plato *Sophist* 263e, but later became part of the philosophical *koinê* of the Empire; cf. Porph. *On Abstinence* 3, 2, vol. 2, p. 153 Bouffartigue/Patillon.

316. *logos spermatikos*, the Stoic concept of an all-pervading, rational divine substance containing, as it were, the blueprints for the development of all beings.

317. *ton hekastou periêgêtikon kai horistikon logon.* The adjective *periêgêtikos* ('guiding') is rare, occurring in only three Greek authors other than Simplicius.

318. *tên hupographikên apodosin.*

319. The highest genera have no genera above them; if they did they would no longer be highest. Individuals, by contrast, as the most specific species (*eidê eidikôtata*), have no differentiae: if they did, then the differentia in question, combined with the new species, would give rise to another lower species; cf. Boethius *In Cat.* 166A; Simplicius below, 45,24. But definitions (*horismoi*) in the strict Aristotelian sense proceed by genus and differentiae (cf. *Topics* 1.8, 103b14-15), so that in the absence of either of these two elements, strict definition is impossible.

320. cf. Boethius *In Cat.* 166A.

321. *viz.* the highest genera and individuals.

322. *to ti ên einai.* an Aristotelian term of art meaning 'essence'.

323. cf. Boethius *In Cat.* 166B1-2.

324. Smith prints the following passage (29,24-30,15) as Porphyry fr. 51, from the *Ad Gedalium.*

325. On this Nicostratian *aporia* cf. K. Praechter 1922, 467 = 1973, 117; P. Moraux 1973, 150-1.

326. This example of ambiguity comes from Arist. *Topics* 1, 107a13-14, where we learn that a 'white noise' (*leukê phônê*) is 'a sound which is easy to hear' (*phônê euêkoos*).

327. i.e. 'of the substance'.

328. i.e. the manuscript of the *Cat.* consulted by Boethus did not read at 1a1-2 'the definition in accordance with the name *of the substance* is different' (*ho de kata tounoma logos tês ousias heteros*), but 'the definition in accordance with the name is different' (*ho de kata tounoma logos heteros*); cf. Dexippus *In Cat.* 21,18-19.

329. cf. above, 26,18 & n. 289. In addition to replacing Aristotle's 'common' (*koinon*) by 'identical' (*tauton*), Andronicus like his disciple Boethus, also omitted 'of the substance' (*tês ousias*) from his text of *Cat.* 1a2.

330. cf. Porph. *In Cat.* 65,4-5.

331. Whereas the definition (*horos, horismos*) is concerned with the essence of a thing (*to ti ên einai*), the description (*hupographê*) merely gives the thing's properties, whether essential or accidental. The description points out a thing's *idiotês*; that is, that property which identifies it and constitutes its individuality.

332. Smith (pp. 41-2) prints the following lengthy passage (30,16-31,21) as Porphyry fr. 52, from the *Ad Gedalium*.

333. This remark is useful for the dating of Nicostratus: If Atticus, whose *floruit* was *c.* 176 AD, enlarged upon an *aporia* first raised by N., then N. must be situated earlier than this date.

334. In other words, two homonyms A and B both participate in the common nature/Platonic Form of homonymity. By virtue of this participation, A and B obtain both the name and the definition (*logos*) of 'homonym', and since their names and *logoi* are the same, they are synonymous.

335. If A and B are considered as having the same name 'Ajax' but not the same nature/*logos*, then they are homonyms.

336. The Greek term for 'two-syllable-word' – *disullabon* – has four syllables.

337. cf. Porph. *In Cat.* 65,18ff; Boethius 166BC; Ammon. 21,16-22,10; Philop. 16,20-17,11; David (Elias) 139,29-140,25. The division in Olympiodorus 34,3-35,14 is rather more complex. The division of homonyms into chance and intentional, the latter being further subdivided into 'by similarity', 'by analogy', and 'by metaphor' (or 'by focal homonymity') goes back to Aristotle *Nicomachean Ethics* 1096b26ff.; cf. Galen *De sophismatis seu captionibus penes dictionem*, vol. 14, 597,10ff. Kühn; Clement of Alexandria *Stromata* VIII,8,24,8-9; Anon. [= Constantinus Palaeocappa?] *In Ethica Nicomachea paraphrasis*, ed. G. Heylbut (= *CAG* 19, 2, Berlin: Reimer, 1889), 10,30ff.

338. *apo tukhês*, literally 'derive from chance'.

339. *apo dianoias*; literally 'derive from the discursive intellect'.

340. Olympiodorus (*In Cat.* 34,13ff.) explains that there can be no division of that which is by chance, only of that which comes about by knowledge or by skill; he quotes as his authority Plato *Gorgias* 448c.

341. Aristotle *Cat.* 1, 1a2.

342. cf. Porph. *In Cat.* 65,30-66,2; Boethius 166B9ff.

343. For puzzles regarding the *arkhai* of the monad and point cf. below, 65,14ff.

344. On the Aristotelian concept of analogy, cf. *EN* 5.6 1131a28ff.; *Poetics* 21, 57b16ff.

345. cf. Porph. *In Cat.* 66,2-12; Boethius 166B12-15.

346. cf. Porph. *In Cat.* 66,12ff., Boethius 166B15-C3.

347. *to aph' henos kai pros hen*; or 'focal meaning'.

348. cf. Porph. *In Cat.* 66,34ff.

349. What follows (Simplicius 32,23-33,11) is a virtual transcription of Porph. *In Cat.* 67,4-31.

350. Homer *Iliad* 20.218.

351. *ibid.* 20,59.

352. Homer *Odyssey* 10.32.

353. Porph. *In Cat.* 67,17.

354. Fragment omitted by A. Smith (1993).

355. cf. above, n. 352.

356. Arist. *Cat.* 1, 1a6-12.

357. cf. Porph. *In Cat.* 68,15-16. For the omission of *kata tounoma* at *Cat.* 1, 1a2, cf. Minio-Paluello's apparatus *ad loc.*

358. Fragment omitted by Smith.

359. Thus, in his lost commentary Porphyry apparently thought it unnecessary to specify which *logos* was the same in the case of synonyms; he therefore deleted '*kata tounoma*' and '*tês ousias*' from the text of *Cat.* 1, 1a7.

360.   What the reader must supply in thought, as intended but not expressed by the author, is presumably the phrase 'in accordance with the name' (*kata tounoma*), since Porphyry's omission of the words 'of the substance' (*tês ousias*) is discussed below, 34,12.

361.   The play on words is untranslatable: the Greek word *korax* means, in the first instance, a crow or a raven; but it also served to designate anything with a hooked structure similar to a crow's beak, such as a siege-engine used for grappling ships, or a hooked door-handle. It is the latter meaning Simplicius has in mind here.

362.   cf. Porph. *In Cat.* 68,18.

363.   Fragment omitted by A. Smith (1993).

364.   According to Porphyry in the *Ad Gedalium*, then, both 'in accordance with the name' and 'of substance/being' should be dropped from Aristotle's text at *Cat.* 1, 1a7. But while 'in accordance with the name' must be supplied, 'of substance/being' should be retained, since a thing's synonymy is unrelated to the question of its being (*ousia*).

365.   'Man' and 'horse' participate to precisely the same extent in their genus 'animal'; therefore 'animal' is predicated of them synonymously. When we consider their species 'man' and 'horse', however, they are different. Simplicius/Porphyry seems to imply here that the genus is linked to substance (*ousia*), while the species is linked to the form (the Greek word for both is identical, *viz. eidos*).

366.   Fragment omitted by Smith.

367.   Porphyry is actually considerably more ambivalent about the correct reading than Simplicius' comments might lead one to believe; what he says in the text as edited by Busse (*In Cat.* 68,15f.) is that the inclusion or omission of 'of being (*ousia*)' does not make any difference. Cf. Strange's n. 75, p. 49 of his translation.

368.   The following table may help to make the commentators' various readings intelligible:

Arist. *Cat.* 1a6-7:	those things are called synonyms of which the name is common and ... the account	In accordance with the name	of being	is the same
Porphyry	✓	✓	✓	✓
Iamblichus	✓	✓	✗	✓
Syrianus	✓	✓	✗	✓
Alexander	✓	✗	✓	✓

369.   With what follows cf. Ammon. 22,14-19; Olympiodorus 38,1-6; Philop. 23,30-24,3; David (Elias) 144,5-17; Arethas 144,22-33.

370.   Homer *Iliad* 14.117. 'Melas', besides being the name of a Homeric character, is Greek for 'black'.

371.   In other words, Savage the savage would be (a) synonymous to other savage men, since Savage both is and is called a savage man; but he would also be (b) homonymous with other savage men, since as a different individual man his definition is different from that of each other man.

372.   *idiôs poion*. For the Stoics, the 'individualizing quality' was that quality which, remaining present throughout a person's existence, individualized him and distinguished him from all other individuals. It is what is designated by proper names like 'Socrates', whereas the 'commonly qualified' (*koinôs poion*) is what is designated by common nouns such as 'man'. Cf. below, 48,15f.; Long and Sedley I, 28, esp. vol. I, pp. 172-5.

373. Arist. *Cat.* 1, 1a8.

374. *ibid.*

375. Smith (42-4) prints the following passage (36,8-31) as Porphyry fr. 53, from the *Ad Gedalium.*

376. *SVF* 2, 105, where the text should be corrected to follow Kalbfleisch's edition. The Stoics would thus seem to have identified synonyms with polyonyms, as Speusippus had done.

377. Arist. *Poet.* fr. 3 Kassel. Kalbfleisch points to Arist. *Rhet.* 3.2, 1404b39, but Simplicius-Porphyry may instead be quoting from the lost Aristotle's *Poetics*, which discussed the sources of verbal humour; cf. R. Janko, *CQ* ii (1982), 323-6.

378. Speusippus fr. 32c Lang = fr. 68c Tarán.

379. Presumably the Stoics.

380. P. Moraux 1973, 151, conjectures that Aristotle's *Poetics* and *Rhetoric*, from which Porphyry draws his counter-examples of Stoico-Speusippian polyonyms, were not available to Boethus, whence his complaint about their omission by Aristotle.

381. Arist. *Cat.* 1, 1a12-15.

382. On paronyms, cf. Porph. *In Cat.* 69,15ff.; Ammon. 23,25-24,12; Philop. 24,4-25,22; Boethius 167D-168D; Olympiodorus 38,13-40,31; David (Elias) 142,16-144,17; Arethas 145,1-146,31.

383. *grammatikos.* Depending on the context, this word can mean either 'elementary school teacher' or 'person who knows how to read and write'.

384. Kalbfleisch indicates a lacuna here, which must have been rather extensive. We need something like <... while the *logos* of *grammatikos* is 'he who knows how to read and write'. The names themselves are also different. Moreover, some people, (not content with this explanation?), say that three things ...> etc., at which point Simplicius picks up Porphyry's explanation once again.

385. Thus, for Simplicius the necessary and sufficient conditions for paronymy are:

(1) participation in the same reality;

(2) participation in the same name (i.e. the fact that the names derive from the same root); and

(3) difference in word-ending. Cf. Porph. *In Cat.* 69,30ff.; Boethius *In Cat.* 168A-B. Most of the other commentators state that four things are necessary for paronymy: similarity of name, difference of name, similarity of object, and difference of object; cf. Philop. 24,26-8; Olympiodorus 38,18-21; David 142,36-143,1; Arethas 145,22-4.

386. *mesotêtês.* A *mesotês* was a subspecies of the adverb, added to the five Stoic parts of speech by Antipatros of Tarsus (D.L. VII, 57). Dionysius Thrax (*Ars Grammatica* ch. 19, 72-3 Uhlig) lists it as the second of his 26 varieties of adverbs, but neither he nor his scholiasts are clear as to the origin and meaning of the term. Cf. J. Lallot, *La grammaire de Denys le Thrace* (Paris 1989), 61, 223 n. 6.

387. *arrhenikê ptôsis.* Apparently, derivation of a masculine noun from a feminine noun (e.g. *hê grammatikê → ho grammatikos*). Conversely, the 'feminine case' indicates the derivation of a feminine noun (e.g. *Alexandria*) from a masculine noun (*Alexandros*).

388. cf. Porph. *In Cat.* 69,20-9; Boethius *In Cat.* 167A (who renders the technical term *metaskhêmatismos* by 'transfiguratio').

389. The musical woman thus meets conditions (1) and (2) above, but not (3). She and 'music' share the same name, since the Greek words for 'musical woman' and 'woman' are the same, *viz. mousikê*; but since there is no difference in word-ending – both are identically called *mousikê* – we have homonymy, not paronymy. Cf. Porph. *In Cat.* 70,8-14; Boethius *In Cat.* 168C.

390. The *spoudaios* meets conditions (1) and (3), but not (2). Cf. Porph. *In Cat.* 70,14-24; Boethius *In Cat.* 168B. The noun *spoudê* ('hurry', 'zeal', 'study'), verb *spoudazein* ('to be busy/eager/studious') and adjective *spoudaios* ('serious') all derive from the same root as the verb *speudein* ('to hurry'). Used as a noun, however, *spoudaios* meant a good man for Aristotle, a Sage for the Stoics, and by Porphyry's time, it had come to be a technical term for a person having attained the first stage in the Neoplatonic scale of values: that of the political/practical virtues based on Aristotelian *metriopatheia*. Since, then, the 'reality' (*pragma*) in which the *spoudaios* participates is virtue (*aretê*), it is an apparent paradox that he is not designated by some term deriving from the word *aretê*. On the Neoplatonic scale of virtues, formulated most influentially by Porph. *Sent.* 32, 31,5ff. Lamberz, cf. J. Pépin 1964, 380-4; I. Hadot 1978, 150-8.

391. The *spoudaios* is not paronymous by derivation from seriousness/*spoudê*. The two terms meet conditions (2) and (3) above, but owing to the ambiguity of the word *spoudê*, it cannot be considered the one *pragma* in which they both participate. Condition (1) above is thus not met, and we do not have paronymy.

392. The brave man (*andreios*) participates not only in the name 'brave' (*andreios*), but also in the reality 'bravery' (*andreia*). Since, in addition, the words *andreios* and *andreia* differ in ending, all three conditions necessary for paronymy are met.

393. Porph. *Ad Gedalium* fr. 54 p. 44 Smith.

394. These are Epic terms, frequently chosen by grammarians to illustrate the suffix *-phi(n)*, used in Homer to express the instrumental, locative and ablative cases (cf. the scholiast to *Iliad* 13.588; Apollonius *Lexicon Homericum* [ed. I. Bekker, Berlin 1833] 87,7-14), and sometimes of the genitive and dative. *Passalophi* (cf. *Iliad* 24.268; *Odyssey* 8.67; 105) means 'from a peg'; *hêiphi* (*Il.* 22.107: *Od.* 21.315) means 'to/in/by means of his own'; while *biêiphi* (cf. *Il.* 4.325; 12.135, 153, 256; 15.614; 16.826; 18.341; 21.367, 501; 22.107; 23.315; *Od.* 1.403; 6.6, 9, 406, 408, 476; 12.210, 246; 21.315, 371, 373) means 'to/in/by means of his strength'.

395. *tois proêgoumenois*. That is to say, derivative things usually come under the same category as that from which they are derived.

396. Etymologically *stasis* is simply the noun formed from *hestanai*, the perfect infinitive of *histêmi*, 'to stand', and thus it means '[the fact of] standing'; yet it may also mean 'rest', in which case there may be an allusion to one of the five Platonic categories of the intelligible (*Sophist* 250a; Plotinus *Ennead* VI,2,8). Thus, by a subtle play on words, Porphyry/Simplicius subordinates an Aristotelian to a Platonic category.

397. For Simplicius/Porphyry the primary reality is the category (*keisthai*); derived from this are abstract nouns denoting states or activities (*stasis*, *klisis*); finally, from this are derived verbal forms, the perfect infinitives *hestanai* and *keklisthai*.

398. cf. Porph. *In Cat.* 70,29-30.

399. cf. above, 23,13-19 (opinion of Syrianus).

400. On the following passage (Speusippus fr. 32a Lang = fr. 68a Tarán); cf., in addition to Tarán's commentary *ad loc.*, J. Pépin 1980, with further bibliography 275 n. 1. Again, it seems that Simplicius has his information from Boethus *via* Porphyry's commentary *Ad Gedalium*.

401. See above, 22,20-3,10.

402. All of which mean, as <Sophonias> reminds us (*Anon. Paraphr.* 4,5), a 'two-edged piece of iron'; i.e. a sword. Cf. Porph. *In Cat.* 69,1ff.

403. Porphyry (69,10ff.) gives a rather different account of heteronyms; he uses different examples (fire/gold; Socrates/bravery) and leaves the reality (*pragma*) out of consideration, speaking only of the *logos* and the name being different.

404. sc. name and *logos*.

405. cf. the following table:

	polyonyms	heteronyms	homonyms	synonyms
logos	same	different	different	same
onoma	different	different	same	same
pragma	same	different		

If the values of a column are different, then the types of words are opposite or 'convertible'; here this is true of the couple polyonyms/homonyms, and of the couple heteronyms/synonyms.

406. For two predicates to be polyonyms, they must fulfil two conditions: (i) they must be the same (*to auto legetai*); and (ii) the subject of which they are predicated must be one and the same (*kath'hen*). 'Partless', and 'least' fulfil both conditions and are polyonyms, as is that of which they are said (e.g. letters of the alphabet); but since 'convex' and 'concave' are different (Simplicius says they have a different *logos*), they do not fulfil condition (i). They therefore cannot fulfil condition (ii), either: for 'convex' and 'concave' cannot be predicated of the *same* circle; rather, they are names for *different* circles. At *De Caelo* 1.4, 270b35f., Aristotle states that convex and concave lines are ('apparently') contrary; yet at *Physics* 4.13, 222b3-4 he says that the concave and the concave are in what is 'in a sense' the same circle. Presumably what Aristotle means in the latter passage is that 'convex' and 'concave' are both said of 'circle' in the abstract and generic sense of the term, although they can never simultaneously characterize the same *individual* circle.

407. This appears to be an imperfect recollection of Plato's *Cratylus* 399c, where the word 'man' (*anthrôpos*) is explained as follows: 'The name "man" (*anthrôpos*) indicates that the other animals do not examine, or consider (*analogizetai*), or look up at (*anathrei*) any of the things that they see, but man has no sooner seen – that is, *opôpe* – than he looks up at and considers (*logizetai*) that which he has seen. Therefore of all the animals man alone is rightly called man (*anthrôpos*), because he looks up at (*anathrei*) what he has seen (*opôpe*)'. Thus, while Plato etymologises *anthrôpos* as deriving from *anathrei* + *opôpe*, Simplicius has recalled *analogizetai* from the same passage, and wrongly thinks that *analogizomai* is connected to the etymology of *anthrôpos*.

408. Simplicius seems to be following here the same school tradition concerning the etymological explanation of *anthrôpos*, *merops* and *brotos*, as that given by Ammon. *In De Interp.* 38,9ff.: man is called *merops* because he uses a divided-up voice (*meristêi opi*), i.e. different languages; while *brotos* refers to 'the fall of his soul into the realm of becoming and the contamination in incurs down here', i.e. to his mortality.

409. By Diogenes; cf. above, 27,19f. and n. 294.

410. There is thus the implication that we always should follow etymology; indeed, since, for the Neoplatonists, names had been imposed by an *onomatothetês*/group of *onomatothêtai*, if not divine then at least extremely wise, to make up names arbitrarily – that is, without regard to the natural consonance of names and realities – would be to fly in the face of nature.

411. Respectively, the Epic/Attic and Doric Greek words for 'day'. Simplicius' point is that dialect variations in the form of a word do not constitute instances of polyonymy.

412. Pindar *Encomium* to Alexander son of Amyntas, fr. 120-1 Schroeder = *Éloges* fr. 2 Puech (Budé) = fr. 126 Tuyrn = fr. 120 Maehler/Snell (Teubner).

413. *homônuma têi progonikêi ê kat'elpida anaphorai*. As we learn from Philoponus (*In Cat.* 22,7ff.), we have hopeful (*kat' elpida*) homonymy when a father names his son 'Plato' in the hope he will turn out to be like the Philosopher, while homonyms by ancestral reference occur when the child is named after his grandfather, so that the latter's memory may be preserved.

414. Since, for the Pythagoreans, one name corresponds to one reality, they had to account for apparent cases of polyonymy. They seem to have done so in at least the following ways: (i) In the case of proper names, polyonymy could be explained by the intentions of the parents (see previous note); such names were definitely *thesei*, not *phusei*. (ii) Some ostensible polyonyms, they claimed, were not words at all. (iii) Finally, if two non-proper genuine names really do designate the same object, then this is not due to arbitrary naming, as in the case of Diogenes' slave; instead, the two apparent polyonyms have two different etymological derivations.

415. The Pythagorean *suzugiai* are the series of contrasting couples of opposed realities such as we find in Aristotle *Metaphysics* 1, 986a22; but how these may be used to explain changes of linguistic form in paronyms is not clear to me.

416. That is, in the *De Interpretatione*.

417. Arist. *Cat.* 4, 1b25-6.

418. *kata seiran*, which Moerbeke rendered as *secundum ramificationem*. Ammon. *In Cat.* 24,15f.; Philop. *In Cat.* 27,28ff. make what is apparently the same point in much simpler terms: since it is things without combination that Aristotle intends to discuss, he mentions them last, so that he can begin teaching about them immediately.

419. On the following fourfold distinction of *ta legomena*, which probably derives from Boethus via Porphyry, cf. P. Moraux 1973, 151-2. Cf. the view of Sosigenes, teacher of Alexander of Aphrodisias, as reported by Dexippus *In Cat.* 7,1ff. Busse.

420. A genuine speech act consists of three elements: (1) language (*logos*); (2) the objects/realities it designates (*pragmata*); and (3) the notions/concepts (*noêmata*) in the speakers' minds. Should any one of these be absent, there is no real speech act. In the case of people talking without thinking (children? idiots? bad philosophers?), element (3) is lacking, so that we can have 'talk' (*logos/lexis*), without anything actually 'being said' (*legomenon*).

421. *ta sumpeplegmena pragmata*. For the Stoics, 'self-complete' propositions were necessarily compound. The word *hêmera* ('day'), taken by itself, is not a proposition (*axiôma*); but when combined with the verb *esti* ('is/exists') the result is a self-complete proposition (*axiôma autotelês*; cf. Sextus Empiricus *Adv. Math.* 8,79).

422. Note Simplicius' correction of Iamblichus here; like a good scholar, he has checked the reference to Alexander he found in Iamblichus' *Commentary on* *the Cat.*, and found that Alexander in fact says something quite different from what Iamblichus maintains. Alexander's *Commentary on the Cat.* was thus available to Simplicius otherwise than *via* Iamblichus. The fact that he never carries out such a check in the case of Porphyry is an additional indication that he had little or no such independent access to Porphyry's works.

423. Arist. *Cat.* 1b25ff.

424. This thesis of the non-intentionality of physical objects has been used by some modern philosophers to refute materialism; cf. Hilary Putnam, *Reason, Truth and History* (Cambridge 1981), 2.

425. *en dianoiais te kai tais tou nou diexodois.* Cf. Dexippus *In Cat.* 9,26: *en dianoiâi kai en diexodois tou nou.* Clearly, these two passages have a common source: no doubt Porphyry, perhaps via Iamblichus (cf. J. Dillon, *op. cit.*, 28 n. 16).

426. cf. Arist. *De An.* 6, 430a26ff.

427. cf. above, 9,4ff.

428. David and Olympiodorus refer to this formulation as 'the Iamblichean *skopos*'.

429. cf. Porph. *In Cat.* 71,3ff., where instead of 'combination by kinship among realities', we read of 'realities which are uttered together (*homou*) because one happens (*sumbebêkenai*) to the other'.

430. *sumplektikos sundesmos.* Cf. Apollonius Dyscolus *De Conjunctionibus* 220,17; 252,22ff. Schneider; J. Lallot 1989, 64-5; 238ff.

431. cf. *SVF* 3.207ff. Dexippus (*In Cat.* 22,12ff.) reports an objection, which he traces to the Stoics, according to which only words connected by a connective conjunction can be said to be in combination; cf. Diogenes Laertius 7, 72. On this view, 'a man is walking' (*anthrôpos peripatei*) would not be in combination. Dexippus replies that Aristotle is not following Stoic doctrine, but older (i.e. Academic?) doctrines, according to which combination (*sumplokê*) is the union (*sunodos*) of the parts of speech.

432. The 'relatively disposed' (*pôs ekhon*) was the third Stoic category; cf. *SVF* 3.369 = Simplicius below, 67,5ff.

433. In a phrase like 'S is P', the *sumplokê* defines which term is S, which is P, and according to what modality P belongs to S.

434. Just as conjunctions can be used to link two or more parts of speech, so, in predication, the verbs 'to have' and 'to be' can be used to link subject and predicate.

435. In 'Socrates is an animal', for instance, 'animal', which is a genus, is predicated of 'Socrates' as though it were a mere accident, like 'white'. In this example, 'Socrates] is 'woven together' (*sumpleketai*) with the genus 'animal'.

436. On the Stoic distinction between complete and deficient sayables (*lekta*), cf. *SVF* 2.166 = Sextus Empiricus *Adv. Math.* 8,80; II.181 = Diogenes Laertius *Lives* 7,63 = Long and Sedley 33F.

437. *poi dê kai pothen.* Part of the opening phrase of Plato's *Phaedrus* (227a1).

438. Plato *Sophist* 253e.

439. i.e. that brought about by conjunctions, and that brought about by predication. My anonymous reader believes the reference here is instead to 'an established Aristotelian position'. I know of no such Aristotelian position, but the reference could well be to an established *Archytean* position; see next note.

440. Simplicius makes frequent use of this dichotomy; cf. below, 114; 117; 157; 237; 235-6 Kalbfleisch. It appears to originate in Iamblichus and the Pseudo-Archytas.

441. Some words appear to have dropped out here (MS L lacks eleven letters); the missing text may have said, for instance, 'at any rate includes the verb "is", and thus consignifies time'.

442. cf. Arist. *De Interp.* 3, 16b6ff.

443. On the Neoplatonic view, the hypostasis Intellect (*nous*) is beyond time, which comes into existence only at the level of Soul; thus noetic activity is atemporal, as opposed to that of the discursive intellect (*dianoia*), which does take place within time (cf. e.g. Porphyry *Sent.* 44). Yet 'the intellect thinks', since it attributes a verb as predicate to the Intellect, seems to ascribe to it a temporal activity. Simplicius' response is typically Neoplatonic: the attribution of temporal activity to the Intellect is only a feature of human language, and is not in the nature of things.

444. The Greek city-name Neapolis appears to consist of two words: *nea*, 'new', and *polis*, 'city'. Yet although the word thus appears multiple, Simplicius' point is that it designates only one object. There were over half a dozen towns in the Roman Empire called Neapolis in Simplicius' time; but it was also the name of a district of Alexandria, and M. Tardieu has argued that this is where the school of Ammonius, one of Simplicius' teachers, was probably located; cf. *Les paysages reliques* (Paris, 1990), 148-50. Counter to this supposition is the frequency with which the Commentators use Neapolis as an example of an apparently compound word with one significatum: cf. Galen *De Sophismatis*, vol. 14, 591,10 Kühn; Ammon. *In De Interp.* 34,3ff.; Philop. *In Cat.* 27,4; David *In Cat.* 145,34.

445. *Agathodaimôn* is the name of a divinity, particularly important in the *Corpus Hermeticum*; cf. Tardieu *op. cit.* 158-9. Yet the worship of the 'Good Demon' as tutelary divinity of the home goes back to Hellenistic times; cf. Nilsson *GGR* II^3 (1974), 187 & n. 7; 213ff. Consisting of the words *agathos* ('good') and *daimôn* ('demon'; 'divinity') the word again appears multiple, but what it designates is one.

446. The Greek word *zô* corresponds both to the English verb 'live' and it implies the personal pronoun 'I'; Simplicius thus considers it to be a compound term, albeit implicitly.

447. In Greek it was possible to say either '*Zeus huei*' ('Zeus is sending rain': Homer *Iliad* 12.25; *Odyssey* 14.457; Hesiod *Works and Days* 486 etc.) or else just *huei*. Simplicius is thus correct to say that the subject 'Zeus' is understood in the phrase 'rains', just as he was in other Greek weather terminology: e.g. [Zeus] *neiphei*: 'It is snowing', [Zeus] *seiei*: 'There is an earthquake', [Zeus] *suskotazei*: 'It is getting dark', etc.

448. 'Categories' and 'Universal Formulae' are merely alternative titles for the same work of Archytas; cf. 21,7-22,5 Thesleff.

449. *hupomnêmatikos.* As we have seen, hypomnematic writings were collections of materials gathered together for the author's own use, and not intended for publication, such as the collections of *theseis* and *protaseis* which Aristotle recommends the student to collect (*Topics* 105aff.). Hypomnematic writings were dismissed by the Neoplatonists as unworthy of study; cf. above, 4,17-18.

450. cf. Ammon. *In Cat.* 24,23ff.

451. There is a typical Greek *Volksetymologie* here, unrecognizable in translation; yet for a Greek speaker it would be obvious that the abstract noun *ousia* is related to one of the participial forms of the verb *einai*, 'to be'.

452. The fact that Aristotle listed *ousia*/substance first in his enumeration of the categories means that, following Archytas, he accords it ontological priority over the other nine categories.

453. These six combinations are arrived at by chiastic logic, which, as was shown by P. Hadot (1954), was popular at least since the time of Porphyry. We start with an enumeration of four terms, in this case substance, accident, universal, and particular. They are then arranged in a square, with each term placed at one of its angles:

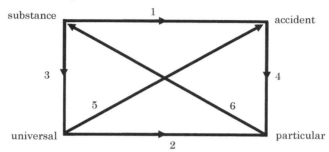

The lines with arrows indicate the possible relationships between these four terms (bearing in mind that in Greek, unlike in English, word order is relatively unimportant). We thus end up with a total of six possible combinations (*sumplokai*): (1) accidental substance; (2) universal particulars; (3) universal substance; (4) particular accident; (5) universal accident; and (6) particular substance. Simplicius will now set out to investigate each of these six possibilities of existence. For examples of the chiastic method, see Ammon. *In De Interp.* 95,13ff.; *In Cat.* 24,22ff.; Philop. *In Cat.* 28,3ff. (cf. *In Anal. Pr.* 39,27ff.; 282,21ff., etc.); Olympiodorus *In Cat.* 43,3ff., etc.

454. *asustatos.* The commentators also use the term *anupostatos.*

455. 'In a substrate' and 'not in a substrate' are, as we shall soon see at some length, equivalent to accidents and substances, respectively. An accidental substance – our combination (1) above – would be empirically impossible, but all Simplicius has to do to eliminate it as a possible combination is to point out that the two terms contradict each other. If P = the property of 'being in a substrate', then (x) ~(Px & ~Px).

456. Again, Simplicius will explain below that '[said] of a substrate' and 'not [said] of a substrate' are equivalent to universals and particulars, respectively. Empirically, there are no universal particulars nor particular universals, but the possibility of their existence can be ruled out *a priori* by the same mechanism used for possible combination (1): if Q = the property of 'being [said] of a substrate', then, (x) ~(Qx & ~Qx).

457. Thus, to return to our diagram above, combinations (3), (4), (5), and (6) – which Ammonius (*loc. cit.* 25,8-9) calls the 'subordinate' and 'diagonal' couplings respectively – are considered real logical possibilities. Simplicius will now attempt to see whether the world actually contains anything corresponding to these possibilities.

458. In other words, Simplicius will translate Aristotle's unusual language into what he 'really' said or meant (*eis ta ... legomena*). On the dialectical *topos* of substituting for a term one which is clearer or more familiar (*metalambanein eis to gnôrimôteron*), cf. Arist. *Topics* 2.4, 111a8-13, with Alexander's commentary *ad loc.* (*In Top.* 156,19-158,7 Wallies).

459. cf., for instance, *Post. An.* 73b3 ff.; *Metaph.* 1007a32ff.

460. i.e. Q = N x (N – 1)/2. In the case in question, 4 x 3 = 12; 12 x ½ = 6.

461. *di'emphantikôterôn onomatôn.* Cf. Ps.-Demetrius *On Style* §283.

462. cf. above, 29,17ff. Porphyry's Latin follower Marius Victorinus enumerates fifteen varieties of definition (*De Definitionibus* 17,5-29,1 ed. Stangl), and adds that there may be more. A *hupographê*, says Victorinus (*op. cit.* 20,6-8 Stangl) is an enunciation 'which does not say what a thing is, but rather, having recourse to a whole gamut of things done and said, declares what each thing is by means of a description'.

463. *eite estin en hupostasei eite mê estin.* As Porphyry had stressed at the outset of his *Isagoge*, the question of the ontological status of universals is not relevant to the study of logic.

464. Arist. *Cat.* 1a20.

465. cf. below, 62,8ff.

466. Arist. *Cat.* 1a24-1b3.

467. 'In something' is analogous to a genus, of which the eleven following meanings are like differentiae. With the following enumeration of the eleven meanings of 'in something', cf. Porph. *In Cat.* 77,22-78,5 (of which Boethius 172B7-C6 is a Latin translation); Ammon. 26,25-27,8; Philop. 32,7-25; David 149,16-34; Olympiodorus 47,3-21; Arethas 151,22-153,25. Porphyry (and therefore Boethius) here enumerate only nine senses of 'in something'.

468. cf. Arist. *Phys.* 4.3, 210a14-25, and the commentaries on this *Physics* passage by Simplicius (*In Phys.*, *CAG* vol. IX, 551,1-553,16 Diels); Themistius (*Paraphr. In Phys.*, *CAG* vol. V.2, 108,6-20 Schenkl), and Philoponus (*In Phys.*, *CAG* vol. XVII, 526,10-529,18 Vitelli). The *Physics* commentators enumerate Aristotle's 'eight or nine' meanings of 'in something', while remarking that the exegetes of the *Cat.* enumerate eleven meanings. Philoponus tells us the two meanings omitted in the *Physics* are 'in time' and 'in a substrate'. As for 'in a substrate', Simplicius explains that in the *Cat.*, there is a difference between form being in matter and accidents being in a substrate, or 'in a substrate' in general; whereas presumably in the *Physics* there is not. Thus, on Simplicius' view, in the *Physics*, Aristotle subsumes 'in a substrate' under the meaning 'form in matter', while in the *Cat.* he treats them as two separate meanings.

469. cf. Arist. *Phys.* 4.3, 210a24 (= meaning no. 8 in Aristotle's enumeration); Simplicius *In Phys.* 552,16.

470. cf. Simplicius *In Phys.* 553,6ff.: Arist. did not include 'in time' in his *Physics* enumeration because at that point in the *Physics*, he had not yet spoken about time.

471. cf. Arist. *Phys.* 4.3, 210a15-16 (= meaning no. 1); Simplicius *In Phys.* 551,18f.

472. cf. Arist. *Phys.* 210a16-17 (= meaning no. 2). Simplicius *In Phys.* 551,21ff. gives as an example 'as a face is in [i.e. consists in] the eyes and the nose and such things'.

473. cf. Arist. *Phys.* 210a17-18 (= meaning no. 3); Simplicius *In Phys.* 551,26.

474. cf. Arist. *Phys.* 210a19-20 (= meaning no. 4). Simplicius *In Phys.* 551,27ff. explains 'as "animal" is in "man" and in "horse", because it is contained within the account (*logos*) of each one'. Cf. Philop. *In Phys.* 528,25-529,7.

475. cf. Arist. *Phys.* 210a22-3 (= meaning no. 7). Simplicius *In Phys.* 552,13ff., explains 'as the things one does for a goal are "in" that goal ... as the virtues are *in* happiness'.

476. cf. Arist. *Phys.* 210a21 (= meaning no. 5). Simplicius *In Phys.* 552,7f. adds that Aristotle [in the *Physics*, that is to say, but not in the *Cat.*] 'appears to place all things which are in a substrate (*panta ta en hupokeimenôi*) in this significatum'.

477. *en tôi kinounti.* Cf. Arist. *Phys.* 4.3, 210a22: 'in the first mover' (*en tôi prôtôi kinêtikôi*). In illustration the *Physics* commentators all (mis-)quote

Homer's 'it lies in [i.e. "depends upon"] the knees of the gods' (*Iliad* 17.514; 20.435; *Odyssey* 1.267, 400; 16.129), which had become proverbial. In his *Physics* commentary, Simplicius regards Aristotle's 'as the affairs of the Greeks are "in" the king' as an illustration as 'in the first mover'; yet here in his *Cat.* commentary, Simplicius clearly separates the meaning 'in the moving cause' from the meaning 'in the ruler'.

478. cf. Arist. *Phys.* 210a21-2 (= meaning no. 6, partim). Cf. preceding note. Hussey in his commentary on *Physics* 3-4 (Oxford: Clarendon 1983) wrongly assumes that by 'king' (*basileus*), Aristotle means the King of Persia. As the Neoplatonist commentators explain, however, the meaning is just that (ancient Greek) kings had power over their subjects. Cf. Philop. *In Phys.* 529,8-9: 'for the ruler (*arkhôn*) is the efficient cause of political affairs'; Boethius *In Cat.* 172C3-4: 'ut in aliquo potente, ut in imperatore esse regimen civitatis'.

479. i.e. Aristotle's meaning no. 5 above. 'As a form in matter' is also Porphyry's candidate for the meaning of 'in a substrate' (*In Cat.* 78,5-6); cf. Boethius *In Cat.* 173C. As often, Simplicius is unaware of Porphyry's view, and attributes it (albeit hesitantly) to Iamblichus. This shows, I believe, that Simplicius knew Porphyry's minor commentary primarily, if not exclusively, *via* Iamblichus.

480. Arist. *Phys.* 4.3, 210a20-1. As Ross notes *ad loc.*, Arist.'s meaning is that health consists in the proper balance of hot and cold elements within the body.

481. The Greek text seems disturbed here, with MS L again presenting a lacuna. The meaning of Iamblichus' difficult Greek is provided by Simplicius *In Phys.*, CAG IX, 552,26-9: 'Thus, he seems to take as one that which is as form in matter and that which is, properly speaking, in a substrate, in accordance with some common nature of that which is shape-giving (*tou morphôtikou*). For both give shape to the substrate (*amphô gar morphôtika tou hupokeimenou esti*)'. Against Iamblichus, Simplicius distinguished between Aristotle's view in the *Physics*, where form is in matter as accidents are in a substrate, and in the *Cat.*, where these two meanings of 'in something' are distinct. Note that Simplicius is not certain he has correctly understood Iamblichus (cf. *dokei legein* at 46,16).

482. In what follows, Simplicius elaborates on objections already made by Alexander (*ap.* Simplicium *In Phys.* 552,18ff.) against the proposed identity of that which is in a substrate and that which is in matter. The former, says Alexander, is an accident, whereas the latter, being form, is substance. That form is not in matter as a substrate is argued in Ps.(?)-Alexander's *Quaestio* 1.8; see the translation in this series by R.W. Sharples (London & Ithaca NY 1992), 43ff. (my thanks go to John Ellis for pointing out this passage).

483. Reading *meros* for Kalbfleisch's *merei* at 46,25; cf. Alex. *ap.* Simplicium *in Phys.* 552,23-4.

484. *horismos*. This is odd; the *horismos* in question ought to be Aristotle's definition of 'in a substrate' at *Cat.* 2, 1a24-5; but this tells us only that what is in a substrate is not a *part* of its substrate, not that it does not *complete* it. The text as it stands lacks the following additional premises: (i) that which completes a substance is a *part* of that substance; but (ii) that which is in a substrate is not a part of the substance (by Aristotle's *horismos*); and therefore (iii) that which is in a substrate cannot *complete* the substance in which it is. The missing axiom that something is a part *iff* it completes a substance (*sumplêroi tên ousian*) must have been traditional and therefore not worth mentioning; Lucius-Nicostratus use it as a premiss below, 48,2-3.

485. i.e. form.

486. Simplicius' argument is as follows: when Arist. talks here in the *Cat.* about what is in a substrate (*en hupokeimenôi*), he cannot be identifying substrate (*hupokeimenon*) and matter (although this identification is frequent, Simplicius might have added, in the *Physics* and the *Metaphysics*). The reason matter is not under discussion in the *Cat.* is that Aristotle is here considering sensible and determinate things, but terms such as 'determinate' (*ti*) and 'individual' (*tode*) cannot be applied to matter. The expression 'in something' (*en tini*) implies presence in something determinate (*tini*, dative singular of *ti*). Yet this determinate something cannot be matter; so 'in something' cannot mean 'in matter'.

487. On the indefiniteness (*aoristia*) of matter cf. e.g. Arist. *De Gen. Animal.* 778a6; *Metaph.* 1037a26; 1049b1-3; 1087a16ff.; *Physics* 207a21ff.; 209b9; 210a8, etc.

488. cf. with Kalbfleisch, Arist. *Physics* 1.9, 192a6.

489. This apparent contradiction may perhaps be explained as follows: when Iamblichus proposed the identification of 'in matter' and 'in a substrate', he will have been quoting Porphyry; when he claims they are different, he will have been expressing his own views. Simplicius has failed to understand his source Iamblichus.

490. Arist. *Phys.* 4.3, 210a14-24.

491. cf. Simplicius *In Phys.* 553,6-8.

492. cf. Simplicius *In Phys.* 552,34-5. Simplicius thus explains the fact that there are eleven meanings of 'in something' in the *Cat.*, but only eight in the *Physics*, by the fact that in the latter work Aristotle eliminated the meaning 'in time', combined together 'in a substrate' and 'in matter', and also combined 'in a vessel' and 'in a place'.

493. In what follows Simplicius will examine the meanings of 'in something', in order to see whether any can be identified with 'in a substrate'. He takes Aristotle to have provided two criteria: in order for a thing to be in a substrate, it must be (i) in something 'not as a part' (cf. *Cat.* 2, 1a24), and (ii) 'incapable of existing apart from that in which it is' (*Cat.* 2, 1a25). Simplicius will first use criterion (i) to eliminate meanings 4, 6, and 7 (cf. 46,5ff. above).

494. Thus, meaning no. 4 is eliminated, for it fails to meet criterion (i).

495. Meaning no. 6 also fails to meet criterion (i). The proof does not come until later: taken with matter (i.e. when it is an *enulon eidos*), the species is a part of composite substance. But in the *Cat.*, Aristotle is *only* concerned with composite substances; i.e. those sensible, phenomenal substances which are composed of matter and form. It follows that the only species Aristotle is concerned with here are engaged in matter. But species engaged in matter are always parts of sensible substances. Therefore species engaged in matter are not as in a substrate.

496. i.e. Aristotle gives as his definition of what is 'in a substrate' 'what is in something, not *as a part*' (*Cat.* 1a24-5). A possible objection may thus be that Aristotle excludes from his definition of 'that which is in a substrate' 'that which is *as* a part' (*hôs meros*), but not that which simply *is* a part.

497. 'As genus in species', meaning no. 7 of 'in something' can also be eliminated. Just as the *Cat.*, since it deals with the sensible world, is only concerned with those species which are enmattered, so the only genera of interest are those which are ranged (*katatetagmena*) or present within sensible objects. But since (enmattered) species consist of (ranged) genera and differentiae, it follows that (ranged) genera are parts of (enmattered) species. Therefore (ranged) genera are not in a substrate.

498. *sc.* other meanings of 'in something'.

499. In what follows, meanings 1, 2, 3, and 8 of 'in a substrate' are eliminated, because they are capable of existing apart from what they are in, and thus fail to meet criterion (ii).

500. Meanings 10 and 11 also thus fail to meet criterion (ii).

501. *sc.* that which is in a substrate.

502. i.e. meanings 4, 6, and 7 of 'in something'.

503. i.e. meanings 1, 2, 3, 8, 10, and 11.

504. Simplicius now considers meaning no. 5 of 'in something': 'as a whole in its parts' (as an example, other commentators adduce 'as ten is in seven and three'). Some claimed that since the whole in parts met criteria (i) and (ii) above, it was in a substrate.

505. Simplicius' response is to introduce a new criterion: Arist. had said that which is in a substrate must be 'in something' (*en tini*, where *tini* is singular). But the whole in parts is in some *things* (*en tisi*, where *tisi* is plural), and thus cannot be in a substrate; cf. Arethas *In Cat.* 154,5-6.

506. cf. Plotinus Enneads VI,3,5 (where Lucius is not named), and on Lucius' *aporia* in general P. Moraux 1984, 537-8; Dexippus *In Cat.* 23,17-24.

507. i.e. accidental qualities.

508. Porph. *Ad Gedalium* fr. 55, pp. 44ff. Smith.

509. This is the first attestation of the concept of a twofold substrate, an idea which was to be developed and systematized by Proclus; cf. *In Tim.* vol. I, 387, 5ff. Diehl, with the commentary by I. Hadot 1978, 81ff.

510. The parallel passage from Dexippus (23,25ff.) has been reproduced by Arnim as fr. 374 in *SVF* 2. Obviously the present passage must also be included, as it is by Long and Sedley; see next note.

511. *hên dunamei kalei ho Aristotelês.* Long and Sedley (28E, vol. I, 168) translate this phrase by 'which Aristotle virtually names', which I believe is incorrect. I prefer to understand *dunamei sôma*; cf. Dexippus *In Cat.* 23,27-8: *hên dunamei sôma Aristotelês phêsi.* The reference is probably to Aristotle *De Gen. et Corr.* 329a33f.

512. *koinôs poion.* One division of the second Stoic 'category', *koinôs poion* designates anything described by a common noun or adjective; cf. Long and Sedley vol. I, 173-4, and following note.

513. *idiôs poion.* The *idiôs poion* is a Stoic concept, corresponding to the essential quality which remains unchanged in an individual person or thing throughout its existence, and constitutes its unique identity; in the case of human beings, it is that which is designated by a proper name (e.g. 'Socrates'). Cf. Long and Sedley § 28, vol. I, 166-76.

514. Porphyry's distinction is thus based on the relativity of the concept of matter, and hence of the concept of 'substrate'. Matter as a substrate can be either 'prime' – the qualityless substrate which in fact never exists as such, but only conceptually; or else it may be such substances as bronze or even Socrates, which, although already provided with qualities, nevertheless serve as substrate for further qualities.

515. My anonymous reader points out that Simplicius' formulation is wrong here: it is not that the division fails to embrace all the categories, but that it fails to embrace all the *properties* within any given category, i.e. it omits the essential ones.

516. Kalbfleisch points to *Cat.* 5, 3a29; more explicit is *An. Pr.* 32, 47a26f.

517. Aristotle's negative definition of substance leaves open the possibility that essential or 'completive' qualities may be substances or semi-substances as well; this will be important when Simplicius comes to investigate the ontological status of the differentia (*Cat.* 5, 3a21-32).

518. On this *aporia* cf. Porph. 79,23-4; Ammon. 28,9ff.; Dexippus 25,8-12;

Philop. 35,16-21; Olympiodorus 48,32-7; David (Elias) 152,5-7; and see J. Ellis, 'The trouble with fragrance', *Phronesis* 35 (1990), 290-302.

519. Since fragrances can be transferred from one substrate to another, it is objected, they can be separated from their original substrate. It is consequently not the case that they are 'incapable of existing apart from that in which they are', as Aristotle's definition required. Simplicius' solution will be that Aristotle did not claim accidents were inseparable from the substrate in which they happen to be at one given moment, but rather that they are incapable of existing separately from *any substrate whatsoever*; in other words, accidents are incapable of separate existence.

520. *melikraton.* Honey mixed with water, used as a sacrificial offering as early as Homer and later as a medicine, particularly against fever.

521. Arist. *Cat.* 1a25; Cf. Porph. 79,23-34; Philop. 35,22ff.; David (Elias) 152,35f.

522. Here Simplicius is warding off another real or possible counter-argument: let us suppose fragrance F leaves incense I at time t_1, in order to transfer over to clothing C at time t_n From t_1 to t_n, F is then an accident which is not in any substrate, but this is the same as to say it is in nothing. Simplicius is the only commentator who draws the conclusion that this implies the existence of a void, which is ruled out by Aristotelian physics. Simplicius' solution is that fragrances and odors are continuous with that from which they emanate. Consequently, for every time t_n, and every place p_n between I and C, there will be a portion of I to occupy p_n at t_n, without there being any time or space in between left unoccupied by some portion of I.

523. *manoumenê.* Cf. Arist. *Phys.* 246a5-9.

524. That apples shrivel up as they emit fragrance proves, according to the commentators, that their fragrance is transmitted to those who perceive it not by itself, but together with slight effluvia of the substance of the apple. The fragrance inheres in these effluvia, and is thus not a counter-example to Aristotle's claim that qualities cannot exist apart from a substrate.

525. P. Moraux 1973, 152f. suggests that this *aporia*, like the preceding one at 48,1ff., comes from Lucius and was found by Simplicius in Porphyry's *Ad Gedalium*.

526. i.e. in Aristotle's *Physics*; Kalbfleisch points to 231b15ff.

527. This was Boethus' own view as well; see the texts cited by P. Moraux 1973, 156 & n. 38.

528. *en tini*, Arist. *Cat.* 1a24-5.

529. Boethus' argument runs as follows:

(1) For Aristotle, a universal is not a determinate thing (*ti*).

(2) Aristotle said that that which is in a substrate is 'in some*thing*' (*en tini*).

(3) therefore that which is in a substrate is not in a universal; and

(4) that which is in a substrate is not in universal *time*.

530. Aristotle defines that which is in a substrate as 'what is in (*en*) something not existing (*huparkhon*) as a part' (*Cat.* 1a24-5), it is suggested we link together he words *en* and *huparkhon*; thus, it is argued, Aristotle defines what is in a substrate as that which is *enuparkhon*, 'inhering within'. Yet things which, like Socrates, are in space and time, are not normally said to 'inhere' (*enuparkhein*) within time. Thus Socrates is not, after all, in a substrate, and is therefore not an accident. Cf. Ammon. 27,27-30.

531. cf. above, 47,1-5.

532. Examples of particular accidents are 'Aristarchus' knowledge' or 'a particular instance of white'; an example of universal substance would be 'man'.

533. What Simplicius has in mind is what Porphyry (*In Cat.* 78,36ff.) refers to as the 'chiastic schema'. Here, we arrange the possible combinations betwen four terms 'substance', 'accident', 'universal' and 'particular' at the four corners of a square. Simplicius appears to be imagining a schema like the following, which appears in the margin of the mansucript Marcianus 224, in a hand of the twelfth or the thirteenth century (cf. Kalbfleisch, p. xx):

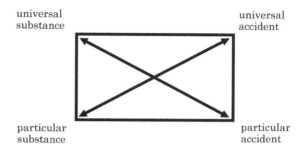

universal substance

universal accident

particular substance

particular accident

Here, the vertical combinations (universal substance and particular substance; universal accident and particular accident) as well as the horizontal combinations (universal substance and universal accident; particular substance and particular accident) are contradictory and therefore impossible, whereas those on the diagonal produce the non-contradictory combinations universal substance and particular accident, and universal accident and particular substance. Aristotle deals only with the last two 'diagonal' combinations.

534. Arist. *Cat.* 1a29-1b1. [Not a separate lemma in *CAG*, but left in text (Ed.)]

535. *ta atoma* (Arist. *Cat.* 1b6).

536. The syllogism envisaged is 'Socrates is a man, man is an animal, therefore Socrates is an animal', in which 'Socrates' is the minor term, 'man' the middle term, and 'animal' the major term.

537. cf. Porph. *In Cat.* 80,32-81,22; Dexippus 26,12-27,2; Ammon. 31,4ff.; Olympiodorus 50,15-21; Boethius 176C-177A.

538. i.e. the problem-raisers construct the following syllogism:
(1) 'man' is an animal
(2) 'animal' is a genus
(3) therefore, 'man' is a genus.
Cf. David *In Porph. Isag.* 135,28ff. where this argument is used by those who claim that the genus cannot be predicated synonymously of the species.

539. In the proposition 'animal is a genus', 'genus' is not predicated of animal as of a substrate; i.e. it is not predicated synonymously and essentially. Predication *kath' hupokeimenou* is essential or 'pragmatic' predication (*ousiôdôs kai pragmatikôs*): cf. Ammon. 31,9-10; Philop. 38,27-8; 39,9-10; but genera are predicated only relationally (*kata skhesin*). A very similar solution is attributed to Alexander in an Armenian *Cat.* commentary: there he specifies that 'genus' is not predicated of 'animal' as of a substrate, but of 'animal' as a universal. 'Animal as a universal', however, is not predicable of particulars. Cf. E. Schmidt, *Philologus* 110 (1966) 282; M. Tweedale, *Phronesis* 29-3 (1984) 295.

540. If 'genus' were predicated essentially of 'animal', then all animals would be genera. But all animals are *not* genera; therefore 'genus' is not predicated essentially of 'animal'. But predication as of a substrate is essential predication; therefore 'genus' is not predicated of 'animal' as of a substrate.

541. If x is predicated of y as of a substrate, and x is subsumed under category C, then y falls under C as well.

542. *epanabibasmôn*. A rare word; cf. Proclus *Platonic Theology* I 9, vol. 1, 39,23 Saffrey/Westerink; Hermias *In Phaedr.* 11,33 Couvreur. The source is Plato's (*Symposium* 211c3) coinage *epanabathmos/epanabasmos* (manuscripts vary).

543. As we learn below (66,6ff.), the *kephalaiôdes* corresponds to the concentrated, gathered-together stage of a reality, designated by the name (*onoma*), whereas the definition (*horismos*) corresponds to the reality in its stage of expansion and self-deployment. As O. Rieth (1933, 177ff.) has shown, this is originally Stoic doctrine, probably transmitted by Porphyry. The term *kephalaiôdes* is used by Porphyry's master Longinus; cf. *On the Short Syllable*, edited among the scholia to Hephaestio by M. Consbruch (Leipzig: Teubner, 1905) p. 88,9.

544. Arist. *Cat.* 3, 1b10.

545. Simplicius' argument seems to claim that universals are not what is predicated *kath' hupokeimenou*, on the grounds that *kath' hupokeimenou* predication implies synonymous predication, but a universal and that of which it is predicated do not have the same *logos*, and so are not predicated synonymously.

546. In the *Ad Gedalium* fr. 56, p. 46 Smith.

547. The interpretation of this fragment is controversial: P. Hadot has proposed an ontological interpretation (cf. 1966, 152; 1968, I, 409ff.) according to which the 'uncoordinated' form is the Platonic Idea; while S. Ebbesen (1981, I, 152) and A.C. Lloyd (at least in his later work; e.g. 1990, 49-66) believe Porphyry was advancing strictly logico-semantic concepts, only subsequently 'contaminated' with ontological implications by the later Neoplatonists.

548. Iamblichus fr. 16, vol. 2, p. 13 Dalsgaard Larsen; cf. vol. 1, p. 247f. Cf. A.C. Lloyd, 'Neoplatonists' account of predication', in *Le Néoplatonisme* (Paris, 1971) 259.

549. The vine is called 'white' because it produces white grapes; similarly, the Form of Man is called 'man' because it produces men. If this is indeed Iamblichus' meaning, he may have been trying to preserve the ineffability of intelligible Forms by claiming they can be named only metaphorically, on the basis of that which participates in them.

550. See, with Kalbfleisch Aristotle's enumerations of the different meanings of 'genus' in *Metaph.* 5.28, 1024a29-b16.

551. *ptôsis*, literally, 'falling'. Perhaps Iamblichus' meaning is that just as, for ancient grammarian, cases other than the nominative were envisaged as 'falling away' from the latter, so the participants in a Form or genus may be seen as 'falling away' from this Form or genus.

552. Arist. *Cat.* 2, 1b6-7.

553. cf. Arist. *Cat.* 3, 1b22.

554. *en tôi ti estin*. Literally, 'in-the-what-it-is'.

555. Knowledge is in soul as its substrate (*Cat.* 1b1-2); but if knowledge were predicated *synonymously* of the soul, knowledge and soul would share the same account (*logos*) and the same name. But soul is not called 'knowledge'; hence they do not share the same name; hence neither is predicated synonymously of the other.

556. The Greek verb *estin* can mean both 'to be' (i.e. it can be used as a copulative) and 'to exist'; here Simplicius is playing upon this ambiguity.

557. Simplicius refers once again to the dispute between Platonists and Aristotelians on the ontological status of universals: although Aristotle does not believe that universals have a separate, independent existence, says Simplicius, he often speaks of them as if they were true beings (Greek *onta*). Cf. above, 45,25ff.

558. cf. Arist. *Cat.* 1b6-7.

559. On this *aporia* of Andronicus cf. P. Moraux 1973, 104.

560. Aristoxenus was a third-century BC writer on musical theory; cf. B. Centrone, 'Aristoxène de Tarente 417', *DPhA* I (1989), 590-2.

561. Again, Simplicius is struggling with the lack of a distinction in Greek between the predicative and copulative uses of 'is': when we say 'P is Q', we sometimes assert a (greater or lesser degree of) identity between P and Q, as in 'Socrates is a philosopher'. No such identity is implied, however, when P = 'Socrates' and Q = 'walking'.

562. i.e. substantial predicates such as 'philosopher', 'Athenian'.

563. Thus, only in cases of predication where the 'is' is held to assert some degree of identity (as in 'Socrates is a philosopher'), will Aristotle's rule hold that whatever is said of the predicate must also be said of the subject.

564. *to kekhrôsmenon* is the genus of which instantiations of a particular colour such as 'a patch of white' (*to leukon*) are the species. On this paralogism, cf. A.C. Lloyd 1990, 62-3.

565. There is a lacuna here; I have translated the text proposed by Kalbfleisch.

566. At *Cat.*, 3, 1b16, the manuscripts of Aristotle and of the commentators, including Simplicius are divided between two different readings: *tôn heterôn genôn* ('of other genera') and *tôn heterogenôn* ('of heterogeneous things'). Kalbfleisch prints the former, and I have followed him in my translation; Minio-Paluello prints the latter in his edition of the *Cat.* Cf. below 56,16ff.

567. Arist. *Cat.* 3, 1b16-24.

568. With what follows cf. Porph. *In Cat.* 82,5ff.; Dexippus 27,3ff.; Ammon. 31-2; Philop. 40ff.; David (Elias) 157,8ff.; <Sophonias> *Paraphr. In Cat.* 7,29ff.; Boethius *In Cat.* col. 177Bff.

569. cf. Porph. *Isagoge* 1,18-3,20 Busse.

570. Porph. *Isagoge* 2,15-16. This formula goes back to Arist. *Topics* 1, 102a31, where Aristotle goes on explain that those things are said to be predicated *en tôi ti esti* which are adequate responses to the question: what *is* a thing? In the case of 'man', for example, the response would be 'an animal'.

571. Porph. *Isagoge* 4, 11-12.

572. Porph. *Isagoge* 11,7-8. In other words, a differentia such as 'rational' is the most adequate response to the question, 'What *kind* (Greek *poion/hopoion*) of an animal is man?'

573. cf. Porph. *Isagoge* 7,22-3; Porph. *In Cat.* 129,2-11; Simplicius *In Cat.* 229,12-20; Boethius *In Isag. 2* 166C; Ammonius *In Porph. Isag.* 56,16ff. Busse. This Porphyrian passage is cited by Proclus *ap.* Olympiodorum, *Commentary on the First Alcibiades of Plato* § 204, p. 128 Westerink: the Peripatetics, says Proclus, wrongly thought the concourse of accidents (*sundromê poiotêtôn*) was the principle of individuation, but this is wrong, for the greater (i.e. substance) cannot be inferred from the inferior (i.e. accidental properties). Dexippus (*In Cat.* 30,23ff.) assimilates the doctrine of individuation by concourse of properties to the Stoic doctrine of the *idiôs poion*: he may have Porphyry in mind.

574. By 'animalian quality', Simplicius here seems to mean a quality which pertains essentially to the genus 'animal'; cf. Boethius *In Isag. 2* 116C, where the difference between a tree and a man is said to be due to 'animalis sensibilis qualitas'. Yet Moerbeke translates '*animalifica*': did he read *zôiopoios* ('animal-making')?

575. *pleustikos.* Among the commentators, only Simplicius and Dexippus

(*In Cat.* 29,6) use this term; as usual, the common source for the two will be Iamblichus (in the first instance), and ultimately Porphyry. 'Capable of sailing', like Porphyry's preferred example *gelastikos* ('capable of laughing') is a *proprium* (Greek *idion*) of 'man', not a differentia.

576. cf. Dexippus *In Cat.* 29,7-9; Boethius *In Isag.* 2 116C, 117D. Strictly speaking, this is true only of the third kind of differentia discussed by Porphyry, that which is such in the most proper sense of the term, and whereby things differ according to a *specific* differentia.

577. cf. Dexippus *In Cat.* 29,9-11. Porphyry does not mention differentiae in his discussion of wholes and parts (*Isagoge* 8,1-3 Busse), where he merely says that the *genus* is to the *individual* as a whole to a part. The species is both a whole and a part, says Porphyry, but he does not specify of what. The differentia contains (*periekhei*) the species (*Isagoge* 13,23-14,3), but neither Porphyry nor Aristotle seems to state that the differentia is part of the species. Yet Alexander (*In Metaph.* 205,22) did make this assertion; and Boethius (*In Ciceronis Topica* III,1096) says the differentia becomes part of the species *in definitions*.

578. *sustatikos*. Cf. Porphyry *Isagoge* 18,22-3.

579. *periekhetai*. Here, for a differentia d to be 'contained' by species S means that (x) (Sx $\rightarrow dx$).

580. We learn later on that this remark dates from the time of Boethus; cf. below 97,30.

581. cf. David, *In Porph. Isag.* 181,24-5 Busse: divisive differentiae belong only to genera, constitutive ones only to species.

582. *kata pantos*. This consideration is absent from the *Isagoge*. On universal predication, cf. Aristotle *Post. An.* 73a28ff.; and on the universality of constitutive differentiae, cf. David *In Porph. Isag.* 182,13ff.

583. In Porphyry's *Isagoge* (9,24ff.), the examples given for divisive (*diairetikai*) differentiae are 'mortal/immortal'; 'rational/irrational'. It is by the combinations of these differentiae that the genus 'living being' is divided into 'man', 'god', or 'animal'. Porphyry's examples of constitutive (*sustatikai*) differentiae are 'animate' and 'sensitive'; it is by the combination of these differentiae that the species 'animal' or 'plant' are formed. In Simplicius' terms, then, 'animate' and 'sensitive' are predicable of each member of the class 'animal' (i.e. they are 'said of every one'), whereas the 'divisive' differentiae 'mortal', 'rational', etc., while they can all be predicated of the *genus* 'animal' 'at the same time', cannot *all* be predicated of any *individual* animal (i.e. they 'are not said separately'); otherwise, the same entity would simultaneously contain contradictory properties. Another way of stating the same point would be to say that the genus contains all its differentiae *potentially* (*dunamei*), but not *in actuality* (*energeiâi*); cf. Porph. *Isagoge* 11,1-5 Busse.

584. *kata to antidiêirémenon*. Each specific differentia (e.g. 'rational') is set out together with its counter-distinguished opposite (e.g. 'irrational') with relation to their common species (here, 'man'). Porphyry says explicitly that both divisive and constitutive differentiae are called 'specific' (*Isagoge* 10,19 Busse); while David (*In Porph. Isag.* 182,22f.) insists that the only differentiae which pertain to species are the constitutive ones, which – unlike the divisive differentiae – are *not* contraries.

585. cf. Porph. *Isag.* 15,4-6, although the context is different (Porphyry is discussing the differences between genus and differentia).

586. *sumplêrôtikas*, literally 'co-fulfiling'. In Porphyrian usage, a 'completive' differentia is one which cannot be removed without the destruction of the substrate, as 'rational' cannot be removed from man or 'hot' from fire; cf.

Porph. *In Cat.* 95,21-96,2 Busse and the *aporia* of Lucius introduced above, 48,1ff.

587. Boethus was also of the opinion that only divisive, and not constitutive, differences should be called 'differentiae'; cf. above, 97,28-34; P. Moraux 1973, 153-9; 1984, p. 368.

588. cf. Porph. *In Cat.* 82,31-2; Boethius *In Cat.* 177C11-13. The idea here is that terms like 'light' and 'heavy' are really predicated, in the proper sense of the term, only of that one of the four basic elements – earth, air, fire and water – of which they are characteristic. Fire is 'light' because it tends to move upwards by nature, and all things other than fire are 'light' only insofar as they contain fire. 'Light' is thus a differentia of other things in a derivative sense, but of fire in the primary sense.

589. The concept of the 'ultimate (*eskhatê/teleutaia*) differentia' has its origin in Arist. *Metaph.* 8.12, 1038a9ff., where it is said to be equivalent to the form (*eidos*) and substance (*ousia*) of a thing. On 'capable of receiving intellect and knowledge' as the ultimate differentia of man, cf. Eustratius *Commentary on Book II of the Posterior Analytics* (= *CAG* 21.1), 75,18ff. Hayduck.

590. cf. Porph. *In Cat.* 82,33-7; Boethius *In Cat.* 177D. The phoenix was a mythological bird who periodically incinerated himself and then, after a certain lapse of time (opinions ranged from one year to five hundred to an entire cosmic cycle), was reborn out of its own ashes. Cf. Rusche, 'Phoenix', *RE* XX, col. 414ff.; J. Hubaux and M. Leroy, *Le mythe du Phénix dans les littératures grecque et latine* (Liège 1939); critically reviewed by M.P. Nilsson, *Gnomon* 17 (1941), 212ff. A colourful description of the phoenix by the Hellenistic Jewish dramatist Ezechiel is preserved by Eusebius *Introduction to the Gospels* 9,29,16; cf. the bibliography given *ad loc.* by É. des Places in his edition of the *Praeparatio* (Livres VIII-IX-X [= Sources Chrétiennes no. 369], Paris 1991), 306-9 & n. 9.

591. cf. Alexander *Quaestio* I.3, 8,22ff. Bruns. Note that Simplicius does not take the easy way out and deny the existence of the phoenix, even though he seems less than totally convinced of it: *hôs historousin*, he says of the mythical bird: 'as it is reported'.

592. *monadikos*. The word goes back to Aristotle, who uses it with regard either to numbers or to solitary animals; here it refers to species of which there is only one member. For heavenly bodies as 'monadic' in this sense, cf. Proclus *Commentary on the Republic* I, 263,26-264,2 Kroll; *Commentary on the Timaeus* I, 435,28-436,1 Diehl, etc.

593. In terminology deriving from Porphyry, *akatataktos* (cf. above, 27,22ff.; 53,7ff.) designates that stage or form of a universal in which it is considered 'in and for itself', apart from any relationship of being 'ordered', 'ranged', or 'coordinated' (*katataxis*) to any of its instantiations. A universal which is *katatetagmenon*, by contrast, is one considered in its relationship to the instantiations which embody it. The heavenly bodies, argues Simplicius, are monadic – they are species having only one instantiation – and they are embodied in matter. What is now under discussion, by contrast, is not embodied in matter (*akatatakton*) and yet has many instantiations (*en pollois theôroumenon*).

594. *eidê*. Since the same Greek word *eidos* can be translated as either 'species' or 'form' (cf. above, n. 35), we should recall that a Greek reader would bear both meanings in mind.

595. In his *Isagoge* (8,7ff. Busse), Porphyry distinguishes between three kinds of differentiae:

(1) Differentiae commonly (*koinôs*) so called; these occur when two entities differ by any kind of alterity; Socrates, e.g. differs by this kind of differentia both

from Plato and from himself [by age, as he grows older; by activity as he works or stops working, etc.];

(2) Differentiae properly (*idiôs*) so called; these occur when two entities differ from each other by an *inseparable* accident, such as 'having-a-snub-nose'; and

(3) Differentiae so called in the most proper sense (*idiaitata*); these occur when one entity differs from another by a *specific differentia*; as e.g. 'man' differs from 'horse' by the specific differentia of 'rational'. Of these three kinds of differentiae, the last-mentioned can obviously *not* be predicated of several species, since they are what *constitutes* (*sumplêrôtikai, sustatikai*) the various species (*Isag*. 10,9-10). There is, by contrast, nothing to prevent common and proper differentiae from being predicated of more than one species. On the fact that the differentia may be predicated of several species, cf. Porph. *Isagoge* 19,11 Busse; *In Cat*. 82,29-31.

596. The present passage (= Iamblichus fr. 17 Dalsgaard Larsen) is a fine example of Iamblichean 'intellective theory' (*noera theôria*). Basically, the idea is that if a differentia is predicable of only one species, this is a contingent fact about the world, not about the nature of the differentia in question.

597. cf. Arist. *Cat*. 3, 1b16, reading *tôn heterôn genôn* instead of Minio-Paluello's *tôn heterogenôn*. In what follows, Simplicius is following very closely Porph. *In Cat*. 83,2ff.

598. *hupallêla*, rendered by Boethius as 'subalterna'; cf. *In Cat*. 177D, 10ff. Here again, there is a divergence between the editors of Aristotle's *Cat*. (Minio-Paluello) and of Simplicius' *Commentary* (Kalbfleisch). The latter prints *hupallêla* as one single word, here and at 54,22, whereas Minio-Paluello prints *hup' allêla* at Arist. *Cat*. 3,1b16, as if there were two separate words. Neither editor indicates any variant readings in the manuscripts. I have followed Kalbfleisch.

599. Substance is what Porphyry would call a *genos genikôtaton*, or 'most generic genus'; cf. *Isagoge* 4,15ff.; via the Latin translation of Boethius, this idea would come down to medieval Scholastics as the *genus generalissimum*. Each of the categories is a *genos genikôtaton*.

600. Porphyry terms this the 'most specific species' (*eidos eidikôtaton*; cf. *Isagoge* 4,17-18); it is the *infima species* of the Scholastics; that species which cannot be further divided into species, but only into individuals.

601. cf. Porph. *In Cat*. 83,36-84,1.

602. cf. Porph. *In Cat*. 84,1-4.

603. Arist. *Cat*. 3, 1b16.

604. cf. Porph. *In Cat*. 84,4-8.

605. Kalbfleisch indicates a lacuna here, suggesting it be filled by 'and "moved by itself" ' or 'moved from within'. William of Moerbeke supplied 'animatum', which is more in accord with Porphyry's *Isagoge*; cf. 10,5 Busse: 'the differentia "animate" and "sensible" is constitutive of the substance of "animal".'

606. In accordance with the rule stated by Aristotle at *Cat*. 3, 1b22: 'the higher genera are predicated of the genera beneath them'. With what follows, cf. Dexippus *In Cat*. 27,10ff. Busse.

607. Thus, the differentiae 'herbivorous', 'seed-eating', and 'carnivorous' can, while remaining the same, be divisive both of the higher genus 'animal' and of the lower genus 'bird'; cf. Porph. *In Cat*. 84,11-17; Dexippus 28,20-7; Boethius 178C. Note that both 'animal' and 'bird' are *subordinate* genera; that is, they have both higher genera above them and lower species beneath them.

608. Arist. *Cat*. 3, 1b16-17. On what follows, cf. Dexippus *In Cat*. 29,29-30,9.

609. *hupopoda*. Cf. Ammonius 31, 25-30; David (Elias) 158, 6ff.; Philoponus

41,22ff.; Olympiodorus 51,24ff.; who inform us that examples of 'footless' furniture include the *thuiskê* ('censer') and the *doidux* ('pestle').

610. Thus, yet another attempt at a counter-example to Aristotle's doctrine has been shot down. The original *aporia*, as Simplicius found it transmitted by his Iamblicho-Porphyrian source, will have been as follows: 'Aristotle says (*Cat.* 3, 1b16-17) that "of those things which are (i) different in genus and (ii) not subordinate to one another, (iii) the differentiae are also different in species". Well, "footed" and "footless" can belong both to the genus "animal" and to "furniture", which are (i) different and (ii) not mutually subordinate. But "footed" and "footless" are *not* different in species, and so they are examples of differentiae which (i) are different in genus; (ii) are not subordinate to one another; and yet (iii) are *not* different in species. Thus Aristotle is wrong.'

Simplicius' reply is simple: (iii) is false. It is *not* the case that the differentiae 'footed' and 'footless' are not different in species; in fact they *are* different, when considered as belonging to 'animal' and 'furniture', and their apparent identity is in fact a mere case of homonymy.

611. i.e. at *Cat.* 1b16, we are to read '*tôn heterôn genôn*', and not '*tôn heterogenôn*'.

612. John Philoponus, Simplicius' Christian opponent, denies the existence of four-footed birds, 'for the multitude of feet would be an obstacle to flight' (*De Op. Mundi* 226,1ff. Reichardt).

613. Herminus' complex argumentation is intended to prove the importance of the qualifier 'in species' in Aristotle's statement that 'The differentiae of things which are other in genera, and whose genera are not subordinate one to the other, differ in species' (*Cat.* 3, 1b16-17). H. imagines the case of two genera, (a) 'winged', and (b) 'footed'. These fulfil Aristotle's criteria of being different and not subordinate one to the other. Yet, H. argues, there are some differentiae, 'two-footed' and 'four-footed', for instance, which can be common to both these genera. This seems contrary to Aristotle's affirmation, but is not: these differentiae *are* different with regard to their *species* (respectively 'winged' and 'footed', and are only identical with regard to their *genus* (i.e. 'animal'). Thus, H. concludes, Aristotle did not mean to exclude the possibility that the differentiae of different, non-subordinate genera could belong to the same *genus*, but only that they could not belong to the same *species*. Cf. P. Moraux 1984, 368-9.

614. In Simplicius' view Herminus is setting up a straw man. Aristotle is not talking about such *huph'hen* as 'winged' and 'footed', but rather – as can be seen from the examples he adduces, 'animal' and 'knowledge' – about genera which *cannot* be brought under a single heading. P. Moraux (1984, 369) agrees with Simplicius in finding Herminus' argument 'wholly superfluous and misleading'.

615. Fr. 57 Smith (from the *Ad Gedalium*).

616. This, presumably, is yet another application of the rule enunciated at *Cat.* 3, 1b22.

617. *mataiologia*; cf. 1 Timothy I,6, which the AV translates as 'vain jangling'.

618. This awkward switch from the plural to singular subject appears to be in Simplicius' Greek (*phêsi*). William Moerbeke appears to have read the plural *phasi*, since he translates 'aiunt' ('they say'). Praechter (1922, 486-7) understands the entire passage 58,15-23 to be a quotation from Nicostratus, but his grounds strike me as inadequate. I take it the Nicostratus quotation ends at 58,17, at which point Simplicius' response begins.

619. Arist. *Cat.* 3, 1b20-1.

620. Arist. *Cat.* 1b23-4. *Pace* Praechter (1922, 486-7), I take this to be another objection of 'the followers of Nicostratus'.

621. This Nicostratian *aporia* is a *reductio ad absurdum*: (i) 'Animal' and 'rational animal' are subordinate genera. (ii) The differentiae of 'animal' are 'rational' and 'irrational'. (iii) (Unstated) <But Aristotle said two subordinate genera can have the same differentiae>, so (iv) The differentiae of 'rational animal' are 'rational' and 'irrational'. (v) (Unstated) <But 'irrational' cannot be a differentia of 'rational animal'>; so (vi) (Unstated) <It is not the case that two subordinate genera can have the same differentiae>.

622. Boethus' solution thus consists in reversing the order of the terms 'subject' (*hupokeimenon*) and 'predicate' (*katêgoroumenon*) in Aristotle's text (*Cat.* 1b23-5).

623. Arist. *Cat.* 3, 1b20-1.

624. On Boethus' remarks, cf. P. Moraux 1973, 153-4 (who sides with Boethus' second solution).

625. On the distinction between differentiae which are constitutive (*sustatikai*) and those which are divisive (*diairetikai*), cf. Porph. *Isagoge* 10,1-21 Busse. Divisive differences are those which serve to distinguish species within a given genus; e. g. 'mortal/immortal' in the case of the genus 'animal'.

626. *sc.* 'the differentiae of subordinate genera from being the same'.

627. *tôi merikôterôi*. 'Man' is conceived of as 'more particular/partial' than 'animal'; it is farther along the road to specificity and more removed from the universal.

628. Arist. *Cat.* 3, 1b22.

629. Arist. *Cat.* 1b20-1.

630. Arist. *Cat.* 1b22.

631. Arist. *Cat.* 1b23-4.

632. Fr. 18, vol. 2, p. 14 Dalsgaard Larsen.

633. *prodiarthrôsis*. This seems to be the only occurrence of the noun, but Simplicius elsewhere uses the verb *prodiarthroô* (cf. below, 8,10; *In Ench. Epict.* 3,18 Dübner = 194,94 Hadot).

634. This is the view of Plotinus; cf. *Ennead* VI, 3,28.

635. A Stoic view; cf. Diogenes Laertius *Lives* VII, 61.

636. We know from Seneca (*Letter to Lucilius* 58) that some Stoics held that the supreme genus was the 'something' (*quid* = Greek *ti*), while others held it was 'that which is' (*quod* = Greek *to on*). On this text, cf. the analyses of W. Theiler 1930, 1-15; P. Hadot 1968, vol. I, 156ff.; V. Goldschmidt 1977[3], 13ff.; and for parallels in Stoic texts cf. *SVF* 2, 329; 333; 334; to 371, cited by M. Pohlenz 1980[5], vol. 2, 37; Long and Sedley 27A-B, vol. I, 162f.

637. cf. Alexander of Aphrodisias *In Top.* 301,19ff. = *SVF* II.329 = Long and Sedley 27B.

638. Arist. *Cat.* 2, 1a15ff.

639. cf. Porph. *In Cat.* 86,5-6; Boethius *In Cat.* 180B.

640. *en tupois* and *en kephalaiois*, when used of knowledge, mean approximately the same thing: they are the rough 'first draft' (the *tupos* metaphor comes from the use of preliminary sketching in painting and clay models in sculpture) which is later filled in with detail; Cf. Arist. *Nicomachean Ethics* 2.7, 1107b14-16, and for further references A. Trendelenburg, *Elementa logices Aristoteleae*[5] (Berlin 1862), pp. 49-50.

641. *kata diexodon*. Cf. Clement of Alexandria *Stromata* 8,4,11,4: 'There are two methods, one by question and answer, the other the method of exposition (*kata diexodon*).' In Galen's *Institutio Logica* (11,2,8-3,1 ed. Kalbfleisch), teaching *kata diexodon* is, as here, contrasted with a preliminary *hupographê*.

642. *holoskherê tên ennoian prolabôn.* Cf. above, 216,4ff.

643. *tais kata diexodon anelixesin. Anelixis* is the process of unwinding or developing of that which is latent, as the multitude develops from the monad in (Neo)-Pythagorean thought; cf. Damascius *Commentary on the Phaedo* I, §15,1-3 Westerink.

644. Reading, with MS A and William of Moerbeke, *tôn aneu sumplokês autôn.*

645. *kata tên onomasian.*

646. *kata tas prokheirous ennoias.* Innate ideas (*ennoiai*) which are *prokheiroi* ('close at hand') are equivalent to the common notions (*koinai ennoiai*) of the Stoics; cf. Gregory of Nyssa *Contra Eunomium* 3,1,40,5-12. While for the Stoics these were simply mental concepts which were the same in all rational beings, the Neoplatonists combined them with Plato's myth of the souls in the *Phaedrus* to make them innate traces of our pre-incarnate visions of the true beings which reside in the Intelligible world.

647. The Stoics distinguished between two kinds of *ennoiai*: those which come about naturally (*phusikôs*) and are also called *prolêpseis*, and those which, through study and instruction, can become 'technical' or scientific; cf. Ps.-Galen *Hist. Phil.* § 92, in Diels, *Doxographi Graeci*, 635,23-636,1 = Aetius 4,11 = Ps.-Plutarch *Placita* 900B8-C2 = *SVF* 2,83, p. 28,19-22 = Long and Sedley 39E.

648. Arist. *Cat.* 4, 1b28-29.

649. In other words, he attempts to make our *ennoiai* about the categories more 'technical'. On the awakening (Gk. *anegeirein/epegeirein*) of our innate ideas as the goal of pedagogy, cf. above, n. 225; Proclus *Platonic Theology* I 7, vol. 1, 32,1-6 Saffrey/Westerink; II 9, vol. 2, 60,6-11; *In Tim.* I, 168,22-7 Diehl, etc. The image may derive from the Ps.(?)-Platonic *Clitophon* 408c3-4; cf. Proclus *Platonic Theology* III 24, vol. 3, 83,17ff. Saffrey/Westerink.

650. *haplôs panta hosa kath' heauta huphestêken,* (Ps.-)Archytas *On the Universal Formula* 22,15-16 Thesleff; cf. T.A. Szlezák 1972, 71. Ps.-Archytas' examples of substances, as preserved in the *Codex Ambrosianus*, are 'man, horse, fire, and water'. On the elements as falling under the categories, cf. (with Szlezák *op. cit.* 101) Philo *On the Decalogue* § 31f.

651. Ps.-Archytas *op. cit.* 22,16-17 Thesleff = p. 35 Szlezák. The examples of quality in the Codex Ambrosianus are 'white, black, morally good (*spoudaios*), bad (*phaulos*)'.

652. *kata to pêlikon.* The word *pêlikos* is associated with Quantity (*to poson*) as early as Philo (*On the Decalogue* 31,5). In second-century AD Neopythagorean authors such as Nicomachus of Gerasa (*Introduction to Arithmetic*, I,3,1, ed. Hoche) – upon whom Iamblichus commented at length – Being is divided up as follows:

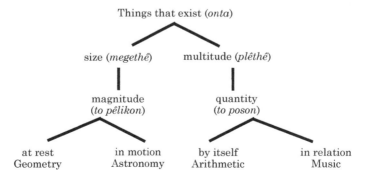

Things that exist (*onta*)

size (*megethê*)   multitude (*plêthê*)

magnitude (*to pêlikon*)   quantity (*to poson*)

at rest — Geometry   in motion — Astronomy   by itself — Arithmetic   in relation — Music

Cf. Proclus *In Eucl.* 35,21ff. Friedlein. As transmitted by Boethius, this division of the mathematical sciences was the origin of the medieval *quadrivium.*

653. Ps.-Archytas' examples of 'weight' are 'one mina' [= 100 drachmae = roughly 1.37 pounds avoirdupois], 'one talent' [= 60 minae = roughly 82 pounds avoirdupois]. For 'magnitude' Ps.-Archytas gives Aristotle's 'two cubits long'; 'three cubits long'.

654. *tôi pros ti.* MS B has *to pros ti pôs ekhon* ('that which is disposed in some way with regard to something else'). Ps.-Archytas' examples of relatives are 'double/half'; 'larger/smaller'.

655. Ps.-Archytas' examples are 'saying, cutting, tuning an instrument, and building'. The reference to 'tuning an instrument' was no doubt added, as Szlezák points out (p. 102), to provide a Pythagorean and specifically Archytean flavour to the enumeration. Archytas' treatises on harmonics were widely known, and quoted by Nicomachus and Porphyry; cf. D-K, I, 431-8.

656. Ps.-Archytas' examples are 'being said, being cut, being composed (*rhuthmizesthai*), and being softened (*malassesthai*)'.

657. For *ekhein*, Ps.-Archytas adduces the Aristotelian examples of 'being armed' (*hôplisthai*), 'being shod' (*hupodedesthai*) as well as one new example: 'having thrown round oneself' (*peribeblêsthai*).

658. Ps.-Archytas' examples of position are 'to be standing' (*hestanai*), 'to be lying down' (*katakeisthai*); 'to be crouching' (*sunkekamphthai*).

659. Ps.-Archytas' examples: 'in Tarentum', 'in Lacedaemonia', 'in a house', 'in the market'. Tarentum was the home of the historical Archytas, while 'Lacedaemonia' was probably chosen to add a Doric touch; cf. Szlezák 1972, 103.

660. Ps.-Archytas' examples of 'time' are 'now' (*nun*) and 'earlier' (*proteron*). On Archytas' theories of time, cf. Ph. Hoffmann 1980.

661. *paradeixis*; apparently a Iamblichean coinage; cf. *De communi mathematica scientia*, Pinax section 35,3.*

662. cf. Porphyry *In Cat.* 86,7ff.; Dexippus 39,8ff.

663. Sextus Empiricus (*Outlines of Pyrrhonism* 2,214ff.) and Alcinous (*Didaskalikos* 5, 156,34-157,10 Hermann), agree that there are three principal types of *diairesis*: that of names into their meanings; that of a whole into its parts; and that of a genus into its species. Cf. Clement of Alexandria *Stromata* VIII.19,1-8. As a fourth type, Sextus mentions the division of a species into particulars; while Alcinous adds two more: that of subjects into accidents and of accidents into subjects. The classification of types of division appears to be of Stoic origin; cf. O. Rieth 1933, 36ff.

664. The Aristotelian principle of the incommunicability of the genera. Cf. Arist. *Metaph.* 5.28, 1024b15; 10.4, 1055a6; 10.7, 1057a26-8; 13.9, 1085a16-19; 35-b4; *Pr. An.* 1.30, 46a17ff.; *Post. An.* 1.7; *Top.* 8.12, 162b7; *Cael.* 1.1, 268a30-b3, etc.

665. In other words, 'being' and 'something' – Stoic candidates for the role of supreme genus; cf. e.g. Plotinus *Enneads* VI,1 [42],8-10 – can be predicated of some of the categories – in particular, substance – to a greater extent than they can of the other nine categories. But genera cannot contain the prior and posterior (cf. Arist. *Metaph.* 3.3, 999a5ff. with Alexander *In Metaph.* 208,28ff. Hayduck; *EN* 1.4, 1096a17-19; *Pol.* 3.1, 1275a34-8; *EE* 1.8, 1218a1-10; etc.), and thus neither 'being' nor 'something' can be a genus.

666. The adjectives *homoiomerês* ('consisting of similar parts'), and *anomoiomerês* ('consisting of dissimilar parts') were understood in Antiquity as originating in the system of Anaxagoras (*c.* 500 – *c.* 428 BC), for whom the *homoiomerê* were fundamental constituents of reality; cf. Arist. *Metaph.* 1.3,

984a11-16 = Anaxagoras fr. A43D-K (vol. II, 17,12-16 etc.). For Aristotle, homoeomerous things were those which, when analyzed, did not contain any constituent parts different either from each other or from the whole; examples would be such organic substances as flesh and bones. Anomoeomeric substances were those which *did* contain different constituents, and included such organs as the hand or the eye. Cf. Arist. *On the Parts of Animals* 2.1, 646a13ff.

667. Homoeomerous wholes are predicated synonymously of their parts, whereas anomoeomerous wholes are predicated homonymously of their parts. In the case of anomoeomerous wholes like a house, the parts of a house are not themselves called 'houses'; similarly, 'beings' could not be the anomoeomerous parts of Being. But beings [*sc.* each individual category] are not homoeomerous parts of Being either, since they are dissimilar. Therefore the ten categories are not the parts of some overarching whole called 'Being'.

668. cf. Dexippus *In Cat.* 39,16-19. In an important paper P. Hadot (1974, 1990, 1999) has attempted to show that this section of Dexippus derives from Porphyry's lost commentary on Arist. *Metaph.* 12. If he is right, the same would hold true of the present text of Simplicius. Yet both passages may instead derive from Iamblichus' interpretation of Archytas; cf. 76,17ff.; 91,14-33.

669. This analogy with the order of an army probably derives ultimately from Arist. *Metaph.* 12.10, 1075a14ff.

670. *touto tên sunekheian kai allêloukhian anairei tês diakosmêseôs.* The phraseology is typically Iamblichean; cf. Dexippus 39,22-3; Proclus *In Remp.* I,288,6ff.; Proclus *ap.* Lydum *De Mensibus* IV,76.

671. *tois aph' henos kai pros hen.* Cf. Dexippus 39,24-40,5. On this type of relation, intermediate between synonymy and homonymy, cf. Arist. *Metaph.* 3.2, 1002a33; 4.2, 1003a33-1003b6; 7.4, 1030a35; *EN* 1.4, 1096b25-31. The exact phrase *aph' henos kai pros hen* does not occur in Aristotle, but cf. for example Proclus *Elements of Theology* prop. 110, 98,11-17, with Dodds's note *ad loc.*; L. Robin 1908, 151-65; J. Owens 1978[3], ch. 3: 'The Aristotelian Equivocals'; G.E.L. Owen in I. Düring and G.E.L. Owen, eds, *Aristotle and Plato in the Mid-fourth Century* (Göteborg 1960), 163-90.

672. Iamblichus fr. 19, vol. II, 14 Dalsgaard Larsen; cf. vol. I, 252.

673. On Herminus' view, cf. P. Moraux 1984, 369.

674. Simplicius is thus ready to agree with Iamblichus that the categories are the result of a relation of derivation (*aph'henos*; cf. Porph. *Isagoge* 1,20-1: one kind of genus is so called 'from the relation of derivation from one thing' (*ek tês aph'henos skheseôs*)). Yet the one thing from which the categories are derived cannot be substance (*ousia*), for substance itself is enumerated as one of the ten categories.

675. *pollakhôs legomenon.* Cf. Arist. *Metaph.* 3.3, 998b27; 4.2, 1003a33ff. In an elementary treatise on logic and semantics like the *Cat.*, Simplicius argues, it is permissible to consider Being (*to on*), in accordance with Aristotle's assertions, as a mere equivocal term, rather than a metaphysical reality. Simplicius here follows the example of Porphyry in the *Isagoge* 6,5ff. Busse.

676. Kalbfleisch cites Arist. *Metaph.* 6.2, 1025b33ff. [presumably a misprint for 1026a33ff.] and 7.1, 1028a10. Yet Hadot (*art. cit.* above, n. 668) has shown the most influential text in this regard was *Metaph.* 12.10; cf. Dexippus 41,12ff.

677. *suntattomenôn.* Cf. Arist. *Metaph.* 12.10, 1075a18-19: '... all things have been coordinated (*suntetaktai*) with regard to one thing.'

678. cf. P. Moraux 1984, 369-70. Herminus believed Aristotle had hedged his bets: if there were as many categories as there were primary genera, then his doctrine was correct; yet if additional genera of being were discovered, his doctrine could accommodate them too.

679. i.e. universal substance, particular accidents, universal accidents, and particular substances; cf. above, 44,6ff.; Boethius *In Cat.* 180B.
680. cf. Porphyry *In Cat.* 86,20ff. Busse. On Athenodorus, see above, 18,28. For the interpretation of what he was objecting to, much hinges on our translation of *eis to toiouton plêthos*. If we translate 'into so *great* a number', then we may be led to conclude that Athenagoras held that Aristotle had come up with *too many* categories (so B.L. Hijmans 1975, 108ff.); perhaps because he held the Stoic belief that there were only four (cf. M. Pohlenz 1984[6], I, 294). If, however, we translate 'into this particular number and no other' (P. Moraux 1984, 588-9 & n. 18), and recall that Athenodorus was one of those who thought the *Cat.* were about words (cf. above, 18,26-19,1; Praechter 1922, 508-10), and thought Aristotle was wrong not to include every kind of word, then he may be reproaching Aristotle with allowing *too few* categories.
681. cf. Porph. *In Cat.* 86,20-5, who adds Cornutus' works an *Art of Rhetoric*. On Cornutus, see above, 18,28.
682. cf. Porph. *In Cat.* 86,31-2. Porphyry's extant commentary only mentions these accusations, before moving to another topic so abruptly that Busse suspected a lacuna (but cf. S. Strange's translation *ad loc.*, 74 & n. 145). Boethius claims he will deal with these objections 'in another work' (180C8-9); might this be a veiled allusion to a more detailed treatment in Porphyry's lost *Ad Gedalium*? On the accusations of excess and deficiency against Aristotle's division of the categories into ten, cf. Ammon. 33,15ff.; Philop. 44,2ff.; David 159,8ff.; Olympiodorus 54,4ff. David, for instance, reports the views of critics who held that the correct number of categories was 1, 2, 3, 4 (Plotinus), 5 (Galen), 6, 8, 9, or 11.
683. *enallaxin*. Cf. below, 66,18ff..
684. *pleonasmon*. Cf. Dexippus *In Cat.* 30,35-31,2.
685. *to kineisthai*. Richard Sorabji suggests the translation 'to be changed', but while this may be the sense here, I have preferred the traditional practice of translating *kinêsis* and related terms by 'movement', leaving 'change' to render *metabolê* and its cognates. For the doctrine, cf. Plotinus *Enneads* VI, I,15-22; VI, 3,1; Plotinus *ap.* Simplicium *In Cat.* 302,5-11; 304,28-32; 306,13-16 Kalbfleisch; Simplicius *In Phys.* 403,9-10; 432,16-17 Diels. Yet Boethus already replied to similar objections (Simplicius *In Cat.* 302,15-17), which must therefore date from near the time of Andronicus.
686. cf. Dexippus *In Cat.* 31,6.
687. cf. Dexippus *In Cat.* 31,7f. Like Aristotle (*Physics* 3.2, 202a5ff.), Simplicius concedes that some sensible agents are moved, presumably because motion in the sensible world is caused by contact (*thixis*), which entails a modification both of agent and of patient.
688. *sundramein eis tauto*, literally, 'because they run together into the same thing'.
689. cf. Plotinus *Enneads* VI, I,17,1-4, quoted by Simplicius *In Cat.* 309,29-32; VI, 3,21,9ff.; David (Elias) *In Cat.* 160,1ff.
690. *hôs men kath'heauta huphestôta*. This, we recall, was the Ps.-Archytas' definition of substance; cf. *On the Universal Logos*, 22,15-16 Thesleff.
691. Simplicius' answer to the suggestion that *paskhein* and *poiein* be subsumed under the Relatives may be understood from the parallel passage in David (160,15ff.), who distinguishes between the neuter singular present participles *poioun* and *paskhon*, which are subsumed under the relatives, and the infinitives *poiein* and *paskhein*, which are not. Similarly, Simplicius concedes that individual things which act and are acted upon (*to poioun*; *to paskhon*), like 'father' and 'son', can be conceived as in relation. Yet just as 'father' and 'son' can

also be conceived of, in their independence, as substances, so the infinitives *poiein* and *paskhein* are not relative, but constitute independent categories.

692. cf. Plotinus *Enneads* VI, 1,24,6-8. David (160,17ff.) reports the view that *keisthai* and *ekhein* should be subsumed under the relatives; since *poiein* and *paskhein* were also thought to belong under the relatives (160,1ff.), it was a small step to suggest, as here, that *keisthai* be subsumed under *paskhein*, and *ekhein* under *poiein*.

693. Thus the suggestion that *keisthai* be subsumed under *paskhein* is refuted by showing that its species (*kathêsthai*; *hestanai*) belong no more to *paskhein* than to its opposite *poiein*. Similarly, *ekhein* ought not to be subsumed under *poiein*, for its species (*hôplisthai*; *hupodedesthai*) belong no more to *poiein* than to its opposite *paskhein*. In fact, argues Simplicius (following Iamblichus?), *keisthai* should be subsumed under the new category of *hidrusis en allôi*; while *ekhein* should come under *to perikeisthai*. Cf. Olympiodorus 56,14: 'having (*ekhein*) is the juxtaposition (*parathesis*) of a substance beside a substance.'

694. cf. Plotinus *Enneads* VI, I,23,10-11; Simplicius *In Cat.* 370,21f.

695. cf. Dexippus *In Cat.* 31,11ff.

696. Fr. 12 Heinze = fr. 95, p. 89 Isnardi Parenti; cf. the editor's commentary *ad loc.*, 327-9. On the Academic division into *kath'hauto/pros ti*, cf. e.g. K. Gaiser 1968², 377 n. 142.

697. P. Moraux 1973, 103-4, judged this information on Andronicus misleading. Simplicius tells us elsewhere that Andronicus *preserved* the ten categories (342,24-5), and often quotes Andronicus' discussion of individual categories without any suggestion they might be reducible to two.

698. *diatemnousin*; cf. Dexippus 31,14.

699. cf. Dexippus 31,19-20. Those who reduce the number of categories to two (cf. Olympiodorus 55,1ff.; David 161,6ff.) are in fact saying the same thing as Xenocrates/Andronicus: the ultimate distinction is between substance/that which is by itself, and accident/that which exists in something else.

700. cf. Dexippus 31,15-19.

701. Simplicius' source objects that since all nine non-substantial categories are accidental, it is therefore abusive to lump them all together as 'relatives'.

702. cf. Dexippus 31,22-30. 'Of' here renders the Greek genitive case.

703. The parallel passage in Dexippus (31,28f.) is for once more clear: if accidents are understood in their relation to their substrate, then they are relative; but taken by themselves they are *per se*.

704. *hoi peri ton Iamblikhon kai Porphurion* = Iamblichus fr. 20, vol. 2, 14-15 Dalsgaard Larsen. It is likely that Simplicius has taken his information Iamblichus' *Commentary on the Cat.*, which in turn was quoting or paraphrasing Porphyry's lost *Ad Gedalium*. The passage should thus be added to Smith's collection of fragments.

705. *oude tên mian autou perilêpsin paralipôn*.

706. cf. Dexippus *In Cat.* 32,5-8. I cannot agree with J. Dillon that Simplicius is here dependent on Dexippus, nor is Simplicius wrongly claiming credit for someone else's doctrine. More probably, both Simplicius and Dexippus are, here as often elsewhere, drawing on a common Iamblicho-Porphyrian source.

707. cf. below, 372,29ff.; Dexippus 32,10ff.; Olympiodorus 53,18-20; 54,28-30; Philop. 43,17-21; David 16,1-4.

708. We learn from David (*loc. cit.*) that this was the solution of Syrianus.

709. *en tôi houtôsi perikeisthai*. In other words, 'has/hold' (the Greek *ekhei* can mean either) cannot be traced back to a further category, but only to the subject who does the having/holding; thus it constitutes a category. 'Being had/held', by contrast, can be reduced to the fact of 'being-positioned-in-a-given-position', and is therefore not a category.

710. cf. Dexippus 32,14-16, who adds that 'position (*thesis*) is thus nothing other than the order (*taxis*) of things which are held'.

711. cf. Dexippus 32,17ff. Elsewhere, Lucius – here, unusually, named in the absence of Nicostratus – seems to suppose that the *skopos* of the *Cat.* was the genera of being; yet here he seems to be adopting the thesis that the *skopos* was meaningful expressions (*lexeis sêmantikai*). P. Moraux perhaps too hastily ascribes this apparent vacillation to philosophical sloppiness (1984, 532f.).

712. There is a lacuna here in the manuscripts of Simplicius as there was already in that used by Moerbeke. In his parallel passage (32,18-29), Dexippus adduces the following reasons for omitting conjunctions: (1) Their use is not a primary, but a secondary use of language (cf. Simplicius 64,20: *oute proêgoumenê autôn estin hê sêmasia*); (2) the conjunction is not complete (*teleia*), but incomplete (*atelês*); and (3) it is not lexical (*lektikê*), but symbolic (*sumbolikê*). Dexippus probably found these points in Porphyry's *Ad Gedalium*.

713. On conjunctions as co-significative (i.e. as non-significant *per se*, but capable of signifying when combined with other parts of speech), cf. e.g. *Scholia in Dion. Thrac.* (= GG I,3) 284,6-10 Uhlig.

714. *diplai* and *korônides*; cf. Dexippus 32,20-4. These were critical signs written in the margins of ancient manuscripts: the *diplê* had the form of a diamond bracket (>), and served to point out notable passages in the text. The *korônis* had various forms, and indicated interruptions in the text, changes of speakers in plays, and crasis.

715. On the meaninglessness *per se* of conjunctions, cf. Ammonius, *In De Interp.* 12,25ff. Busse; Boethius *In De Interp.*[2], PL 64, col. 394-395; *On the Categorical Syllogism*, PL 64, col. 796: Poseidonius *ap.* Apollonium Dyscolum *On Conjunctions* (= GG II,1) 214,4f. Schneider; *On Adverbs* (= GG II,1,1) 133,25f. Schneider; *On Syntax* (= GG II,3), 27,10 Uhlig; *Schol. in Dion. Thrac.* (GG I, 3) 436,2-3 Hilgard.

716. cf. Dexippus 32,23ff.; Ammonius *In De Interp.* 12,25ff., where the distinction between essential parts of speech (nouns and verbs) and accessory/non-essential parts (articles, prepositions, conjunctions and adverbs) is illustrated by the example of a ship: nouns and verbs correspond to the planks out of which the ship itself is built, but conjunctions etc. correspond to the hinges, linen and pitch which hold the ship together. The latter could not properly be called *parts* of the ship, according to Dexippus and Ammonius; like prepositions, their function is to ensure the coherence of the whole, but they are insignificant in themselves.

717. On the *logos/lexis* distinction cf. Arist. *Poet.* 20, 1456b20-1; *Rhet.* 3, 1404b26; Theophrastus, cited above, 10,25f.; Ammonius *In De Int.* 12,30ff. Busse. The view that conjunctions are part of the *lexis* but not of the *logos* is that of Boethus (cf. above, 11,27f.), as quoted by Porphyry in the *Ad Gedalium*.

718. According to Simplicius the Greek verb *legein* ('to say') denotes the saying of a *meaningful* expression; if it is meaningless expressions which are uttered, then we must use another verb than 'to say'.

719. cf. Dexippus 32,30ff.

720. cf. Dexippus 33,1ff. It was the Stoics who called articles 'indefinite-formed' (*aoristôdê*); cf. Apollonius Dyscolos *On Pronouns* 6,30; 7,3-6, Schneider; *On Syntax* 68,18; Priscianus *Grammatical Institutions* 11,1,1; 2,16; 17,52 Hertz/Kiel.

721. The negation was one of the 26 varieties of adverb recognized by Dionysius of Thrace (*Tekhnê Grammatikê* 19,18,9 Uhlig); they correspond to the

Greek negative particle *ou*, whose function is to deny the action denoted by the verb before which it is placed.

722. *sterêseis*. Expressions *kata sterêsin* are those turned negative by the addition of an alpha privative; cf. Dionysius Thrax fr. 8 Link; Apollonius Dyscolos *On Adverbs* 144,17; *On Conjunctions* 231,7, etc.

723. *ekklisis* denotes the mood of a verb (*rhêma*), i.e. indicative, imperative, optative, and subjunctive; some grammarians also included the infinitive. Cf. Dionysius of Halicarnassus *On Literary Composition* 6,38; 25,190; Dionysius Thrax *Tekhnê Grammatikê* 13,5; 47,3ff.; with the scholia *ad loc.*

724. cf. Dexippus 33,8ff., with J. Dillon's translation, 67 n. 119.

725. The following passage = fr. 116 in V. Rose, ed., *Aristotelis qui ferebantur librorum fragmenta* (Leipzig 1886 [reprinted 1967]), 107-8; cf. W.D. Ross, ed., *Aristotelis Fragmenta Selecta* (Oxford 1955), 102-3. The passage is translated and amply commented upon by P. Moraux 1951, 67ff.

726. *en tois Methodikois*. The title *Methodika* is attested as no. 52 in the list of Aristotle's writings preserved by Diogenes Laertius; cf. I. Düring 1957, 44. Moraux (*loc. cit.* 66f.) argues for its identity with the *Topics*.

727. *en tais Diaresesin*. Aristotle's *Diaireseis* are no. 42 in the list of Diogenes. Several apocryphal writings with this title were in circulation in Antiquity (cf. H. Mutschmann, *Divisiones quae vulgo dicuntur Aristoteleae*, Leipzig 1906), yet Moraux believes they are not to be identified with the lost work here mentioned by Simplicius.

728. *ta peri tên lexin*. While the Aristotelian work entitled *Peri lexeôs* (= Diog. no. 87) is generally agreed to be identical with Book III of the *Rhetoric* (cf. P. Moraux 1951, 103-4), the fact that Simplicius indicates there were doubts as to its authenticity led Moraux to believe this lost work was different from the one known to the source of Diogenes (*op. cit.* 67 n. 104).

729. cf. Dexippus 33,13-14, where the rare verb *anupodetein* also occurs.

730. In other words, negative terms like 'going barefoot' (*anupodetein*) should subsumed under the same category as the positive state of which they are the denial, *viz.* 'wearing shoes'. Cf. Dexippus 33,15-21, who gives as examples of his meaning the fact that 'corpse' and 'living being' will fall under the same category, as will 'blindness' and 'the possession of sight'. <Sophonias> in his *Paraphrase* (10,32-7 Hayduck) adds that 'not-man' (*ouk anthrôpos*) will be ranged under the same category as 'man' (*anthrôpos*).

731. cf. Dexippus *In Cat.* 33,21-34,2.

732. Since Aristotle states (*Cat.* 4b20) that the quantified is either discrete or continuous, that which is neither discrete nor continuous cannot be a quantified.

733. Aristotle claims Plato distinguished between mathematical and intelligible numbers in his unwritten doctrines; cf. L. Robin 1908. Plotinus devoted *Ennead* VI,6 to the question of intelligible numbers; while Syrianus distinguished between eidetic/intelligible, mathematical, and formal numbers. The other *Cat.* commentators explain that intelligible number is that which counts, and is in the soul; corporeal number is that which is counted, and is in the objects which are counted. Cf. Ammon. 59,20-60,8; Philop. *In Phys.* 718,24-5; 740,8-9; Olympiodorus *In Cat.* 89,9-10; 143,12-13; etc.

734. Kalbfleisch points to *An. Post.* 1.27, 87a26, where the monad is said to be a substance without place (*ousia athetos*), while the point (*stigmê*) is a substance *with* place (*ousia thetos*). Yet Simplicius' reference may instead be to Aristotle's lost work *On the Good*; see following note.

735. *hê duas pros ta duo*. Similar distinctions between the two dyads – one intelligible, the other numerical and deriving from the coming together of the intelligible dyad with the One – are attributed both to the Pythagoreans (cf. Sextus Empiricus *Adv. Mathem.* 10,276) and to Plato himself in his unwritten teachings (cf. Alexander *In Metaph.* 56,20f. Hayduck, citing Aristotle's lost work *On the Good* [= fr. 2, in *Aristotelis Fragmenta Selecta*, 113-15 Ross]). Cf. the bibliography given by W.E. Dooley to his translation of this passage (*Alexander of Aphrodisias: On Aristotle Metaphysics 1* [London & Ithaca NY 1989]), 84 n. 176. On the Dyad in Neopythagorean speculation cf. e.g. Anatolius in Anon. *Theologoumena Arithmeticae* 7,14-14,12 De Falco; Johannes Lydus *De Mensibus* II,7.

736. Boethus' discussion of intelligible numbers, a two-fold monad and the nature of the dyad – all Academic/Neo-Pythagorean doctrines – is surprising, considering Boethus' denial of the Platonic Forms. P. Moraux (1973, 155) attempts to explain Boethus' position by the influence of Speusippus, whom B. elsewhere quotes (above, 36,29-30; 38,19; cf. L. Tarán, 'Speusippus and Aristotle on Homonymy and Synonymy', *Hermes* 106 [1978], 75ff.). But these doctrines may go back to Plato himself; with the passage cited from Sextus above cf. Hermodorus, *On Plato*, quoted *via* Derkyllides and Porphyry by Simplicius *In Phys.* 247,30-248,20; 256,14-257,4 Diels.

737. cf. Alexander *Commentary on Book I of the Prior Analytics* (= *CAG* 2.1, Berlin 1883) 81,22-4 Wallies.

738. cf. Anon. *Theol. Arith.* 1,4 De Falco. Yet the doctrine is pre-Aristotelian; cf. *Topics* 1.18, 108b27ff.

739. cf. below 153,32ff. The parallel in Macrobius *Dream of Scipio* II.14,24 is presented as an Aristotelian argument, but it *may* derive from Porphyry.

740. On 'father' as a relative (*pros ti*), cf. 166,9-10.

741. Since number is defined as a multiplicity (*plêthos*) composed of monads (Arist. *Metaph.* 1.1, 1053a20), Alexander had claimed that the monad is part of the Quantified. The reply of his critics – presumably Porphyry and/or Iamblichus – was twofold: (i) the monad is not a *part* of number, but its principle (*arkhê*); the monad is therefore different from number, and does not fall under the category of the Quantified, as does number. (ii) Rather than the Quantified, the monad and the point should be subsumed under the Relative (*pros ti*), for as principles they are necessarily principles *of* something, as a father is necessarily a father *of* his children, and that which has such a necessary relation to something other is a relative.

742. *suntetagmenê, exeirêmenê*. This contrasting pair of terms occurs frequently in Proclus and in Damascius, but seems to appear only here in Simplicius' writings. John Dillon points out its origin in Iamblichus; cf. fr. 52 Dillon = Proclus *In Tim.* II,142,27ff. The meaning of the terms is probably identical to Porphyry's contrast between what is 'coordinated' (*katatetagmenon*) and 'uncoordinated' (*akatatakton*); cf. above, 27,23ff.; 53,8; 56,2.

743. On the triad *arkhê-meson-peras* cf. Plato *Parmenides* 165a6-7; Theon *On the Usefulness of Mathematics* 46,15 Hiller; Timaeus Locrus *On the Nature of the World and the Soul* 80, 148,13 Marg. Cf. Arist. *De Caelo* 1.1, 268a11ff.: '... the Pythagoreans say the all and everything in it are limited by the number three, for end (*telos*), middle (*meson*) and beginning (*arkhê*) give the number of the whole, and their number is the triad'. Cf. Plato *Laws* 715e (which the scholia *ad loc.* explain as an Orphic saying); Alexander *ap.* Simplicium *In De Caelo* 42,29ff. Heiberg.

744. On the monad as contracted number cf. Damascius *On Principles* I, 120 Ruelle = vol. I, 52,24-5 Westerink/Combès; *On the Philebus* §64.

745. Simplicius' reasoning runs as follows: (i) the coordinated (*suntetagmenê*) principle is in the same genus (*viz.* Quantity) as the limit and the middle;

(ii) the transcendent (*exêirêmenos*) monad of number is a contracted (*sunêirêmenos*) number; (iii) but the opposite to contracted number is discrete (*diôrismenos*) number; (iv) discrete number is under Quantity (*Cat.* 6, 4b22-2); hence (v) since opposites fall under the same genus, contracted number is also under Quantity. But (vi) since contracted number = transcendent number, transcendent number is therefore also under Quantity.

746. *SVF* II.225. Cf. above, 52,32.

747. i.e. as equivocal, or having different senses.

748. Once again, Simplicius supposes that for the purposes of a beginner's logical treatise like the *Cat.*, Aristotle's nominalist view that the One has no substantial existence but rather, like Being, is just a hononymous expression, is acceptable. Refuting Aristotle and establishing the existence of the One and the Forms will be the task of metaphysics or theology; cf. Syrianus' commentary on the *Metaphysics*.

749. i.e. Plotinus (*Ennead* VI, 3,21,3-9; cf. Dexippus *In Cat.* 34,3-10), who may in turn have been following Lucius-Nicostratus.

750. cf. above, 63,6ff.

751. cf. Alexander *ap.* Simplicium *In Phys.* 416,27ff.; Plotinus *Ennead* VI, 3,23,3-4.

752. i.e. as Richard Sorabji points out, qualitative change.

753. Far from being a category, argues Simplicius, movement (defined as the path from potentiality to actuality) is a *pollakhôs legomenon* or homonymous term, present in different form in all the categories, like Being or the One.

754. On rest as a possible category-candidate, cf. Plotinus *Ennead* VI, 3,27,1-4; Dexippus *In Cat.* I, 39, 34,17-19.

755. *SVF* 2,369 = Long and Sedley 27F. Together with Plotinus *Ennead* VI, 1,25ff. (= *SVF* 2,371), this passage constitutes our main testimony on the Stoic categorical doctrine. It has given rise to an extensive bibliography: to the works listed by Long and Sedley (vol. 2, 495-6) add O. Rieth 1933, 70ff.

756. I suspect this remark may be a marginal gloss.

757. i.e. to the difference? This page of Simplicius' commentary is full of awkward constructions, but the awkwardness seems to have appeared in the oldest manuscripts, since Moerbeke faithfully translates them word for word into Latin.

758. *sic*; see previous note.

759. With the following *diairesis* of the categories, cf. the similar – but not identical – division given by David 159,9-33; Olympiodorus 54,3-24; Arethas 165,29-37.

760. I know of no parallel to this initial division between *huparxeis* and *energeiai*, but, as an anonymous reader points out, the division *huparxis-dunamis-energeia* is Iamblichean (*De Myst.* I,4; I,5). David and Olympiodorus first divide beings into things in a substrate (*hupokeimenon*) and things not in a substrate; cf. Ps.-Archytas *On the General Formula* 31,6-7 Thesleff with Th. A. Szlezák 1972, 143; Plotinus *Ennead* VI, 1,25,29-30 (of the Stoics).

761. cf. Proclus *Commentary on the Republic* I,226,13-14; *Platonic Theology* III,25; *In Parm.* 1238,6-9; etc.

762. David and Olympiodorus by contrast, claim that all members of the branch of things in a substrate which is not *per se* are 'in relation' (*en skhesei*). Of things in relation, they say, some are in pure relation, and these fall under the category Relative (*pros ti*); some are in relation to other things, and they form the last six categories.

763. *kata huparxin*. This awkward phrase simply summarizes the steps covered by the *diairesis* up to this point: the Qualified and the Quantified are

(a) existences (*huparxeis/kata huparxin*, as opposed to activities); which (b) exist in something other (as opposed to being *per se*); and they are 'unrelated' (*askhetoi*), as opposed to things in relation.

764. *pros antistrephonta.* Cf. Arist. *Cat.* 7, 6b128.

765. *kata tên pros asômata.* The designation of time and place as incorporeals is of Stoic origin.

766. For David and Olympiodorus the categories 'Where' and 'When' are formed by the combination of Substance (*ousia*) and Quantity (*poson*).

767. *eph' hôn hidrumetha.* The subsumption of Position (*keisthai*) under 'establishment in something other' (*hidrusis en allôi*) appears to be Iamblichean; with Simplicius 63,15-21 above, cf. Iamblichus, quoted below, 336,25f.

768. *pros ta perikeimena.* On the subsumption of Having (*ekhein*) under 'Lying-around' (*to perikeisthai*), see above, 63,15-21, and especially Iamblichus, quoted below, 337,15f.

769. Fr. 21, vol. 2, 15 Dalsgaard Larsen.

770. Reading *pantôn* for *pasas*, with Moerbeke. The decade or number ten, sum of the first four numbers, was sacred in the Pythagorean tradition; cf. W. Burkert, *Lore and Science in Ancient Pythagoreanism* (Cambridge, Mass. 1972), 72ff.

771. *tetagmenon ti kai hôrismenon pragma*, 32,17-20 Thesleff; cf. Aristotle *Protrepticus* B33, 42 Düring. In the koinê-version of Ps.-Archytas discovered in the Codex Ambrosianus, Ps.-Archytas states that there are two kinds of human life: one called 'existence' (*to einai*) and a higher one called 'existing well' (*to kalôs einai*); the *tekhnai* were invented for the former, while *epistêmê* helps towards the latter. These distinctions go back to Aristotle's *Protrepticus*, fragmentarily preserved by Iamblichus; cf. Szlezák 1972, 150-1, with parallels from Pseudo-Pythagorean literature.

772. *eidêtikous arithmous.* As Szlezák points out (*op. cit.* 151), Archytas' mention of ideal numbers indicates that he had 'some knowledge, however rudimentary, of that Plato who was not to be found in the Dialogues'.

773. cf. Aristotle *Topics* 1.12, 105a13-14: 'Induction (*epagôgê*) is a passage from particulars to universals.' This text is quoted by Alcinous *Didaskalikos* 5, 158,1ff. Hermann, who adds that induction 'is most useful for setting in motion our innate ideas (*phusikas ennoias*)'.

774. Arist. *Cat.* 4, 1b25-6.

775. To claim that no reality corresponds to commons and universals is, of course, to claim that they have no real existence, a claim made by both Stoics and Peripatetics. Simplicius' unnamed opponent may be Alexander; cf. below, 82,22ff.

776. On the difference between 'transcendent' (*exêirêmena*) and 'coordinated' (*katatetagmena*) genera, cf. P. Hadot 1968, vol. I, 408ff; the present passage is translated *ibid.*, 413. Cf. Simplicius' comments on the triple nature of the common, *In Cat.* 83,25ff.: there are (i) the transcendent (*exêirêmenon*) common; cause of both the commonality and the differentness in individuals. An example is the 'Animal-in-itself' (*autozôion*), which provides their commonality to all individual animals, and gives rise to the diverse species of 'animal'. (ii) second is the common 'animal' which inheres within each member of each animal species; and (iii) third is the common animal which arises in our conceptions (*ennoiais*) by abstraction, and is last in origin (*husterogenês*).

777. cf. Proclus *Platonic Theology* II,3, 30,7-9 Saffrey-Westerink.

778. cf. Simplicius *In Phys.* 144,12ff. Diels.

779. *adiaphoron.* It is the third of the three kinds of common described by Simplicius, not the first, which is 'undifferentiated' (83,9) in the sense that, like the *atomon eidos* (cf. Aristotle *Posterior Analytics* 2.13, 97a37) it does not have differentiae in the proper sense of the term. Cf. Anon. *In Anal. Post. II* (= *CAG* 13.3), 586,25-6; 588,9-10 Wallies.

780. Presumably, what is meant is that common substances such as 'soul' and 'body' come into being already equipped with differentiae which render them compatible with the things in which they are instantiated. Soul, for instance, comes 'pre-equipped', as it were, with differentiae which allow it to exist and function as an incorporeal psychic entity.

781. *tou sumpephurmenou.* A reminiscence of Plato *Phaedo* 66b: 'as long as we have a body and our soul is mixed together (*xumpephurmenê*) with such a great evil, we will never possess that which we long for.'

782. i.e. the second of the three kinds of universal/common described above, which is the *enulon eidos* or inherent form. It is 'differentiated' as a result of its contact with matter, the principle of differentiation and individuality (cf. C. Baeumker 1890, 281ff.).

783. cf. *Phaedo* 74a, where the 'equal in itself' is discussed; *Republic* 5, 476b.

784. Kalbfleisch points to *Republic* 7, 537c; but Simplicius' use of the verb *periagein* ('to make a person turn his head around'; 'to rotate'; said of the soul and of the prisoners in the Cave) indicates he is rather thinking of *Republic* 7, 518c-e; cf. 514b2; 515c7; 521c6-7.

785. *en methexei.* Forms 'in participation' are those which are participated; cf. Proclus *In Tim.* 3.32,10-11; Simplicius *In Phys.* 720,36; 766,21-2; In the Neoplatonic hierarchy of intelligible Forms or Ideas, the highest level is the 'unparticipated' (*amethekton*); followed by the 'participated' (*metekhomenon*); and then the 'participant' (*metekhon*). The first of these three terms correspond to the first two kinds of common enumerated by Simplicius; but while the third kind of common is the abstract universal which subsists in our conceptions, the third Idea/Form is matter, according to Proclus (*In Parm.* 797,23-798,10). Cf. S. Gersh, *From Iamblichus to Eriugena* (Leiden 1978), 90ff.

786. Arist. *Post. An.* 1.11, 77a5-9.

787. Simplicius has one long sentence here (71,2-10), which I have broken into two to facilitate understanding. As is clear from the other Commentators, Simplicius' comments are in answer to the *aporia* 'Why did Aristotle say "of things which are said in accordance with *no* combination" (*kata mêdemian sumplokên*)? Is there more than one type of combination?' Simplicius' response is affirmative: Aristotle wished to exclude from consideration not only that combination between nouns and verbs which gives rise to affirmations and denials, but also the 'potential' combination implied by prepositions and conjunctions, which require combination with other parts of speech in order to be significant.

788. Above, 43,25.

789. As we have seen (above, n. 447), the Greek verb *huei*, meaning '(it) rains' was a shortened form of *Zeus huei*, 'Zeus is sending down the rain'. Thus, argues Simplicius to say '*huei*' is to indicate a substance (*viz.* Zeus) and an activity (his sending forth of the rain), just as the statement *zô* ('I live') indicates both a substance ('I') and an activity (living). Cf. Porph. *In Cat.* 87,38-40.

790. The verb *aikizomai*, 'to assault, damage, torture' is chosen here not because of its meaning, but as an example of verbs in the middle voice (*ta mesa rhêmata*).

791. Greek *boreas* meant both 'the north wind' and 'the North'.

792. cf. Porph. *In Cat.* 87,3-5; Boethius *In Cat.* 181C.

793. Presumably, what Simplicius means is that although homonyms, synonyms and paronyms involve and are defined by their relation to at least two kinds of thing (*viz.* name and reality), since the things they relate to are not *complete* categories, they are still to be considered as simple/not in combination.

794. On *huposunthetai* words, see above, n. 147.

795. Arist. *Cat.* 2, 1a16-17.

796. cf. Ps.-Archytas, above, 68,25. The numbers ten and four play an important role in Pythagoreanism and early Academic doctrine (cf. e.g. K. Gaiser 1968², 110ff.); and in late Neoplatonism (cf. Gersh *op. cit.* 98) − in exegesis of an Orphic fragment (no. 315 Kern), it was determined that the Forms were four in number at one level of the spiritual world, and ten at another − and in the Gnosticism of Ptolemy, Marcus, and the Valentinians (cf. B. Layton, *The Gnostic Scriptures* [New York 1987], 138, 225, 302).

797. On the fourfold combination, cf. above, 44,1ff.

798. Arist. *Cat.* 5, 2a13-14.

799. It makes no difference whether I say 'man' or 'one man': both are simple entities and are subsumed under the category of Substance. Likewise, both singular and plural 'man' are simple and fall under the same category, as do both universal and particular 'man'; for singular and plural, universal and particular are present in all the categories.

800. *Cat.* 4, 2a4-6.

801. The syllogism thus runs as follows: (i) 'Being true' and 'being false' are not properties of simple words; but (ii) 'being true' and 'being false' *are* properties of declaratory statements. Therefore (iii) simple words are not identical with declaratory statements. Cf. Aristotle *De Interp.* 4, 17a2ff.

802. On the rhetorical figure of 'assertion and denial' ['not x (*arsis*), but y (*thesis*)'], cf. e.g. Hermogenes *On Types of Style* I,11,394ff. (= trans. C.W. Wooten 1987, 52), with the commentary *ad loc.* of Syrianus 62,11-16 in Rabe's edition (Leipzig 1892). As Philoponus remarks (*In Cat.* 52,13f.), 'not in a substrate' is an *arsis*; 'in a substrate' a *thesis*; cf. Sextus Empiricus *Outlines of Pyrrhonism* 1,192.

803. cf. Aristotle *De Interp.* 7, 17a38-18a12.

804. Most of the following *aporiai* can be found in Plotinus *Ennead* VI,1,1,19-30. Cf. P. Moraux 1984, 542-3. P. Henry 1987, 123ff. believes the passage is a sample of Plotinus' oral teaching as noted down by Porphyry; but it is likely that transmission via Porphyry's *Ad Gedalium* and (probably) Iamblichus' *Commentary on the Cat.* is enough to explain the differences between Simplicius' text and that of the *Enneads*.

805. i.e. sensibles and intelligibles will have the same name, and the same *logos*; cf. Arist. *Cat.* 1, 1a6-12.

806. For Aristotle, there can be no genus or universal among entities standing towards each other in a relation of prior to posterior; cf. above n. 711.

807. cf. Dexippus *In Cat.* 40,14-18; Simplicius 76,13-17.

808. More, that is, than the ten enumerated by the Peripatetics; cf. Plotinus *Ennead* VI,1,1,25; Dex. *In Cat.* 42,13. P. Henry 1987, 137-8, 141.

809. cf. Plotinus *Ennead* VI,3,5,6-7.

810. cf. Arist. *EN* 1.4, 1096a21-3.

811. cf. Dex. *In Cat.* 40,19-21.

812. This passage presupposes the theory − probably Porphyrian − of the imposition of names (*thesis onomatôn*). At the dawn of history, human beings got together and imposed names first on sensible objects such as 'man', 'rock', and 'white'; this was the first imposition. Subsequently, they considered the names so imposed and divided them into nouns, verbs and the other grammatical categories. Aristotle's *Cat.* deals with first of these two impositions; cf. Porph. *In Cat.* 57,18-35; Boethius *In Cat.* 159A7-160A3.

813. Those philosophers who have been able to contemplate the Forms realized they could not express them directly in human language. They therefore made slight alterations in language to designate the Forms: in the case of the Form of man, for instance, they altered the word 'man' (*anthrôpos*) to 'humanness' (*anthropôtês*) or 'man-in-himself' (*autoanthrôpos*). Without taking these as actual designations of the Forms, then, true philosophers will henceforth use such coinages as ladders or stepping-stones, and by means of analogy progress from them to the noetic perception of the Forms themselves, which are beyond all names. According to Proclus (*In Tim.* I,33,7ff.) it was above all the Pythagoreans 'who tracked down the similarities of true beings by means of analogies, and passed from images (*eikones*) to models (*paradeigmata*)'; cf. Proclus *In Tim.* I,432,22f.

814. *dianoêtê*. Late Neoplatonism made a tripartite division of reality, into sensibles, intelligibles, and 'discursives' (*dianoêta*). The latter, intermediate between sensibles and intelligibles, corresponded to mathematical entities – and to forms engaged in matter, according to Proclus (*In Parm.* 1057,27) – and the human reasoning faculty (*dianoia*) which perceived them. This concept can be traced to Plato's allegory of the Divided Line: cf. Iamblichus *On Common Mathematical Knowledge* 8,1-94, 32,8ff. Festa; Proclus *Elements of Theology* Proposition 123, 108,33-110,1 Dodds, etc.

815. i.e. the intelligibles.

816. The threefold division of substance is frequently mentioned by Aristotle; cf. *Metaph.* 7.3, 1029a2-3; 8.1, 1042a26-31, etc.

817. Kalbfleisch indicates a lacuna here. The missing text must have explained that Aristotle here is speaking of composite (*sunthetos*) substance, perhaps adding a justification of Aristotle's choice.

818. *aph' henos kai pros hen*, or 'focal homonymity'. Cf. above, 32,12ff.; 62,4ff. with notes.

Bibliography

Ballériaux, O., 1989, 'Thémistius et l'exégèse de la noétique aristotélicienne', *Revue de philosophie ancienne* 7 (1989), 199-233.

────── 1994, 'Thémistius et le néoplatonisme. *Le nous pathêtikos* et l'immortalité de l'âme', *Revue de philosophie ancienne* 12 (1994), 171-200.

────── 1996, 'Eugénios, père de Thémistios et philosophe néoplatonicien', *L'Antiquité classique* 65 (1996), 135-60.

Baeumker, C., 1890, *Das Problem der Materie in der Griechischen Philosophie, eine historisch-kritische Untersuchung* (repr. Frankfurt: Minerva GMBH, 1963).

Beutler, R., 1953, 'Porphyrios', *RE* XXII, 1, cols 275-313.

Bidez, J., 1913, *Vie de Porphyre, le philosophe néo-platonicien, avec les fragments des traités 'Peri Agalmatôn' et 'De Regressu Animae'*, Gand (repr. Hildesheim: Georg Olms Verlagsbuchhandlung, 1964).

Blumenthal, H.J., 1979, 'Photius on Themistius (Cod. 74.): did Themistius write commentaries on Aristotle?' *Hermes* 107, 168-82.

────── 1979, 'Themistius, the last Peripatetic commentator on Aristotle?' in *Arktouros: Hellenic Studies Presented to Bernard M.W. Knox on the Occasion of his 65th Birthday*, Berlin 1979 = R. Sorabji, ed., 1990, ch. 5, 113-23.

Brisson *et al.* 1982 = Brisson, L., Goulet-Cazé, M.-O., Goulet, R. and O'Brien, D., *Porphyre, La Vie de Plotin, I. Travaux préliminaires et index grec complet* (= Histoire des doctrines de l'antiquité classique 6), Paris: Vrin.

────── *et al.* 1992, = Brisson, L., Cherlonneix, J.-L., Goulet-Cazé, M.-O., Goulet, R., Grmek, M.D., Flamand, J.-M., Matton, S., O'Brien, D., Pépin, J., Saffrey, H.D., Segonds, A.-Ph., Tardieu, M. and Thillet, P., *Porphyre, La Vie de Plotin, II. Études d'introduction*, texte grec et traduction française, commentaire, notes complémentaires, bibliographie (= Histoire des doctrines de l'antiquité classique 16), Paris: Vrin.

Burkert, W., 1962, *Weisheit und Wissenschaft – Studien zu Pythagoras, Philolaos und Platon* (= Erlanger Beiträge zur Sprach- und Kunstwissenschaft, 10).

────── 1972, [Eng. translation], *Lore and Science in Ancient Pythagoreanism*, Cambridge, Mass.: Harvard University Press.

Cardullo, R.L., 1995, *Siriano, esegeta di Aristotele: introduzione, testo, traduzione, note e commento* (= Symbolon, Universita di Catania, Dipartimento di studi antichi e tardoantichi, 14), Firenze: La nuova Italia.

Corrigan, K., and O' Cleirigh, P., 1986, 'The course of Plotinian scholarship from 1971 to 1986', *ANRW* II.36.1, 571-623.

Dalsgaard Larsen, B., 1972, *Jamblique de Chalcis, exégète et philosophe*, thèse présentée par B.D.L., 2 vols, Aarhus: Universitetsforlaget.

Dillon, J., 1973, *Iamblichi Chalcidensis in Platonis dialogos commentariorum fragmenta*, edited with translation and commentary. (= Philosophia Antiqua 23), Leiden: E.J. Brill.

—— 1977, *The Middle Platonists*, London: Duckworth (repr. with a new Afterword, 1996).

—— 1987, 'Iamblichus of Chalcis (*c.* 240-325 AD)' in W. Haase, ed., *ANRW* II.36.2, Berlin, 862-909.

—— 1997, 'Iamblichus' *Noera theôria* of Aristotle's Categories', *Syllecta Classica* 8, 65-77.

Dörrie, H., 1959, *Porphyrios' 'Symmikta Zetemata'. Ihre Stellung in System und Geschichte des Neuplatonismus nebst einem Kommentar zu den Fragmenten* (= Zetemata Heft 20), München.

Düring, I., 1957, *Aristotle in the Ancient Biographical Tradition* (= Acta Universitatis Gothoburgensis, Göteborgs Universitets Årsskrift 63, 2, Studia Graeca et Latina Gothoburgensia 5), Göteborg.

Ebbesen, S., 1981, *Commentators and Commentaries on Aristotle's Sophistici Elenchi*, 3 vols (= *CLCAG* 7.1-3), Leiden: E.J. Brill.

—— 1987, 'Boethius as an Aristotelian scholar', in J. Wiesner, ed., 1987, 286-311.

—— 1990, 'Porphyry's legacy to logic: a reconstruction', in Sorabji, ed., 1990, 141-71 (= *CLCAG* vol. 7 part 1, 133-70).

Erler, M., 1987, 'Interpretieren als Gottesdienst. Proklos' Hymnen vor dem Hintergrund seines Kratylos-Kommentars', in G. Boss and G. Seel, eds, *Proclus et son influence* (Zürich), 179-217.

Evangeliou, C., 1988, *Aristotle's Categories and Porphyry* (= Philosophia Antiqua vol. XLVIII), Leiden/New York/Copenhagen/Cologne: E.J. Brill.

Festugière, A.-J., 1971, 'L'ordre de lecture des dialogues de Platon aux Ve/VIe siècles', *Études de philosophie grecque*, Paris: Vrin.

Fortenbaugh, W.W. et al., eds, 1992, *Theophrastus of Eresus: Sources for his Life, Writings, Thought, and Influence*, 2 vols (= Philosophia Antiqua LIV 1-2), Leiden/New York/Cologne: E.J. Brill.

Foulkes, P., 1992, 'Where was Simplicius?', *Journal of Hellenic Studies* 112, 143.

Gaiser, K., 1963, *Platons ungeschriebene Lehre: Studien zur systematischen und geschichtlichen Begründung der Wissenschaften in der Platonischen Schule*, Stuttgart: Ernst Klett Verlag, repr. 1968.

Gätje, H., 1982, 'Simplikios in der arabischen Überlieferung', *Der Islam*, 59.

Gersh, S., 1978, *From Iamblichus to Eriugena*, Leiden: E.J. Brill.

Glucker, J., 1978, *Antiochus and the Late Academy* (= Hypomnemata Heft 56), Göttingen: Vandenhoek & Ruprecht.

Goldschmidt, V., 1977, *Le Système stoïcien et l'idée de temps*[3], Paris (1st ed. 1953).

Gottschalk, H.B., 1987, 'Aristotelian philosophy in the Roman world from the time of Cicero to the end of the second century AD', *ANRW* II.36.2, 1079-174; 1089-112; 1150-1. Reprinted in R. Sorabji, ed., 1990, 55-81.

Gutas, D. 1999. 'The Alexandria to Baghdad complex of narratives', *Documenti e Studi sulla Tradizione Filosofica Medievale* 10, 155-93.

Goulet-Cazé, M.-O., 1986, *L'ascèse cynique: un commentaire de Diogène Laërce, VI, 70-71*, Paris.

———— 1990, 'Le cynisme à l'époque impériale', *ANRW* II.36.4, 2720-833.

Hadot, I., 1969a, *Seneca und die griechisch-römische Tradition der Seelenleitung*, Berlin.

———— 1969b, 'Épicure et l'enseignement philosophique hellénistique et romain', *Actes du VIIIe Congrès de l'Association Guillaume Budé*, Paris 1969, 347-53.

———— 1978, *Le Problème du néoplatonisme alexandrin*, Paris.

———— 1986, 'The spiritual guide', in A.H. Armstrong, ed., *Classical Mediterranean Spirituality, Egyptian, Greek, Roman*, New York: Crossroad, 436-59.

———— ed., 1987a, *Simplicius: sa vie, son oeuvre, sa survie*. Actes du Colloque international de Paris (28 Sept. – 1 Oct. 1985), organisé par le Centre de Recherches sur les Oeuvres et la Pensée de Simplicius (RCP 739 – CNRS) (= Peripatoi Band 15), Berlin/New York: Walter de Gruyter, 1987.

———— 1987b, 'La vie et l'œuvre de Simplicius d'après des sources grecques et arabes', in 1987a, 3-39.

———— 1987c, 'La division néoplatonicienne des écrits d'Aristote', in J. Wiesner, ed., *Aristoteles Werk und Wirkung, Paul Moraux gewidmet. Zweiter Band: Kommentierung, Überlieferung, Nachleben*, Berlin/New York: Walter de Gruyter, 1987, 249-85.

———— 1987d, 'Les introductions aux commentaires exégétiques chez les auteurs néoplatoniciens et les auteurs chrétiens', in M. Tardieu, ed., 1987, 99-122.

———— 1990, *Simplicius, Commentaire sur les Catégories*, traduction commentée sous la direction de Ilsetraut Hadot, Directeur de Recherche au CNRS, fasc. I: Introduction, première partie (1-9,3 Kalbfleisch, traduction de Ph. Hoffmann (avec la collaboration de I. et P. Hadot), commentaire et notes à la traduction par I. Hadot avec des appendices de P. Hadot et J.-P. Mahé (= Philosophia Antiqua vol. L), Leiden/New York/Copenhagen/Cologne: E.J. Brill.

———— 1991, 'The role of the commentators on Aristotle in the teaching of philosophy according to the prefaces of the Neoplatonic commentaries on the *Categories*', in H.J. Blumenthal and H. Robinson, eds, *Aristotle in the Later Tradition* (= *Oxford Studies in Ancient Philosophy*, suppl. vol. 1991), Oxford, 175-89.

———— 1992, 'Aristote dans l'enseignement philosophique néoplatonicien,' *Revue de Théologie et de Philosophie*, 124, 407-425.

———— 1996, *Simplicius, Commentaire sur le Manuel d'Épictète*. Introduction et édition critique par Ilsetraut Hadot (= Philosophia antiqua vol. LXVI), Leiden/New York/Köln: E.J. Brill.

Hadot, P., 1954, 'Cancellatus respectus. L'usage du chiasme en logique', *Archivum Latinitatis Medii Aevi* (Bulletin du Cange) 24, 277-82.

———— 1966, 'La métaphysique de Porphyre', *Entretiens Hardt sur l'antiquité classique* XII), Vandoeuvres-Genève 1966, 127-63 = 1999, 317-53.

———— 1968, *Porphyre et Victorinus*, 2 vols, Paris: Études Augustiniennes.

———— 1974, 'L'harmonie des philosophies de Plotin et d'Aristote selon Porphyre dans le commentaire de Dexippe sur les *Catégories*', in *Plotino e il Neoplaton-*

ismo in Oriente e in Occidente (= Problemi attuali di scienza e di cultura 198), Rome: Accademia Nazionale dei Lincei Anno CCCLXXI, 31-47, repr. in id., 1999, 355-82, and in English translation in R. Sorabji, ed., 1990.

———— 1980, 'Sur divers sens du mot *PRAGMA* dans la tradition philosophique grecque', in P. Aubenque, ed., *Concepts et catégories dans la pensée antique*, Paris: Vrin, 309-19.

———— 1993, *Plotinus or the Simplicity of Vision* (translated by Michael Chase), Chicago: University of Chicago Press.

———— 1995, *Philosophy as a Way of Life* (translated by Michael Chase), Oxford: Blackwell.

Happ, H., 1971, *Hyle: Studien zum aristotelischen Materie-Begriff*, Berlin/New York: Walter de Gruyter.

Henry, P., 1987, 'Apories orales de Plotin sur les *Catégories* d'Aristote', in J. Wiesner, ed., 120-56.

Hijmans, B.-L, Jr., 1975, 'Athenodorus on the Categories and a pun on Athenodorus', in *Kephalaion: Studies in Greek Philosophy and its Continuation offered to C.J. de Vogel* (= Philosophical Texts and Studies 23), Assen, 105-14.

Hoffmann, P., 1980, 'Jamblique exégète du Pythagoricien Archytas: trois originalités d'une doctrine du temps', *Les Études Philosophiques*, 307-23.

———— 1984-85 'Sens et dénomination. Homonymie, analogie, métaphore selon le commentaire de Simplicius sur les Catégories d'Aristote', *AEPHE* 93, 343-56.

———— 1987a, 'Catégories et langage selon Simplicius – la question du 'skopos' du traité aristotélicien des Catégories', in I. Hadot, ed., 1987a, 61-90.

———— 1987b, 'Sur quelques aspects de la polémique de Simplicius contre Jean Philopon: De l'invective à la réaffirmation de la transcendance du ciel', in I. Hadot, ed., 1987b, 183-221.

———— 1992-3, 'Sur la doctrine néoplatonicienne des Universaux', in *Théologies et mystiques de la Grèce hellénistique et de la fin de l'Antiquité*, *AEPHE, Ve section* 101, 241-5.

———— 1994, 'Damascius', in R. Goulet, ed., *Dictionnaire des philosophes antiques*, vol. 2, Paris, 541-93.

———— 1999, 'Les analyses de l'énoncé: catégories et parties du discours selon les commentateurs néoplatoniciens', in Ph. Büttgen, S. Diebler, M. Rashed, eds, *Théories de la phrase et de la proposition, de Platon à Averroès* (coll. Études de littérature ancienne, 10), Paris: Éditions rue d'Ulm, 209-48.

Isnardi Parente, M., 1982, *Senocrate-Ermodoro, Frammenti* (= La Scuola di Platone, vol. 3), Napoli: Bibliopolis.

Kustas, G.L., 1973, *Studies in Byzantine Rhetoric*, Thessalonica.

Lallot, J., 1989, *La grammaire de Denys le Thrace*, Paris.

Lameer, J., 1997, 'From Alexandria to Baghdad: reflections on the genesis of a problematical tradition', in G. Endress and R. Kruk, eds, *The Ancient Tradition in Christian and Islamic Hellenism* (Leiden: Research School CNWS), 181-91.

de Libera, A., 1996, *La Querelle des universaux. De Platon à la fin du Moyen Âge*, Paris: Seuil.

———— 1999, *L'Art des généralités, théories de l'abstraction*, Paris.

Lloyd, A.C., 1971, 'Neoplatonists' account of predication', in *Le Néoplatonisme*, Paris.

——— 1990, *The Anatomy of Neoplatonism*, Oxford: Clarendon Press.

Long, A.A. and Sedley, D.N., 1987, *The Hellenistic Philosophers*, vol. 1: Translations of the principal sources, with philosophical commentary; vol. 2: Greek and Latin texts with notes and bibliography, Cambridge: Cambridge University Press (repr. 1988).

Luna, C., 1990, *Simplicius, Commentaire sur les Catégories*, traduction commentée sous la direction d'Ilsetraut Hadot, Directeur de Recherche au CNRS, fasc. III: Préambule aux *Catégories*. Commentaire au premier chapitre des *Catégories* (p. 21-40,13 Kalbfleisch), traduction de Ph. Hoffmann (avec la colloboration d'I. Hadot, P. Hadot et C. Luna, commentaire et notes à la traduction par C. Luna [= Philosophia Antiqua vol. LI], Leiden/New York/Copenhagen/Cologne: E.J. Brill.

——— 2001, Review of R. Thiel, 1999, *Simplikios und das Ende der Neuplatonischen Schule*, *Mnemosyne* 54-4, 482-504.

Lynch, J.P., 1972, *Aristotle's School*, Berkeley/Los Angeles/London: University of California Press.

Moraux, P., 1951, *Les Listes anciennes des ouvrages d'Aristote*, Louvain.

——— 1973, *Der Aristotelismus bei den Griechen von Andronikos bis Alexander von Aphrodisias*. Erster Band: Die Renaissance des Aristotelismus im 1. Jh. v. Chr. (= Peripatoi 5), Berlin/New York: Walter de Gruyter.

——— 1984, *Der Aristotelismus bei den Griechen von Andronikos bis Alexander von Aphrodisias*, Zweiter Band: Der Aristotelismus im I. und II. Jh. n. Chr. (= Peripatoi 6), Berlin/New York: Walter de Gruyter.

Müller, C.W., 1969, 'Die neuplatonischen Aristoteleskommentatoren über die Ursachen der Pseudepigraphie', *Rheinisches Museum* 112, 120-6.

O'Meara, D.J., 1989, *Pythagoras Revived: Mathematics and Philosophy in Late Antiquity*, Oxford: Clarendon Press.

Owens, J., 1951, *The Doctrine of Being in the Aristotelian Metaphysics*, Toronto: Pontifical Institute of Mediaeval Studies, 1963[2], 1978[3].

Pelletier, A., 1984, 'De la culture sémitique à la culture hellénique: rencontre, affrontement, pénétration', *Revue des études grecques* 97, 404-5.

Pépin, J., 1964, *Théologie cosmique et théologie chrétienne*, Paris.

——— 1974, '*MERIKÔTERON – EPOPTIKÔTERON* – Proclus en *In Tim.* I, 204,24-7. Deux attitudes exégétiques dans le néoplatonisme', *Mélanges d'histoire des religions offerts à H.-C. Puech*, Paris, 323-30.

——— 1980, 'Clément d'Alexandrie, les *Catégories* d'Aristote et le fragment 60 d'Héraclite', in P. Aubenque, ed., *Concepts et Catégories dans la pensée antique*, Paris, 271-84.

Peters, F.E., 1968, *Aristoteles Arabus*, Leiden.

Pohlenz, M., 1984[6], *Die Stoa*, 2 vols, Göttingen.

Praechter, K., 'Richtungen und Schulen im Neuplatonismus', *Genethliakon für Carl Robert*, Berlin, 1911, 105-56 (= 1973, 165-216).

——— 1912, 'Christlich-neuplatonische Beziehungen', *Byzantinische Zeitschrift* 21, 1-27.

——— 1922, 'Nikostratos der Platoniker', *Hermes* 57, 481-517 (= 1973, 101-37).

—— 1973, *Kleine Schriften*, herausgegeben von Heinrich Dörrie (= Collectanea 7), Hildesheim/New York: Georg Olms Verlag.

Prantl, K., 1855-67, *Geschichte der Logik im Abendlande*, I, 1855, II, 1861, 1885², III, 1867, Leipzig: S. Hirzel, reprinted Graz: Akademische Druck-U. Verlaganstalt, 1955.

Rahner, H., 'Die seelenheilende Blume. Moly und Mandragore in antiker und christlicher Symbolik', *Eranos-Jahrbuch* 12 (1945), 117-239.

Rieth, O., 1933, *Grundbegriffe der stoischen Ethik. Eine traditionsgeschichtliche Untersuchung* (= Problemata 9), Berlin.

Robert, L., 1937, *Études anatoliennes*, Paris.

Robin, L., 1908, *La Théorie platonicienne des idées et des nombres d'après Aristote*, Étude historique et critique, thèse Paris: Félix Alcan, repr. Hildesheim: Georg Olms Verlag, 1984.

Rutten, Chr., 1961, *Les Catégories du monde sensible dans les Ennéades de Plotin* (= Bibliothèque de la Faculté de Philosophie et Lettres de l'Université de Liège, fasc. 160), Paris: Les Belles Lettres.

Saffrey, H.D., 1990, *Recherches sur le néoplatonisme après Plotin* (= Histoire des doctrines de l'antiquité classique 14), Paris: Vrin.

Sharples, R.W., 1987, 'Alexander of Aphrodisias: scholasticism and innovation', *ANRW* II.36.2, 1176-243.

Sheppard, A.D.R., 1980, *Studies on the 5th and 6th Essays of Proclus' Commentary on the Republic* (= Hypomnemata 61), Göttingen: Vandenhoeck & Ruprecht.

—— 1987, 'Proclus' philosophical method of exegesis: the use of Aristotle and the Stoics in the commentary on the Cratylus', in J. Pépin and H.D. Saffrey, eds, *Proclus: lecteur et interprète des anciens* (= Actes du Colloque sur Proclus, organisé par le CNRS à Paris au mois d'octobre 1985), Paris: Presses du CNRS, 137-51.

Smith, Andrew, *Porphyrii Philosophi Fragmenta*, Leipzig/Stuttgart: Teubner, 1993.

Sorabji, R.R.K., ed., 1987, *Philoponus and the Rejection of Aristotelian Science*, London/Ithaca NY: Duckworth/Cornell University Press.

—— 1990a, *Aristotle Transformed: The Ancient Commentators and their Influence*, London/Ithaca NY: Duckworth/Cornell University Press.

—— 1990b, 'The Ancient Commentators on Aristotle', in Sorabji 1990a, 1-30.

—— (forthcoming.) 'Magical names and the fate of the Alexandrian Neoplatonist School', in Andrew Smith, ed., *Proceedings of the conference on Neoplatonism and Society*, Dublin.

Strange, S.K., 1987, 'Plotinus, Porphyry, and the Neoplatonic interpretation of the "Categories" ', *ANRW* II.36.2, 955-74.

Szlezák, T.A., 1972, *Pseudo-Archytas über die Kategorien. Texte zur griechischen Aristoteles-Exegese*, herausgegeben, übersetzt und kommentiert (= Peripatoi 4), Berlin/New York: Walter de Gruyter, 1972.

Tarán, L., 1981, *Speusippus of Athens: A Critical Study with a Collection of the Related Texts and Commentary* (= Philosophia Antiqua vol. XXXIX), Leiden: E.J. Brill.

Tardieu, M., 1986, 'Sabiens coraniques et "Sabiens" de Harran', *Journal Asiatique* CCLXXIV, 1-44.

————— 1987, 'Les calendriers en usage à Harran d'après les sources arabes et le commentaire de Simplicus à la *Physique* d'Aristote', in I. Hadot, ed., 1987a, 40-57.

————— 1987, ed., *Les Règles de l'interprétation* (Centre d'études des religions du livre; patrimoines, religions du livre), Paris: Cerf.

————— 1991, *Les Paysages reliques: routes et haltes syriennes d'Isidore à Simplicius* (= Bibliothèque de l'École des hautes études. Sciences religieuses, vol. 154), Louvain/Paris: Peeters.

Theiler, W., 1930, *Die Vorbereitung des Neuplatonismus*, Berlin.

Thesleff, H., 1965, *The Pythagorean Texts of the Hellenistic Period* (= Acta Academiae Aboensis, Ser. A: Humaniora. Humanistika-Vetenskaper, Social-vetenskaper, Teologi, 30, 1), Åbo.

Todd, Robert B., tr., 1996, *Themistius: On Aristotle On the Soul* (The Ancient Commentators on Aristotle), London/Ithaca NY: Duckworth/Cornell University Press.

van Riet, S., 1991, 'A propos de la biographie de Simplicius', *Revue philosophique de Louvain* 89.

Wehrli, F., 1955-69, *Die Schule des Aristoteles: Texte und Kommentar* (10 vols) Basel/Stuttgart: Benno Schwabe & Co.

Westerink, L.G., 1990, 'Introduction', *Prolégomènes à la philosophie de Platon*, texte établi par L.G. Westerink et traduit par J. Trouillard, avec la collaboration de A.Ph. Segonds, Paris: Les Belles Lettres, vii-xcix.

Wiesner, J., ed., 1987, *Aristoteles Werk und Wirkung, Paul Moraux gewidmet. Zweiter Band: Kommentierung, Überlieferung, Nachleben*, Berlin/New York: Walter de Gruyter.

Wurm, K., 1973, *Substanz und Qualität: ein Beitrag zur Interpretation der Plotinischen Traktate VI.1-3* (= Quellen und Studien zur Philosophie 5; diss. phil. Münster 1969), Berlin.

English-Greek Glossary

abstract: *exaireô*
abstraction: *aphairesis*
accident: *sumbebêkos*
accomplish: *draô*
accomplish: *sumperainô*
accord: *sumphônia*
account: *apodosis, logos*
acquainted with, be: *sungignomai*
acquired: *epiktêtos*
active, be: *energeô*
activity: *energeia*
actual, the: *energeiâi*
actuality: *entelekheia*
add: *prostithêmi*
added, be: *proskeimai*
address: *agoreuô, prosphôneô*
adduce: *pherô*
adjacent/next to, be: *parakeimai*
admirable: *thaumasios*
admit: *homologeô*
adorn: *kosmeô*
advance reservation: *prokatalêpsis*
affect: *pathos*
affirmation: *kataphasis*
affirmative: *kataphatikos,*
    kataphatikon
agree: *sunomologeô*
agreement, be in: *sumphôneô*
akin: *sungenês*
alter slightly: *hupallattô, parenklinô*
alter: *alloioô*
alteration: *alloiôsis*
analogy: *analogia*
analyse: *analuô*
analysis: *analusis*
ancestral: *progonikos*
ancient: *palaios, presbus*
anhomoeomerous: *anomoiomerês*
animate: *empsukhos*

appear: *phainomai*
appellation: *prosêgoria*
apply: *prosagô*
apprehension: *antilêpsis*
appropriate, be: *prosêkô*
appropriate: *oikeios*
architect: *oikodomos*
argue: *epikheireô*
argument: *epikheirêma*
art: *tekhnê, tekhnai* (pl.)
article: *arthron*
articulate: *diarthroô*
articulation: *diarthrôsis*
assimilate oneself: *exomoioô*
associate with: *homileô*
assume the appearance of:
    hupoduomai
at random: *sumpephorêmenos*
attribute: *apodidômi, paradidômi*
autonomous: *autokratês*
awestruck, be: *sebomai*
axiom (geometrical): *axiôma*

bad things: *ta kaka*
bare: *psilos*
beautiful: *kalos*
become: *kathistêmi*
being: *einai, on,* (pl.) *onta*
believe: *dokeô*
belong: *huparkhô*
belonging: *huparxis*
bewitched, be: *thelgomai*
blame: *memphomai*
blessed: *olbios*
body: *sôma*
bond: *desmos*
boundary: *horos*
bring forth: *propherô*
bring forward: *proagô*

bring round: *periagô*
bring together: *sunagô*
bronze: *khalkos*
brought about, be: *perigignomai*

calculation: *logismos*
call on as a witness: *marturomai*
call: *kaleô, prosagoreuô*
capable of, be: *sunoida*
carnivorous: *sarkophagos*
case: *ptôsis*
cast down: *hupoballô*
cause: *aition*
celestial: *ouranios*
chain: *seira*
change (n.): *metabolê*
change (v.): *methistêmi, paralassô*
change in form: *paraskhêmatizô*
character: *êthos, kharaktêr*
characteristic particularity: *idiôma*
characteristic property: *idiotês*
choose: *haireô*
citizen: *politês*
clarify: *saphênizô*
clarity: *saphêneia*
classify: *diatattomai*
close to hand: *prokheiros*
coincide: *suntrekhô*
co-indicate: *prosdêloô*
cold: *psukhros*
coldness: *psukhrotês*
colour: *khroa, khrôma*
colour (v.): *khrôzô*
colourless: *akhroos*
column: *kiôn*
combination: *sumplokê*
combine: *sumplekô*
come to be within: *enginomai*
come to light: *prophainô*
commensurate: *summetros*
commentator: *exêgêtês*
common, make: *koinoô*
common: *koinos*
commonality: *koinônia, koinotês*
commonly qualified thing: *koinôs
     poion*
compact: *sustrephô*
comparative: *sunkritikos*
complete (adj.): *autotelês, entelês*
complete (v.): *sumplêroô*
completing: *sumplêrôtikos*
composed, be: *sunkeimai*
composite: *sunthetos*

composition: *sungramma, suntaxis,
     sunthesis*
compound: *sumpeplegmenos,
     sunkrima*
comprehension: *katalêpsis,
     katanoêsis, perilêpsis*
comprehensive: *perilêptikos*
conceive (of): *ennoeô, epinoeô*
concentrate: *suspeiraô*
concentration: *sunairesis*
concept: *ennoia, epinoia*
concern: *spoudê*
concise: *suntomos*
concision: *suntomia*
conclude by syllogism: *sullogizomai*
conclusion: *sumperasma*
concourse: *sundromê*
concur: *epipsêphizô*
condemn: *katêgoreô*
condensed: *sunestrammenos*
condition: *sustasis*
confidence: *pistis*
configuration: *skhêmatismos*
confirmed, to be: *pistoomai*
confuse: *sunkheô*
confused: *adiarthrôtos*
confusion: *sunkhusis*
conjoined: *suzugos*
conjunction: *sundesmos, suntukhia*
connatural: *sumphutos*
connective: *sumplektikos*
consequent upon, be: *sunakoloutheô*
consider: *hêgeomai, nomizô, theôreô*
consist of, constitute: *sunistêmi*
constitutive: *sustatikos*
constraining force: *anankastikon*
contemplate: *theaomai*
contend against: *prosphiloneikeô*
continuity: *sunekheia*
continuous: *sunekhês*
contract: *sunaireô*
contradict: *antilegô, antiphaskô*
contradiction: *antiphasis*
contrast: *antidiastellô*
contribute: *sunteleô*
converse: *dialegomai*
convert: *epistrephô*
convertible, be: *antistrephô*
convex: *kurton*
coordinated: *katatetagmenos*
coordination: *katataxis*
co-pertain: *sunuparkhô*
copy: *apographê*

corporeal: *sômatikos*
correct: *orthos*
co-signify: *prossêmainô, sussêmainô*
count: *arithmeô*
count: *katarithmeô*
counter-argument: *enantiologia*
country: *patris*
coupled with, be: *sunduazomai*
coupling: *suzugia*
create within: *empoieô*
criterion: *kritêrion*
curved line: *korônis*
customary: *sunêthês*
cut: *temnô*
cutting/being cut: *temnesthai*

deficiency: *elleipsis*
define: *aphorizô, horizô*
definition: *diorismos, horismos,*
  horos, logos
demonstrate: *apodeiknumi,*
  deiknumi, epideiknumi
demonstration: *apodeixis, paradeixis*
demonstrative: *apodeiktikos*
density: *puknotês*
depend upon: *artaô, exartaô*
derivative form: *enklisis*
derivative: *paragôgon*
describe: *hupographô*
description: *hupographê*
desire (v.): *potheô, epithumeô*
destruction: *phthora*
detached, be: *apartaomai*
develop: *diexodeuô*
development: *diexodos*
diagonal: *diagônios*
dialectical: *dialektikos*
dialectics: *dialektikê*
dialogue: *dialogos*
differ: *diapherô, parallattô*
differentia: *diaphora*
differentiated, be: *diaphoreomai*
differentiation: *diastolê*
diminution: *meiôsis*
discovery: *heuresis*
discrete: *diôrismenos*
disdain (v.): *kataphroneô*
disperse together: *sundiaphoreô*
disperse: *diaspaô*
disposed, be: *diakeimai*
disposition: *diathesis*
dissimilar: *anomoios*
distinction, make a: *diastellô*

distinction: *diakrisis*
distinguish: *diakrinô, diistêmi,*
  diorizô
distinguished: *ellogimos*
distinguishing (adj.): *diakritikos*
divide: *diaireô*
divine: *theios*
divisible: *diairetos*
division, make a: *diatemnô*
division: *diairesis*
do, make: *poiein*
doctrine: *dogma, mathêma*
drug: *pharmakon*
dyad: *duas*

element: *stoikheion*
elementary teaching: *sullogê*
elementary: *stoikheiôdês*
emend: *metagraphô*
encounter: *entunkhanô*
encourage: *paramutheomai*
encouragement: *paramuthia*
ending: *katalêxis*
endow with form: *eidopoieô*
engage in: *pragmateuomai*
engaged in matter: *enulos*
enter into: *epeiseimi*
entirely: *pantei, pantodapôs, pantôs*
entitle: *epigraphô*
enumeration: *diarithmêsis*
enunciate: *ekphôneô*
epistemological: *gnôstikos*
equivalent, be: *exisazô*
essence: *ti ên einai*
essential: *ousiôdês*
establish: *hidruô*
establishment: *hidrusis, kataskeuê*
ethical: *êthikos*
etymology: *etumologia*
even/odd: *artioperissos*
even: *artios*
evidence: *tekmêrion*
exact, be: *akribologeomai*
exact: *akribês*
examine: *episkeptomai, skopeô*
example: *hupodeigma, paradeigma*
exceed: *huperballô, huperekhô*
excess: *huperbolê*
exchange: *anatallagê*
exegesis, carry out an: *exêgeomai*
exhaustive: *aparaleiptos*
exhortation: *parainesis*
exist: *huphistêmi*

impose [a name]: *epitithêmi*
impossible: *adunatos*
impression: *phantasia*
in conformity with correct opinion:
    orthodoxastikôs
in serial fashion: *kata seiran*
in summary form: *en kephalaiois*
inaccessible: *abatos*
incense: *thumiama*
include together with:
    sumperilambanô
include: *perilambanô*
incorporeal: *asômatos*
indeclinable: *monoptôtos*
indefinite: *aoristos*
indefinitely quantified: *aprosdioristos*
indefiniteness: *aoristia*
indicate: *hupodeiknumi*
indicative of: *dêlôtikos*
indifferent: *adiaphoros*
individual: *atomos, idios*
individualizing quality: *idiôs poion*
indivisible: *ameristos*
induction: *epagôgê*
ineffable: *aporrêtos*
infallible: *aptaistos*
infinite: *apeiros*
infinity: *apeiria*
inhere: *enuparkhô*
innate by nature: *autophuês*
inquiry: *skemma*
instruct: *prostattô*
instrument: *organon*
instrumental: *organikos*
intellect: *nous*
intellection: *noêsis*
intellective power: *dunamis noera*
intellective: *noeros*
intelligible: *noêtos*
interconnection: *allêloukhia*
intermediary: *mesotês*
internal: *endiathetos*
interval: *diastêma*
interweaving: *epiplokê*
introduce: *eisagô, epagô*
introduction: *eisagôgê*

join forces in combatting:
    sunagônizomai
join together: *episunaptô, sunaptô*
joined together, be: *sunartaomai*

keep silent: *hêsukhazô*

kinship: *sungeneia*
know: *ginôskô*
knowledge: *gnôsis*
knowledgeable: *epistêmôn*

labours: *ponoi*
lack: *leipomai*
lacking, be: *elleipô*
lacking: *katadeês*
language: *dialektos*
lay bare: *paragumnoô*
lead: *agô*
learn: *manthanô*
lengthy: *polustikhos*
letter: *epistolê*
letter: *stoikheion*
lexical: *lektikos*
licence: *adeia*
light (adj.): *kouphos*
light (n.): *phôs*
limb: *morion*
limit (n.): *peras*
limit (v.): *perainô*
line: *grammê, stix*
linkage: *sunartêsis, suzeuxis*
logic: *logikê*
long-windedness: *makrologia*
lover of contemplation: *philotheamôn*
lover of learning: *philomathês*

magnitude: *megethos, pêlikon*
main point: *kephalaion*
maintain: *diasôizô, paraphulattô*
majesty (quality of style):
    megaloprepês
major: *meizôn*
make: *poiein*
mantle: *pharos*
manuscript: *antigraphon*
master: *despotês*
mathematician: *mathêmatikos*
matter: *hulê*
mean (adj.): *mesos*
mean (v.): *sêmainô*
meaningless expression (example of):
    'blituri'
meaningless: *asêmos*
measure: *metron*
mechanical: *mêkhanikos*
mention: *mimnêskô, mnêmoneuô*
metaphor: *metaphora*
metaphorical(ly): *kata metaphoran*
method: *methodos*

tetragon: *tetragônon*
theological: *theologikos*
theorem: *theôrêma*
things said: *legomena, ta lekta*
think over: *dianoeomai*
think: *noeô*
thorough study of, make a:
 diapragmateuomai
thought: *dianoia*
throw stones: *lithoboleô*
time: *khronos*
title: *epigraphê*
token: *gnôrisma*
touch: *haphê*
trace: *ikhnos*
transcendent: *exêirêmenos*
transcription: *paragraphê*
transfer: *metabainô, metagô*
transform: *metaballô*
transformation: *metaskhêmatismos*
transformed in order to accord, be:
 susskhêmatizomai
transition: *metabasis*
translate: *metalambanô*
transmission: *paradosis*
transmit: *paradidômi*
treatise: *pragmateia*
truth: *alêtheia*
try: *peiraomai*
two-syllable word: *disullabon*
type: *idea*

unanimity of thought: *homonoia*
unaware, be: *agnoeô*
uncombined: *asumplektos*
uncommon: *asunêthês*
uncoordinated: *akatataktos*
undemonstrated: *anapodeiktos*
undergo: *paskhô*
underlie: *hupokeimai*
understand: *akouô, exakouô, suniêmi*
undertaking: *epikheirêsis*
undifferentiated: *adiakritos*
undivided: *adiairetos*
ungraspable: *aperilêptos*
unification: *henôsis, monoeidês*

universal: *holikos, katholou*
universe: *kosmos*
unknown: *agnôstos*
unmoved: *akinêtos*
unwritten: *agraphos*
usage: *khrêsis, sunêtheia*
use in an extended/improper sense:
 katakhraô
use: *proskhraomai*
useless verbiage: *mataiologia*

variegated: *poikilos*
veil: *parapetasmos*
verb: *rhêma*
vie: *philotimeô*
view: *opsis*
virtue: *aretê*
virtuous: *spoudaios*
voice: *phônê*
void: *kenon*
vote: *psêphos*

watch closely: *paratêreô*
weight: *rhopê*
when: *pote*
where: *pou*
white: *leukos*
whiteness: *leukotês*
whither: *poi*
winged: *ptênon*
wisdom: *sophia*
without a beginning: *anarkhos*
without any change: *aparallaktôs*
without language: *aphônos*
without matter: *aülos*
without relation: *askhetos*
witness: *martus*
word: *phônê*
write down: *apographomai*
write: *graphô, paragraphô*
wrong opinion, be of the: *pseudodoxeô*

younger: *neôteros*

zealous: *prothumos*

Greek-English Index

metalambanô, translate, 27,11;
44,27
metapherô, refer to metaphorically,
32,24; 33,10
metaphora, metaphor, 33,7; *kata
metaphoran*, metaphorically,
32,20; 33,10; 57,19
metaskhêmatismos,
transformation, 37,17
metatithêmi, substitute, 1,11; 39,27
metekhô, participate, 6,30; 17,21;
30,31
meterkhomai, pursue, 74,16; 20
methexis, participation, 31,17;
37,29; 70,21-2
methistêmi, change, 50,1
methodos, method, 4,29; 5,27;
6,3.17; 45,9; *hê apodeiktikê m.*,
16,6
metokhê, participle, 25,12
metrios, moderate, 1,14
metron, measure, 65,18
mimeomai, imitate, 8,26
mimnêskô, mention, 18,9; 19,18;
41,7
mnêmoneuô, mention, 18,11; 74,6
monadikos, monadic, 55,29-30; 56,3
môlu, moly (mythical plant), 5,14
monas, monad, 32,1; 65,14
monoeidês, uniform (adj.), 4,16;
kata to monoeides, in its
uniform aspect, 22,18; 28,17
monon, only, 26,3ff.
monoptôtos, indeclinable, 25,26
monôs, exclusively, 17,19
morion, limb, 8,27
morphê, shape, 46,13; 67,35
morphôtikos, shape-giving, 46,21
mousikê, music, 37,21; 58,10
mousikos, musical, 37,19
muthos, myth, 6,30; 7,4.7
muthikos, mythical, 7,10

naiô, dwell, 32,28
neos, new; *neôteros*, younger, 36,29;
67,19
noêma, notion, 7,34; 9,32; 10,2-5;
34,6; 72,3
noeros, (of style) intellective, 2,13;
6,20; *dunamis noera*,
intellective power, 18,8-9
noêsis, intellection, 12,17; 15,9;
41,28-9

noeô, think, 41,9; 43,18
noêtos, intelligible, 65,20; *en tois
noêtois*, among the intelligibles,
66,31
nômaô, handle, 33,3
nomizô, consider, 7,3; 39,10
notheuô, reject, 18,11
nothos, spurious (of books), 8,22
nous, intellect, 3,6; 6,23; 7,31; 12,17;
nou kai epistêmês dektikon
(as ultimate *differentia* of man),
55,28

oikeios, appropriate, proper, 12,11;
18,2
oiketês, slave, 27,19; 39,27
oikia, house, 14,7
oikodomikos, pertaining to
architecture, 5,20
oikodomos, architect, 20,12
olbios, blessed, 40,3
on, being, 33,24; 60,6; 61,22
onoma, noun, 10,25; 22,19; 25,26;
onoma idion, particular name,
21,10; 32,23; 33,5-6;
(Pythagorean view), 40,6-7;
onoma kurion, proper name,
35,26
onomasia, nomenclature, 3,21; 36,26
onomatikos, pertaining to a name,
27,21
onomatopoieô, make up names,
17,32
onomatothetês, namer, 20,5
onomazô, name, 25,6; 32,11
onta, beings, 9,22.25-6.28; *ta onta
hêi o.*, being *qua* beings, 9,29;
hê peri tôn ontôn theôria,
ontology, 15,34
organon, instrument, 5,17-18;
14,21; 32,6
organikos, instrumental, 4,23.29;
5,5; 20,8-9
orthodoxastikôs, in conformity
with correct opinion, 5,22
orthos, right; correct, 8,14
opsis, view; sight, 12,26
orophê, roof, 14,14
ouranios, celestial, 69,27
ousia, substance, 9,14.26.27; 11,8;
21,11.20; 22,29; 29,20.30; 31,31;
35,7; 42,17
ousiôdês, essential, 55,6; 72,1

Subject Index

accident, 42,14; 43,8f.; 44,27ff.;
  46,30; 49,32f.; 50,10ff.; 62,5f.;
  63,25; 64,8ff.
 as particular nature, 64,1
 concourse of, 55,5
 defined, 42,17; 44,16
 form as, 74,23ff.
 particular, 50,16ff.
 universal, 50,25ff.
accord
 between Aristotle and Archytas,
  2,22ff.; 13,23ff.
 between Aristotle and Plato,
  7,30ff.; 71,1ff.
activity/actuality (*energeia*), 63,12ff.;
  66,23; 67,27f.
affection (*pathos*), 63,13ff.
affirmation, 72,25ff.; 73,5ff.
 differentiae of, 73,12ff.
alla mên, 27,18; 39,27
analogy, 31,33ff.; 32,21ff.; 39,20;
  74,4.24ff.; 75,20
'animate': defined, 28,22ff.
aph' henos kai pros ti, 62,7; 74,31ff.
apples, fragrance of, 49,10ff.
Aristotle, works of
 Categories
  title of, 8,12.17f.; 9,1f; 15,26ff.;
   16,31ff.
  authenticity of, 8,12.18ff.; 9,3f.;
   18,7ff.
  chapter-headings of, 3,29; 8,11ff.
  division of, 3,20f.; 4,10ff.;
   8,13.25ff.; 18,22ff.
  part of philosophy it belongs to,
   8,13.30f.; 20,7ff.
  form of expression of, 3,25; 6,19ff.
  goal of (*skopos*), 1,8; 3,24f.; 6,6ff.;
   8,12.14f.; 9,5ff.; 20,3; 44,5; 62,15;
   69,1ff.
  hypomnematic, 4,16ff.

  obscurity of, 3,26; 6,31ff.
  order of study of, 3,23; 5,3ff.; 8,13
  qualities of exegete of, 3,26 ; 7,23ff.
  qualities of student of, 3,28; 7,33ff.
  usefulness of, 8,12.16ff.; 13,26ff.
  where to begin study of, 5,3ff.
 article, significance of, 25,20ff.;
  64,29ff.; 71,5

being (*to on*), beings, 44,12ff.; 60,6;
  61,22ff.; 69,5f.; 73,30ff.
 a genus or not, 21,26f.
 as homonymous, 33,23f.; 66,13
 divided into ten categories, 62,13f.
 community between, 43,7ff.
being acted upon (*paskhein*), 61,13ff.;
  63,5ff.17; 66,17; 67,32
being moved (as genus), 63,6ff.
blituri (as example of meaningless
  word), 12,31; 27,17.32; 41,13f.

case, 37,9ff.; 65,7ff.
 masculine and feminine, 37,14ff.
categories
 as homonymous (Iamblichus),
  22,2ff.; 24,2
 arguments against number of,
  62,30ff.
  as deficient, 64,13ff.
  as excessive, 63,4ff.
  as substituted, 66,16ff.
 Simplicius' division of, 67,25ff.
 Stoic, 67,1ff.16ff.
categorization, 21,10ff.
concepts/notions (*ennoiai*; *noêmata*),
  innate, 5,24; 12,28ff.; 13,9;
  60,26ff.
combination (*sumplokê*), 44,21f.;
  72,25ff.
 in vs. without c., 42,8ff.; 60,12.23ff.;
  71,20ff.

Lightning Source UK Ltd.
Milton Keynes UK
UKOW06f1300070815

256552UK00005B/51/P